JOBS FOR PEOPLE
WHO LOVE TRAVEL

Books and CD-ROM by Drs. Ron and Caryl Krannich

The Almanac of International Jobs and Careers
Best Jobs for the 1990s and Into the 21st Century
Change Your Job, Change Your Life
The Complete Guide to International Jobs and Careers
The Complete Guide to Public Employment
The Directory of Federal Jobs and Employers
Discover the Best Jobs for You!
Dynamite Answers to Interview Questions
Dynamite Cover Letters
Dynamite Resumes
Dynamite Salary Negotiations
Dynamite Tele-Search
The Educator's Guide to Alternative Jobs and Careers
Find a Federal Job Fast!
From Air Force Blue to Corporate Gray
From Army Green to Corporate Gray
From Navy Blue to Corporate Gray
High Impact Resumes and Letters
Interview for Success
Job Search Letters That Get Results
Job-Power Source CD-ROM
Jobs and Careers With Nonprofit Organizations
Jobs for People Who Love Computers and the Information Highway
Jobs for People Who Love Health Care and Nursing
Jobs for People Who Love Hotels, Resorts, and Cruise Ships
Jobs for People Who Love to Work From Home
Jobs for People Who Love Travel
Mayors and Managers
Moving Out of Education
Moving Out of Government
The New Network Your Way to Job and Career Success
The Politics of Family Planning Policy
Re-Careering in Turbulent Times
Resumes and Cover Letters for Transitioning Military Personnel
Shopping and Traveling in Exotic Asia
Shopping and Traveling in Exotic Hong Kong
Shopping and Traveling in Exotic India
Shopping and Traveling in Exotic Indonesia
Shopping and Traveling in Exotic Morocco
Shopping and Traveling in Exotic Singapore and Malaysia
Shopping and Traveling in Exotic Thailand
Shopping and Traveling the Exotic Philippines
Shopping in Exciting Australia and Papua New Guinea
Shopping in Exotic Places
Shopping the Exotic South Pacific

JOBS FOR PEOPLE WHO LOVE TRAVEL

Opportunities At Home and Abroad

Second Edition

Ronald L. Krannich, Ph.D.
Caryl Rae Krannich, Ph.D.

IMPACT PUBLICATIONS
Manassas Park, VA

JOBS FOR PEOPLE WHO LOVE TRAVEL:
Opportunities At Home and Abroad

Library of Congress Cataloging-in-Publication Data

Krannich, Ronald L.

Jobs for people who love travel: opportunities at home and abroad / Ronald L. Krannich, Caryl Rae Krannich—2nd ed.
    p. cm.
Includes bibliographical references and index.
ISBN 1-57023-031-5
1. Vocational guidance. 2. Travel. 3. Employment in foreign countries. I. Krannich, Caryl Rae. II. Title
HF5381.K688 1995
331.7'02—dc20   95-16791
                                                             CIP

For information on distribution or quantity discount rates, call 703/361-7300 or write to: Sales Department, Impact Publications, 9104-N Manassas Drive, Manassas Park, VA 22111-5211, Tel. 703/361-7300 or Fax 703/335-9486. Distributed to the trade by National Book Network, 4720 Boston Way, Suite A, Lanham, MD 20706, Tel. 301/459-8696.

CONTENTS

NOTE TO USERS

While we have attempted to provide accurate and up-to-date information in this book, please be advised that names, addresses, and phone numbers do change and that organizations do move, go out of business, or change management. This is especially true for organizations located in the New York City and Washington, DC metropolitan areas. Application deadlines, fees, prices, and product and service orientations may also change. We regret any inconvenience such changes may cause to your job search.

If you have difficulty contacting a particular organization included in this book, please do one or all of the following:

- Consult the latest edition of *The National Directory of Addresses and Telephone Numbers* (Omnigraphics: Detroit, MI).

- Contact the Information or Reference section of your local library. They may have online services or directories which include the latest contact information.

- Call Information for current phone numbers.

Inclusion of organizations in this book in no way implies endorsements by the authors or Impact Publications. The information and recommendations appearing in this book are provided solely for your reference. It is the reader's responsibility to take initiative in contacting, evaluating, and following-through with employers.

The names, addresses, phone numbers, and services appearing in this book provide one important component for conducting a successful job search. Placed within the larger context of an effective job search, this component should be carefully linked to your self-assessment, research, networking, and resume writing and distribution activities.

JOBS FOR PEOPLE
WHO LOVE TRAVEL

1

SO YOU WANT TO TRAVEL AND WORK AT THE SAME TIME

*L*et's be honest. You have the travel bug. It's hard to shake or even explain to others. But you're not alone. It's a common affliction or obsession you either overcome or soon succumb to.

You love to travel. But unlike most people, you would like to travel and earn a decent living at the same time. You've come to the right place. You're ready to explore some job and career options that would allow you to pursue your passion for travel. That's what this book is all about—finding jobs that enable you to travel to your heart's content. Like you, we decided to succumb to the travel bug!

JOIN THE CLUB

Welcome to the wonderful world of work and travel, or travel and work—which ever order fits you best. You're joining a growing club of traveler-workers who want more out of life than just another job. While many jobs enable you to take a trip or two each year, other jobs offer more frequent and exciting travel. Like many others, you're probably afflicted with that unexplained urge to travel—see new places, meet new people, experience new environments, or just be in motion, going from one place to another. You may even be a travel junky, requiring a "travel fix" every two months or so!

LIFE AS WORK AND PLAY

Unlike most people, you have a lifestyle preference that combines work and travel. Put another way, you want to work and play at the same time—the ultimate worklife. You would like to travel on a regular basis rather than just during your annual vacation. If you could create your ideal job, you would probably design one that avoids a regular 9 to 5, Monday through Friday, office routine. You would probably be working in your favorite country, traveling to and from your favorite cities, or just roaming a country or the globe in pursuit of meaningful work and play. You might even start your own business, one which would permit you to frequently travel.

Some critical observers might say you have an attitudinal or a motivational problem. Others would say you have the ideal job in mind! You might say you have a bad case of wanderlust that needs to be satisfied in some type of meaningful travel-work setting.

You and millions of other individuals share a common bond or affliction—that unexplained urge to travel and keep traveling on a regular basis. For some people, the love of travel is one of those important seasons of life—they did it when they were young, perhaps as a student or when they were single, but they have since resigned themselves to a more stationary lifestyle. For others, the continuing urge to travel is part of their basic motivational pattern for work—they need to travel and constantly change their environments in order to remain motivated, enthusiastic, and productive.

Rather than confine travel to a season of life, you recognize that travel is an important part of your life; you have a need to place it at center stage in your worklife. Better still, you should find jobs that incorporate the type of travel you find both personally and professionally rewarding. In other words, you're someone who needs to find a worklife that is synonymous with a lifestyle.

> *You're someone who needs to find a worklife that is synonymous with a lifestyle.*

TAKE THE RIGHT ACTION

Fortunately for you and thousands of other individuals, numerous jobs do combine work and travel. They enable you to pursue a particular lifestyle that rewards you both professionally and personally.

If you want to land one of these jobs, you'll have to do three things:

- Identify what jobs are most compatible with your desired work-travel lifestyle.

- Know where these jobs can be found and whom to contact for vacancy information.

- Acquire the necessary job search skills for landing the right job for you.

Our task in the following pages is to guide you in acquiring sufficient information and knowledge to make your worklife dreams come true. Like us, you probably would love a job—perhaps even pursue a career—that permits you to regularly engage in travel.

Welcome to the club. You'll be joining millions of other individuals who seek jobs that enable them to pursue their passion for travel. Let's have some fun putting together a job portfolio that may indeed combine work and play into an exciting worklife/lifestyle.

WHERE ARE THEY GOING, WHAT ARE THEY DOING?

Stroll through any airport or visit a railway or bus station and you'll observe hundreds of people on their way to somewhere. Some are in the pursuit of pleasure; others are fulfilling family and friendship obligations; and still others operate these major transportation hubs for the benefit of all types of travelers. But the majority are working— going to and from work sites that define their occupations. Many look happy; others look anxious to complete this transportation process; and some look tired, probably hoping to be going somewhere else soon.

We've always wondered what all those other people on our plane or train do for a living. As soon as our plane lands or our train stops, many fellow passengers head for the row of pay phones or pull out their cellular telephone to begin conducting business. Lugging fat briefcases and lightweight computers, most of these phone hounds are probably salespeople making their first connections to what hopefully will become a successful deal.

If it weren't for our work, we might not enjoy travel!

For years we have traveled both at home and abroad for pleasure, family, and business. Our fat passports testify to our ambitious work and lifestyles. They have become so full of immigration stamps that we now have difficulty locating evidence of our last stop. Like others, we carry a laptop computer wherever we go—the ultimate office-on-the-go. Be it San Francisco, Chicago, Boston, New York, London, Amsterdam, Prague, Casablanca, Moscow, Bombay, New Delhi, Beijing, Tokyo, Hong Kong, Bangkok, Kuala Lumpur, Singapore, Jakarta, Bali, Melbourne, Sydney, Christ Church, Auckland, Papeete, or Honolulu, we're never really away from our Virginia-based business. And we love what we do—traveling and working at the same time. Indeed, if it weren't for our work, we might not enjoy travel!

FROM ADDICTION TO HABIT
TO AN EXCITING CAREER

Travel is analogous to prostitution—you first do it for fun, and then you decide to do it for money! We simply love to travel. At one time, like many other people, we dreamed of finding enough free time and money to indulge our travel fantasies. A job was something we did most of the year; travel was something we did in our free time. Our first taste of travel came early in life—the ubiquitous annual family vacation and summer camps. Next came college and those wonderful semester breaks, foreign language classes, study abroad programs, a round-the-world college choir tour, Peace Corps, and graduate research abroad. High school and later college teaching jobs enabled us to use our two to three-month summer breaks for pursuing interesting work and play abroad as well as enjoying travel adventures at home.

Travel is analogous to prostitution—
you first do it for fun, and then
you decide to do it for money!

We were, and still are, discriminating worker-travelers. We had a bias for working in exotic places, knowing some day soon these developing areas would graduate to the status of not-so-exotic places. One year it was Tokyo and Beirut, another year Hawaii and Thailand, and the next year Mexico and the Caribbean—all part of study and work. Travel seemed to easily merge with education and work. It was enjoyable, enlightening, and profitable.

After being teachers, freelance researchers/writers, and development workers/consultants abroad, we eventually turned our travel addiction into the ultimate work/travel combination—inaugurated a new travel guide series on shopping in exotic places. Making three to four trips abroad each year for periods of two to four months, we're now into our tenth travel volume. We have plans to further expand our travel research and writing activities in the decade ahead.

We have an unabashed addiction to travel which we can't shake even if we tried. Returning exhausted from our latest travel/work adventure—and vowing not to travel again for another year—within two months we get that unexplained urge to hit the road again.

Ours is a hopeless addiction we share with thousands of other people, perhaps including yourself. Admitting, and finally succumbing to our addiction, we decided to turn it into a strength that also become a financially rewarding habit and career.

We love to combine travel with our work. Indeed, many of our earlier career choices were conscious decisions to marry what we loved to do professionally with interesting travel experiences. And we are not alone. We've met numerous people who have a similar addiction to travel. Using their two to four weeks of vacation each year to satisfy their travel needs, many people would love to turn their vacation experiences into some type of full-time avocation. Others have been able to fashion careers that enable them to work and travel at the same time. Some have even been fortunate enough to turn their yearly vacations into long-term careers that enable them to work, live, and travel in exciting places.

A LOVE/HATE RELATIONSHIP

Travel is not for everyone. Nor is it something you may love all of the time or for all seasons of your life. In fact, many people have a love/hate relationship with travel. They love the fond memories surrounding the positives of travel, but they frequently forget the negatives associated with many travel problems. They may love arriving at and experiencing a new and unfamiliar destination, but they often hate the transportation process involved in getting there. Long waiting lines at taxi queues and airports, traffic jams, delayed schedules, crowded planes and trains, and bad food, accommodations, and service quickly take the excitement out of travel.

For others, travel and work changes with the seasons of life. At one time—especially when you are young and single—you may enjoy living and traveling abroad or being on the road two or three days a week. But at other times, age, marriage, children, and family preferences modify your free-wheeling work-travel lifestyle.

A new scenario might go something like this. After living and working abroad for several years, your spouse lands a great job he or she really loves, one involving little or no travel; your children attend good schools which they and your spouse prefer they attend until graduation; or you've become a comfort-creature—prefer frequenting five-star hotels and restaurants—who can gladly live without another uncomfortable Third World experience. You now prefer a more settled life at home with an occasional trip abroad for short periods of time. You still love to travel, but it should no longer consume your lifestyle and negatively affect your personal life. Your new season in life puts travel and work in a much different perspective.

PURSUE YOUR PASSION

Whatever your present season in life, you should at least explore job and career options that best appeal to your lifestyle values, interests, skills, and abilities. Get ready to join thousands of other individuals who pursue their career passions by landing jobs that are both professionally and personally rewarding.

During the past decade we have spoken with many people who simply love to travel but feel stuck in jobs that offer little or no opportunities for travel. We're often reminded of the divorce lawyer who attended a summer-abroad program in Europe and majored in international studies as an undergraduate. For years he had dreamed of working abroad. Instead, he went on to law school and became a successful divorce lawyer—his mother approved. He made lots of money, but he disliked his work, especially the people he worked with and the ethics surrounding his daily work. His interests and values no longer were conducive to a healthy career in divorce law. What he really wanted to do was to find a more personally rewarding job that involved international work, especially international travel. It was his undergraduate international experience, rather than his successful legal practice, that really gave him personal and professional satisfaction.

We're also reminded of the high-paid, over-stressed physician who had a successful practice working fourteen hours a day with little time for enjoying vacations. She really wanted to work in rural Africa providing basic health care services. Even though she expected a dramatic reduction in income and very basic living conditions, she preferred this international lifestyle to what was considered by her peers as a model of success for a physician.

Our divorce lawyer and physician are by no means atypical. We've encountered numerous lawyers, physicians, nurses, teachers, salespeople, secretaries, engineers, architects, entrepreneurs, and retirees who really want to find jobs that would incorporate their love for travel. For them, travel is the missing link in what is ostensibly a successful career. Some of these people have been able to find jobs within their present career that enable them to travel more. Others have changed careers in order to pursue what has been a lifelong passion—travel.

> *Thousands of jobs involve different types of travel, and some of those may be the perfect fit for you.*

Whatever you are doing or planning to do with your life, you should at least explore job and career options for people who love travel. If your passion is travel, see if you can find the perfect career marriage—a job that incorporates your occupational interests, skills, abilities, and values with your love of travel. You need not pursue jobs in the travel industry nor ones that require living abroad for long periods of time. Thousands of jobs involve different types of travel, and some of those may be the perfect fit for you.

The following chapters explore numerous job options for people who love travel. They include descriptions of jobs as well as information—names, address, and phone numbers—for contacting potential employers. The book concludes with a listing of additional career and travel resources which should prove useful for pursuing your passion.

WHERE DO YOU GO FROM HERE?

We wish you well as you pursue your career and travel interests. While we are primarily concerned with outlining job and career options for people with a passion for travel, we also recognize the need to examine other important concerns central to conducting an effective job search. Indeed, knowing your job and career options will only take you so far toward landing the job you want. You must also possess capabilities to land a job. This involves using effective job search skills for opening the doors of employers.

We examine the most important job search skills required for landing jobs in today's job market in several other books: *Change Your Job Change Your Life*, *High Impact Resumes and Letters*, *Dynamite Resumes*, *Dynamite Cover Letters*, *Job Search Letters That Get Results*, *Dynamite Answers to Interview Questions*, *Interview for Success*, *Dynamite Tele-Search*, *Discover the Best Jobs For You*, *The New Network Your Way to Job and Career Success*, and *Dynamite Salary Negotiations*. We also address particular job and career fields in the following books: *The Best Jobs for the 1990s and Into the 21st Century*, *The Complete Guide to Public Employment*, *Find a Federal Job Fast*, *The Complete Guide to International Jobs and Careers*, *The Directory of Federal Jobs and Employers*, *The Almanac of International Jobs and Careers*, *Jobs for People Who Love Hotels, Resorts, and Cruise Ships*, *Jobs for People Who Love Computers and the Information Highway*, *Jobs for People Who Love Health Care and Nursing*, *Jobs for People Who Love to Work From Home*, and *The Educator's Guide to Alternative Jobs and Careers*. These and many other job search books are available in bookstores and libraries. For your convenience, they also can be ordered directly from Impact Publications by completing the order form at the end of this book ("Career Resources") or by acquiring a copy of the publisher's comprehensive catalog.

Contact Impact Publications to receive a free copy of the most comprehensive annotated career catalog available today—*"Jobs and Careers for the 1990s."* For the latest edition, write to:

IMPACT PUBLICATIONS
ATTN: Job/Career Catalog
9104-N Manassas Drive
Manassas Park, VA 22111-5211

They will send you, via fourth-class mail (expect four weeks for delivery), one copy upon request; for additional copies, or requests for first-class mailing, send $2.95 per copy. This catalog contains almost every important career and job finding resource available today, including many titles that are difficult if not impossible to find in bookstores and libraries. You will find everything from additional travel-related career books to books on resume writing, interviewing, government and international jobs, military, women, minorities, students, entrepreneurs as well as videos, audiocassettes, computer software, and CD-ROM programs. This catalog puts you in touch with the major resources that can assist you with every stage of your job search.

DISCOVER WHAT YOU REALLY LOVE TO DO

The following pages are designed to assist you in pursuing one of your work and lifestyle passions—travel at home or abroad. Once you identify jobs most appropriate for your interests and skills, be sure to follow through with a well organized job search campaign designed to put you in contact with potential employers. This will involve conducting further research, writing resumes and letters, networking for information and advice, and conducting informational and job interviews. If you do this, you too can find a job involving the type of travel you love!

2

TEST YOUR
LTQ AND ICQ

*J*ust how prepared are you for finding and doing jobs that involve travel? While many people may be high on desire and motivation to find jobs permitting travel, many of these same people lack the necessary knowledge and skills for landing such jobs.

Let's examine how you orient yourself to jobs involving travel as well as probe your level of knowledge and skills for landing the perfect job. Just how realistic, motivated, and prepared are you for finding a job involving travel? What exactly are your qualifications? What about your educational level, training, and experience? What job search and travel skills do you possess? If you are interested in international travel and relocation abroad, are you prepared to travel abroad for an interview as well as quickly move abroad if necessary?

YOUR LTQ

While the chapters that follow will help you answer many questions about the "what" and "where" of jobs involving both domestic and international travel, here we want to examine your motivation and ability to find and do those jobs. The following exercise identifies your "Love to Travel Quotient" (LTQ). Respond to each of the statements according to the instructions and then compile your composite LTQ score at the end of the exercise.

INSTRUCTIONS: Respond to each statement by circling which number at the right best represents your level of knowledge, skill, attitude, experience, or behavior.

SCALE: 0 = not at all   3 = maybe, uncertain
1 = strongly disagree   4 = agree
2 = disagree   5 = strongly agree

1. I love to travel.   0 1 2 3 4 5

2. When traveling for pleasure, I often think
   about having a job that would enable me
   to make the same or similar trip.   0 1 2 3 4 5

3. Each year I take ___ trips for at least
   3 days each. (circle the number of trips)   0 1 2 3 4 5

4. After returning from a trip, within three
   months I'm usually ready to take another trip.   0 1 2 3 4 5

5. I prefer a job that enables me to spend at
   least 20% of my work time traveling.   0 1 2 3 4 5

6. I have a resume designed for a job involving
   travel.   0 1 2 3 4 5

7. I have skills that are highly sought after
   in jobs involving travel.   0 1 2 3 4 5

8. I know how to locate companies and
   employers that have jobs involving travel.   0 1 2 3 4 5

9. I know how to get potential employers
   interested to contact me for a job interview.   0 1 2 3 4 5

10. I know at least 5 people who have jobs
    involving travel and who are willing to
    give me job leads.   0 1 2 3 4 5

11. I have set aside at least 20 hours per week
to conduct my job search.   0 1 2 3 4 5

12. I'm good at networking for information,
advice, and job referrals.   0 1 2 3 4 5

13. I'm prepared to move to a new job location
within 30 days.   0 1 2 3 4 5

14. I have a particular city, region, or country
in mind where I would like to work.   0 1 2 3 4 5

15. I have a clear idea of what type of
organization and employer I want to
work with.   0 1 2 3 4 5

16. I have a clear idea of what I want to do
and have stated this at the beginning of
my resume.   0 1 2 3 4 5

17. I know how to conduct a long distance
job search campaign.   0 1 2 3 4 5

18. I know how to conduct a long distance
job search campaign.   0 1 2 3 4 5

19. I am a flexible person who can easily
adapt to different situations and changing
circumstances.   0 1 2 3 4 5

20. I'm usually successful at what I do.   0 1 2 3 4 5

21. I welcome and thrive on adventure, challenges,
and changing and unique situations.   0 1 2 3 4 5

22. I'm not like most other people I meet back
home in terms of my motivations, goals, and
career pattern.   0 1 2 3 4 5

23. I'm generally a very happy and contented
person.   0 1 2 3 4 5

24. While money is important to me, it's not
the driving force behind my desire to seek
a job involving travel.   0 1 2 3 4 5

25. I have a sense of commitment and
responsibility to what I do.   0 1 2 3 4 5

26. I usually make a favorable impression
on employers.   0 1 2 3 4 5

27. I try to keep my knowledge and skills
    as current as possible in my profession.   0 1 2 3 4 5

28. I'm strongly motivated to work hard at
    finding the right job involving travel.   0 1 2 3 4 5

29. I'm generally a very patient person.   0 1 2 3 4 5

30. I'm also a very persistent and tenacious
    person.   0 1 2 3 4 5

31. I have a good sense of humor.   0 1 2 3 4 5

32. I don't take myself too seriously.   0 1 2 3 4 5

33. I'm interested in learning more about others.   0 1 2 3 4 5

34. I believe I'm a realistic person—I do my
    research, analyze situations in terms of
    pros and cons, and arrive at sensible and
    successful decisions.   0 1 2 3 4 5

35. I know how to get my first job interview
    within 4 weeks and the first job offer
    within 60 days.   0 1 2 3 4 5

36. I know how to negotiate salary and benefits.   0 1 2 3 4 5

TOTALS FOR EACH COLUMN   _____

GRAND TOTAL FOR ALL COLUMNS   _____

If your composite score (Grand Total) is above 140, you may well be on your way to quickly finding a job involving travel. If your score is between 110 and 140, you need to work on those items on which you scored between 0 and 3. If your score is below 110, you need to get yourself well organized for the job market by following this and several other job search book.

YOUR ICQ

While most of the 36 statements relate to jobs involving travel, as well as the job search in general, several others specifically relate to finding an international job. Indeed, the knowledge and skills required for finding an international job differ in many ways from finding jobs in general. If you are interested in international jobs, respond to the following statements. Add your score to your previous score to get your ICQ—"International Career Quotient":

37. I've traveled to 0, 1, 2, 3, 4, or 5 countries
    (circle the number at the right)   0 1 2 3 4 5

38. I know whom to contact abroad for
    information on international jobs.   0 1 2 3 4 5

39. I'm willing to wait 6 to 18 months before
    landing an international job.   0 1 2 3 4 5

40. I can read, write, and speak fluently at
    least one foreign language.   0 1 2 3 4 5

41. I've taken 0, 1, 2, 3, 4, or 5+ college
    level courses in international business,
    finance, marketing, and economics. (circle
    number to right)   0 1 2 3 4 5

42. I have a high school diploma (1), B.A. (2),
    M.A. (3), Ph.D. (4), or Post-Doctorate (5).
    (circle number to right representing your
    highest education)   0 1 2 3 4 5

43. I've lived abroad for 0, 1, 2, 3, 4, or
    5+ years. (circle number to right)   0 1 2 3 4 5

44. I already have held international jobs for
    0, 1, 2, 3, 4, or 5+ years. (circle number
    to right)   0 1 2 3 4 5

45. I know what I should and should not do when
    looking for an international job.   0 1 2 3 4 5

46. I know what is the best educational background
    for landing an international job.   0 1 2 3 4 5

47. I know what international skills employers
    are most looking for in today's international
    job market.   0 1 2 3 4 5

48. Many of my friends and acquaintances are
    from other countries.   0 1 2 3 4 5

49. I keep abreast of international developments
    and thus consider myself knowledgeable about
    the international arena.   0 1 2 3 4 5

50. I know how the international hiring process
    works in most organizations.   0 1 2 3 4 5

51. I'm willing to travel abroad at my own
    expense to interview for a job.   0 1 2 3 4 5

52. I'm generally tolerant of others and
    their ways of life.   0 1 2 3 4 5

53. I'm a good listener who empathizes
    with others.   0 1 2 3 4 5

54. I tend to get along well with people
    from other societies and cultures
    without going "native."   0 1 2 3 4 5

55. Ambiguities don't bother me much.   0 1 2 3 4 5

56. Within 30 minutes I can get 3 international
    job leads by phone.   0 1 2 3 4 5

57. I love living and traveling abroad.   0 1 2 3 4 5

TOTALS FOR EACH COLUMN   _____

GRAND TOTAL FOR ALL COLUMNS   _____

If your composite score (Grand Total) for all 57 items is above 225, you may well be on your way to quickly finding an international job. If your score is between 170 and 224, you need to work on those items on which you scored between 0 and 3. If your score is below 170, you need to get yourself well organized for the international job market by following this and several other books on finding an international job.

IMPROVING YOUR SCORE AND SKILLS

Now review each of the above items on which you scored below 3. Make notes as to what you need to do to move your score on these items into the 4 and 5 columns. Some of the following chapters will assist you. You may also want to consult our *Change Your Job, Change Your Life* and *The Complete Guide to International Jobs and Careers* which may help you develop specific job search skills. Other items may require additional education, experience, skills, and patterns of behavior as well as effective job search skills—things that are beyond the scope of this book but within your control.

Once you finish this book as well as work on your job search skills, complete these exercises again. You should increase your score by 20 percent. If you put this book into practice over the coming weeks by spending 20 hours each week on your job search, you should improve your score by another 20 percent. Better still, you should eventually land the job you want!

3

FINDING YOUR RIGHT JOB AND LIFESTYLE

*I*f you love to travel, you'll probably love a job that lets you travel on a regular basis to places you really enjoy visiting. But travel is not for everyone. Nor do most people seek jobs involving travel.

You're different. Only certain types of people love travel as well as seek employment that incorporates their love for travel. These people have a particular motivational pattern that affects how they relate to the world of work. Some pursue predictable career paths with a single company or industry. Others engage in a great deal of job hopping as they pursue their passion for travel.

18

For those who do love travel, the positives of travel tend to out-weight the negatives. At the same time, many people are very particular about where they want to travel. Some prefer jobs that take them away from the office for several hours a day or a few days each week or month. Others enjoy living abroad for lengthy periods of time or traveling abroad several weeks or months each year.

HEADING FOR THE LAST FRONTIER

Whatever your travel preferences, be sure you understand where you are coming from in terms of your motivations. Indeed, individuals seeking jobs that incorporate their love for travel exhibit motivational patterns that are different from other job seekers. Few are able to clearly separate their personal and professional lives. Many wish to pursue a lifestyle which merges both lives into one. Rather than seek just any job, they want jobs that enable them to pursue a unique and enjoyable lifestyle where travel plays a central role.

The international employment arena is the last great frontier for striking out on one's own.

International job seekers are some of the most extreme cases exhibiting a passion for travel. In many respects, the international employment arena is the last great frontier for striking out on one's own. It's filled with myths, martyrs, misfits, and missionaries—a particular breed of job seeker that is simultaneously fascinating and frustrated. We can think of few other employment arenas—other than perhaps the film culture of Hollywood—that generate so many unrealistic job seekers who are high on fantasies and motivation but low on information and skills. Individuals pursuing jobs in this arena defy most career counseling advice on how to best find a job.

IT'S OKAY TO BE UNREALISTIC

But being unrealistic is not necessarily negative for people who love to travel, and especially for those who seek international jobs. Ironically, it is the dreams, fantasies, and unrealistic expectations—coupled with an unending drive, persistence, and entrepreneurial spirit—that successfully lead many such job seekers into the international job market. They often confound career counselors with their restlessness, sense of mission, and commitment to "go international" despite all odds and their general lack of goals, skills, and information. Setting goals based upon dreams—rather than on an established pattern of motivations, skills, and experience—these people tend to defy standard career planning and job search methods.

WE DID IT OUR WAY

Travel plays a central role in motivating international job seekers. Indeed, for over 25 years we've pursued our own international jobs and careers. We've lived and worked abroad, counseled others on how to find international jobs, and assisted international workers in re-entering the U.S. domestic job market.

We've fashioned an exciting career and lifestyle that enables us to regularly work abroad while maintaining our career base in the U.S. Indeed, we spend approximately two months a year working abroad.

We've met our share of interesting and intelligent international entrepreneurs; social dropouts; those possessed with a cause; individuals obsessed with becoming culturally neutral and linguistically competent; and a wide range of expatriates, short-termers, tourists, and travelers who are all doing something interesting in the international arena. Many are passionate people pursuing vague career goals.

We've served as employees to others' organizations as well as freelanced and engaged in our own form of entrepreneurship.

We've frequently wondered how others ever got involved with international jobs, and what continues to drive them in such careers.

And we regularly hear from numerous individuals who seek to break into the international job market after having been struck with the travel bug, a case of wanderlust, a sense of mission, or a yearning to do something different, challenging, unique, or exotic. Travel seems to give special meaning to their lives.

CAREER RISK-TAKERS
PURSUING A LIFESTYLE

In contrast to most job seekers we encounter, the international job seeker is a very different type of individual in terms of motivation, goals, skills, and lifestyles. While the typical job seeker is usually motivated by money, career advancement, and "success" within some organizational structure, more often than not, the international job seeker is motivated by a certain degree of restlessness to do something different; a need to travel and change their work environment; a commitment to pursue an important cause or idea; or a desire to experience a different culture, society, and lifestyle.

International job seekers are the ultimate career risk-takers who are seldom obsessed with their careers. Many reject the conventional model of the "successful job seeker" that assumes you must have clear-cut goals and accumulate marketable skills that lead to career advancement and career success. Instead, such job seekers often take any job they can get, willingly compromise their career goals and skills to the requirements of particular jobs, and are always on the lookout for new job opportunities that may well become their next job jump within a highly unstable and unpredictable international job market.

The desire for an international lifestyle is often the driving force for seeking a job.

While many international job seekers are looking for jobs and potentially satisfying international careers that allow them to frequently travel, they also seek to fashion a particular lifestyle that takes priority over any particular job or career. Indeed, the desire for an international lifestyle is often the driving force for seeking a job—any type of job—in order to "stay" abroad. Many are hopelessly addicted to international life and travel. As a result, many international job seekers are less concerned with formulating clear job and career objectives and developing marketable skills than with finding a job in their favorite part of the world, be it Europe, Australia, Africa, Asia, or the Middle East. Many have a passion or obsession for returning to their favorite regions, countries, or cities. Their self-indulgent dream is to live and work in Europe, Asia, Africa, or the Middle East—or London, Paris, Rome, Madrid, Casablanca, Bangkok, Singapore, Hong Kong, Sydney, or Tokyo—and they act accordingly by seeking jobs that will put them into their desired places. They are impatient with such basic career planning questions as *"What do you really want to do?"*, because they've already answered this question with a lifestyle answer: *"Get out of my present confining job and go work in France or, more specifically, in Paris."* Rather than deal with the fundamentals of career planning and the job search process—developing an objective, identifying skills, conducting research, writing resumes, networking for job leads, and interviewing for jobs—many of these people are preoccupied with locating job vacancies which they hope they can "fit" themselves into. They are more concerned with finding out *"where are the jobs"* than with *"what are the jobs"* and *"how to go about finding a job."* They are especially interested in acquiring names, addresses, and telephone numbers of potential international employers so they can contact them directly for a job.

ADVICE FROM THE EXPERTS?

Not surprising, international job seekers pose a basic dilemma for career counselors: What kind of career advice do you give someone whose primary concern is to find a job that will support an international lifestyle or a passion for travel rather than to find a job they do well and enjoy doing and which leads to career advancement? How does one deal with the fundamentals of motivation and goal setting when such individuals do not fit into the conventional pattern of successful career planning?

The very nature of the international job market challenges many conventional career planning and job search methods. Career planning approaches, for example, requiring job seekers to first assess their skills, abilities, and work values and then formulate a career objective that guides their job search toward satisfying long-term careers and progressive career advancement do not work well for people who just want to job so they can continue to pursue their travel passion.

The international employment arena simply is not structured to permit the success of such models and methods. Rather, this is a highly fragmented and segmented job market; access is often difficult if not impossible for many types of jobs; employment is frequently short-term—with a three-year contract considered an excellent job opportunity; job-hopping among many disjointed jobs requiring different mixes of skills is a common pattern for those intent upon continuing employment abroad; and geographic location and cultural settings of employment blur the more traditional skill requirements for job performance. This structure forces international job seekers into a particular pattern for finding and maintaining jobs; they quickly learn the art of networking for developing professional relationships as well as for accessing job vacancy information. In short, those committed to seeking international jobs must be prepared to address both the lifestyle and career questions simultaneously.

Other job seekers with a passion for travel, but not necessary for living and working abroad, pose a similar dilemma for career counselors. They are often more concerned with satisfying their obsession with travel than with pursuing a successful career. What they most need is an ideal job that permits them to simultaneously engage in on-the-job travel while pursuing a successful career.

YOU'RE DIFFERENT FROM OTHERS

Over the years we have met and worked with hundreds of individuals who love travel. Many pursued international jobs and careers. We've encountered our share of journalists, corporate executives, bankers, missionaries, educators, researchers, lawyers, artists, writers, development workers, medical personnel, government bureaucrats, politicians, tour operators, military personnel, soldiers of fortune, volunteers, contractors, consultants, and entrepreneurs to write a separate book on interesting international personalities! We regularly hear from hundreds of other individuals who are interested in breaking into the international job market, re-entering it after a lengthy absence, or changing international jobs and careers. We also have conducted job search seminars abroad for those interested in re-entering the U.S. job market or finding other international employment.

We've always been fascinated with the international arena and the many interesting people who work abroad. We wonder how and why they got involved with international work rather than stay home to follow traditional careers or pursue a standard American lifestyle complete with a home mortgage and stable community life.

What we've learned over the years is that these people are different from the people we know back home in terms of motivations, personalities, and lifestyles. While some go international for the money, most are simply restless, curious, or stricken with that unexplained addiction to travel and a desire to pursue an idea, cause, or lifestyle that cannot be satisfied in some job back home. Some are international junkies who thrive in the international arena. Others literally dropped out of their own societies and work-driven lifestyles back home for more easy-going and personally rewarding lives abroad. Some are social misfits who attempt to build new identities in other cultures. For many of these people, getting ahead and achieving career success means moving on to another interesting, challenging, and satisfying international job. Someday they may have to return home to "settle down," but in the meantime many believe they are having the time of their lives; they want to continue this lifestyle indefinitely—as long as they can remain employed abroad in some type of job. Many work in jobs that are not particularly glamorous nor interesting, but their jobs enable them to do what they most enjoy— living abroad. Most are successful in changing jobs to continue their international lifestyles.

MOTIVATION AND REALITY

What concerns us most are the motivations and job search behavior exhibited by individuals who have never worked abroad but who want to "break into" the field. Many of these people are students who have some foreign language competency, have traveled or studied abroad, or pursued an international course of study. Others are ex-military personnel who have lived abroad but now want to become international consultants or literally "make big bucks" abroad to compensate them for their many lean years working for Uncle Sam. Many are ex-Peace Corps volunteers and medical personnel who have worked in health care and rural development for a few years and now want to find another interesting and personally rewarding international job. Some are frustrated State Department and USAID employees who work in organizations most recently noted for low morale and blocked career advancement opportunities. And some are construction workers —heavy equipment operators, electricians, carpenters—who have never worked abroad but who heard they can make big money in a hurry working abroad. We also hear from numerous entrepreneurs who seek our advice on developing contacts for importing products from the Asian and Pacific regions—unexpected contacts with individuals who have become attracted to our travel guides.

What motivates these people to pursue international jobs and careers or strike out on their own into an unfamiliar employment frontier? What is it they really want to do? How do they differ from the ordinary job seeker? The career and motivation patterns for experienced international workers are fairly evident. Many, for example, got started by accident rather than by design. They lived abroad as children of international workers or were military brats. Some signed up for the military or Peace Corps and received interesting assignments that convinced them that they should pursue an international career. Many began as students who took a course, joined a study program abroad, or just traveled abroad during their summer break. They found the international experience and lifestyle interesting, so much so that they wanted to do it full-time. Many journalists, corporate executives, and business people also got involved accidentally; many were transferred abroad as part of the corporate promotion process. Missionaries, Peace Corps Volunteers, development workers, and many government personnel seem to initially pursue international jobs and careers by design.

We also see patterns among those who are interested in "breaking into" the international jobs market. Many have totally unrealistic expectations and questionable motivations. Like perceptions of Hollywood, they see international jobs as being glamorous and high profile jobs that are well paid and result in major changes in peoples' lives and relations between nations. And as in Hollywood, there are a few such international jobs, but they are few and far between the many other types of less glamorous, low profile, and low to average paying jobs most commonly found abroad.

Let's take a look at some of the most common myths that motivate individuals to pursue jobs involving travel. Many of these same myths prevent individuals from achieving job search success. Several of the myths relate to the international job market and various steps in the job search process. By examining these myths and corresponding realities, we should get a clearer picture of our motivations and how to best organize ourselves for finding jobs involving travel.

MYTHS AND REALITIES

Jobs involving travel have a certain lure and mysticism which was once reserved for itinerant missionaries, anthropologists, and soldiers of fortune of decades ago. Indeed, there are probably more myths about such jobs than of any other type of work.

Most job seekers are unprepared and naive in approaching the job market; some might be best termed "job dumb." They play around the periphery of this job market with little success in penetrating it successfully. They muddle-through the job market with questionable perceptions of how it works. Combining facts, stereotypes, myths, and folklore—gained from a mixture of logic, experience, movies, nightly news reports, and advice from well-meaning friends and relatives— these perceptions lead job seekers down several unproductive paths. They are often responsible for the self-fulfilling prophecy and lament of the unsuccessful job seeker: *"There are no jobs available for me."*

Travel-Related Jobs

Some of the more important myths preventing individuals from finding jobs involving travel include:

MYTH 1:   **Jobs involving travel generally pay well.**

REALITY: It depends on the job. For example, many jobs in the travel industry, especially travel agents, are relatively low paying jobs. Even owners of a typical travel agency have relatively low earnings. But individuals in these jobs often receive numerous travel perks, such as free ("fam") trips and discounts on transportation and accommodations, to compensate for their low earnings. On the other hand, many sales positions involving travel pay well, depending on the sales performance of the individual.

MYTH 2:   **Jobs involving travel normally go to individuals with a great deal of work experience and numerous skills.**

REALITY: Again, it depends on the particular job. Many jobs involving travel are entry-level sales or marketing positions—new employees are required to travel in order to familiarize themselves with a regional, national, or international organization, clientele, and territory. Other jobs will be reserved for experienced personnel. This is particularly true in organizations with international offices. Generally only the most experienced personnel receive overseas assignments.

MYTH 3: **Jobs involving travel are generally more exciting and challenging than non-travel jobs.**

REALITY: This may be true for some jobs, but the excitement and challenge of jobs largely depends on the individual. Many jobs involving travel are boring—involve lots of airports, taxis, and hotels that all look the same after a few trips. After a while, many people in these so-called glamorous jobs yearn for a job involving little or no travel!

MYTH 4: **Most jobs involving travel are either in sales or international business.**

REALITY: The range of jobs involving travel is extremely large. Almost every occupation, be it teaching, accounting, engineering, or health care, has jobs involving different degrees of travel—both domestic and international.

MYTH 5: **Jobs involving travel are more difficult to find than jobs involving little or no travel.**

REALITY: You'll discover thousands of jobs involving travel. Indeed, at least one of every three jobs involves some degree of travel. If you develop a well organized job search focused around your major interests, skills, and abilities, you'll likely find the right travel-related job for you.

MYTH 6: **Individuals with extensive travel experience are more likely to get travel-related jobs than those with little or no travel experience.**

REALITY: Not necessarily so. Those who get these jobs generally have other important job-related skills. Travel is merely one of many means by which they are expected to perform their job or it becomes a job perk associated with certain types of positions.

MYTH 7: **Most jobs involving travel relate to international work and require traveling abroad.**

REALITY: The large majority of jobs involving travel are found at home rather than abroad. While many of these jobs may not seem as exotic or exciting as those involving international travel, they nonetheless provide numerous on-the-job travel opportunities.

International Jobs

Several other myths and realities relevant to jobs involving travel specifically focus on international jobs:

MYTH 8: **International employment pays extremely well compared to salaries in the States.**

REALITY The financial rewards of international employment vary greatly. Some jobs—especially international consulting—can pay very well. Jobs with many non-profit organizations as well as teaching English positions often pay poorly. For those living abroad, special financial benefits are often offset by additional expenses incurred in trying to maintain a certain lifestyle as well as lost opportunities for supplementing income, such as appreciation on property in the States or job opportunities for one's spouse.

MYTH 9: **International jobs are very challenging and interesting.**

REALITY Some international jobs are exciting, but many are dull and boring. The excitement tends to come from the lifestyle which involves traveling and learning about other cultures, eating different foods, meeting new and different people, and encountering unique events. Foreign Service Officers often end up stamping travel documents in some dreadful, hot and dirty capital city where the most exciting things to happen are to receive a letter from home, take a trip outside the country, acquire a new videotape, or check into a first-class hotel which has hot water and air conditioning. These are the events that make working and living abroad interesting for many people. They are often the subjects of peoples' "war stories" about *"how it was when we lived and worked abroad."*

MYTH 10: **International work involves exciting and sometimes exotic travel.**

REALITY: Travel is definitely a benefit for many individuals who have international jobs. However, the excitement of travel often wears off after age 40; after children reach high school age; after the third move in five years; after the tenth flight in a single year; and after the third lost suitcase and another terrifying taxicab ride from another chaotic airport. On the other hand, young, single people tend to disproportionately enjoy the novelty of international travel. Like all novelties, this one can wear off after awhile.

MYTH 11: **International development work is personally rewarding because of the positive changes one is able to make in the lives of others.**

REALITY: International development work is personally rewarding for individuals who can make a difference in the lives of others. But development work also is one of the most frustrating areas of international work. Few changes actually take place; the process tends to be very political; and development work

fails more often than it succeeds. Individuals working for the USAID missions in Third World countries, for example, are more likely to be preoccupied
with obligating funds and putting out brush fires on
problematic USAID projects than in making progress in development. For many people, development
work becomes more of a personal ego trip than one
of concrete long-term accomplishments. Satisfaction
comes more from "mingling with the locals"—
speaking the local language, eating the local foods,
laughing at the local jokes, and receiving the exaggerated status accorded to well-educated foreign
development workers.

MYTH 12:   **International lifestyles are better than back home.**

REALITY: International lifestyles vary considerably. Living
abroad can mean a large and comfortable home with
servants and a good international school for one's
children. But such comforts are often offset by daily
inconveniences of transportation and communication,
by poor health and recreation facilities, by cultures
which are best remembered rather than lived, and by
the unemployed spouse situation. In many countries
one spends a great deal of time on the basics of
living, such as shopping for food and getting from
point A to point B. Local health facilities may be
rudimentary or downright dangerous. And one's
spouse is likely to be unemployed—a recurring and
serious problem for two-career couples who have
chosen to live abroad and then find international
living a tremendous strain on their marriage, often
ending in divorce. Local cultures may place con-
straints on women. Consequently, adverse living
conditions may result in a low level of work output
and little professional development. For families
with teenage children, the international lifestyle
often becomes a serious liability because excellent
international high schools are only found in a few
countries. At this point in life, many people are

anxious to return home or be transferred to a country which has a good international school. Others get tired of international living. Added to these adverse conditions are safety considerations attendant with the continuing rise of international terrorism and anti-Americanism. Consequently, the international lifestyle is not for everyone nor is it for some people at particular stages in their lives.

MYTH 13: **It's easier to find an international job while traveling or living abroad than by networking or applying from the U.S.**

REALITY: From where one should best look for an international job depends on several factors. Expatriates living in-country often have an advantage in landing short-term contract jobs because of their location. Many companies prefer hiring someone already in the field for small jobs that may only involve $10,000 to $30,000 in labor expenses. It's cheaper to recruit such people than to transport someone from abroad to do these jobs. Consequently, expatriates will be in a good position to find many of these short-term jobs. On the other hand, many government agencies and companies prefer hiring their long-term field personnel from the States because they find a larger pool of qualified candidates based there. They have a bias for hiring individuals who are one-step removed from the local situation and who are more involved in the professional mainstream which is based back home rather than in some isolated location abroad. Most important of all, recruitment and hiring decisions tend to be centralized with headquarters staff. They publicize vacancies, interview candidates, and select the finalists. Living and working abroad tends to place one outside this centralized recruitment process. Ironically, expatriates living abroad are well advised to make regular trips back home in order to better position themselves in the international job market.

MYTH 14:   **One must have a great deal of international experience to get an international job.**

REALITY: It depends on the situation and the job. Many jobs require little or no international experience—only a specific or exotic skill that is difficult to find.

MYTH 15:   **Travel experience and language competency are essential to finding an international job.**

REALITY: This is one of the great myths of finding an international job. While travel, foreign languages, and international education may help you find a job, they are not necessarily prerequisites for entering the international job market. Indeed, many people break into this job market without such backgrounds. They possess other more important skills which are in demand. In many countries, English is the working language of international jobs. Knowing a foreign language may be crucial to one's job in some countries, such as Japan, China, Indonesia, and France, but not so for many jobs in other countries, such as Germany, Hong Kong, Singapore, the Philippines, or India.

MYTH 16:   **An international-related educational background is essential for finding an international job.**

REALITY: An international education may be helpful in better understanding the international arena, but it is no guarantee of gaining entrance to the job market. At best such an education will better help you network with others you meet in the international job market. The most important international courses to take will be business, especially in accounting and marketing, and foreign languages. History, art, culture, sociology, education, interdisciplinary Third World courses, and even international business may be interesting to take and will definitely enrich your stay abroad. But few such courses will directly help you find an international job since they have little skill content other than teaching the same courses to others either at home or abroad. At the same time, education in general is important for many international jobs, especially in cultures where "qualifications" are equated with higher educational degrees—regardless of the particular field of study. Education and qualifications have different meanings in different cultures. Thus, the higher one's educational level—measured as the possession of a B.A., M.A., or Ph.D.—the better your chances of landing an international job. In fact, international jobs are more sensitive to educational credentials and how they translate into status in other countries than to specific performance skills. All things being nearly equal, a candidate with an M.A. is more likely to be hired than someone with only a B.A. Therefore, the more educational credentials you can accumulate, the better positioned you should be in the international job market. Even a B.A. degree does not mean a great deal abroad these days.

MYTH 17: **Living and working abroad is dangerous.**

REALITY: It can be dangerous, but it seldom is. Living and working abroad may actually increase your safety quotient. It's much safer to work abroad than in many places in the U.S. where your chances of being in an accident, mugged, or killed are some of the highest in the world. However, some countries in the Middle East and Latin America have reputations as being dangerous for foreigners and particularly for Americans. If you work in one of these countries, you should take sensible precautions to ensure your safety, such as hiring guards and a driver, locking your doors, changing your daily routines, avoiding strange places, and never walking alone at night.

MYTH 18:   **There are few international jobs available today.**

REALITY: There are numerous international jobs available
today for those who know where they are and how
to find them. In fact, we expect to see the number of
international job opportunities increase steadily over
the next decade as the world economy becomes even
more interdependent, national boundaries become
more open, and populations move more easily
between countries. The basic problem is breaking
into what often appears to be a relatively closed job
market. If you shed many of your preconceptions of
the international job market, examine your motivations, develop an intelligent plan of action, and
simply persist with a well organized and focused
international job search, you should be able to join
millions of others who work in this fascinating job
and career arena.

MYTH 19:   **It's best to use an international job placement
service to get an international job.**

REALITY: You should be able to do just as well in finding an
international job on your own than by hiring some-
one to help you. In fact, many of these so-called
placement firms have bad reputations for exploiting
clients and engaging in fraudulent practices. Some
misrepresent their services by convincing vulnerable
job seekers that they have some special access to
international job vacancies and employers. Many
require up-front fees for the promise of helping you
find a job. Few do much more than mail your
resume to different organizations that have overseas
operations. This you can easily do on your own by
spending a few hours in your local library surveying
international directories and with the same results—
few if any invitations for interviews. The most
reliable firms are the "headhunters" and "executive
search" firms that are paid by employers to hire
specific types of individuals. If you follow the

advice of this book, you should have no problem penetrating the international job market and finding the job that best fits your interests, skills, and motivations. You will do much better than many firms that try to get you to buy into their questionable placement services. In the meantime, if you decide to use such a firm, be sure you carefully examine their performance record rather than accept their promises of performance. Paying up-front fees is a sure sign you are buying promises rather than paying for performance.

MYTH 20: **One has to have "connections" in order to break into the international job market. Whom you know is more important than what you can do.**

REALITY: While "connections" and knowing people are important to finding any job, and especially important when seeking an international job where information on job vacancies and opportunities is difficult to access, they are by no means essential. Your most important asset will be your marketable skills in a job market that places high value on unique job skills. How well you communicate your skills, experience, and motivations to employers—be it through resumes, letters, application forms, word-of-mouth, headhunters, executive search firms, classified ads, or contacts and "connections"—will largely determine your success in getting the job. You should use contacts and "connections" not because they are **the** way to get an international job. They are some of the most efficient and effective ways of communicating your availability and qualifications in a job market noted for being highly decentralized, fragmented, and chaotic. The system, or lack thereof, is not organized well for efficiently and effectively communicating job vacancy information nor linking qualified candidates with job vacancies. Therefore, your job is to organize your own system for best communicating your qualifications to

potential international employers. Contacts, "connections," and networking strategies should become
a few of your many methods for organizing this job
market around your qualifications.

MYTH 21:   **Most international jobs involve a great deal of
travel. An international job will enable me to see
and experience the world.**

REALITY: Many international jobs involve very little travel.
The most traveling you may ever do is when you
move from your home base to the job site abroad,
and then return for a home visit once or twice in a
two to three year period. Some international jobs
involve working in one location, sometimes isolated,
for one to two years at a time. If you are looking for
an international job because you particularly like to
travel, you may be better off looking for a job that
involves a great deal of travel. These jobs are most
likely found with headquarters staff, in international
sales, or in the travel industry. This is one of the
major mistakes some individuals make when choos-
ing to "go international" with their career. Their
major motivation for wanting an international job is
travel. They assume that international jobs involve
a great deal of travel to many interesting places or
such a job will give them an opportunity to do more
travel. They quickly learn they may have greater
opportunities for international travel had they stayed
home and found a good paying job with generous
vacation time or one that involved periodic travel
abroad. Whatever you do, don't assume an international job will give you more opportunities to travel.
It may or may not. If you really want to travel
abroad to many places, make international travel
your career or start your own international business.
An international job may result in getting stuck is
some undesirable location that neither gives you the
income nor time to do the travel you dreamed of
doing while living and working abroad. Always start

by examining your motivations for seeking an international job.

MYTH 22: **Most international jobs require moving and living abroad.**

REALITY: Many do but many others don't. Many international jobs are based in the United States and involve periodic travel to work sites abroad. International consultants and contractors, for example, may spend one to two months at a time on projects abroad, but their work base is back home. Educators, researchers, foundation employees, and business people often spend only a few weeks a year working abroad. Even employees of the State Department and USAID will spend much of their career in Washington, DC. City and state government employees involved in promoting tourism and trade are based in their home communities from where they conduct international business. In fact, many people enjoy their international jobs, careers, and lifestyles precisely because they have the best of both worlds— based at home and regularly travel and work abroad. They can still remain a part of their own society and communities while maintaining an exciting international career. In so doing, they avoid many of the hassles involved in full-time living and working abroad. Ironically, some of these people might change careers if their international jobs required lengthy residence abroad!

MYTH 23: **If one wants to work in the international arena, it's best to work for government or a multinational corporation.**

REALITY: Government agencies and multinational corporations do offer numerous international job opportunities, but they are only a few of the many players in the international job market. In fact, you may find some of the most interesting and rewarding jobs are found

with nonprofit organizations or nongovernmental
organizations (NGOs) and small or medium-size
businesses in the travel and hospitality industries. On
the other hand, you may discover being an international entrepreneur—either as some type of free-
lancer, independent consultant, or importer-export-
er—to be much more interesting than working for
others who will largely determine your work agenda
and your future in the international arena.

MYTH 24:   **The best international jobs are found within the
U.S. State Department and USAID or with the
United Nations.**

REALITY: These may be great jobs for some people, but they
aren't for others, including many present employees
who are looking for other more rewarding alternatives. While these high-profile organizations appear
to offer many international glamour jobs, in reality
competition is keen for these jobs and many are
disappointing, boring jobs. Morale is especially low
in the State Department and USAID because of
recent changes in the personnel systems that do not
reward international expertise and experience; career
rewards are given to those who can demonstrate
managerial expertise—a skill that requires little or
no demonstrated international or area expertise.
Benefits continue to erode as these agencies cutback
on traditional perks. Furthermore, many of the jobs
primarily involve the procurement process—from
obligating funds to monitoring contracts. Individuals
who go into these organizations with the expectation
of doing significant international work often are
disappointed in discovering they are primarily
pushing paper, stamping passports, monitoring
problematic projects, and financing contractors. The
"hands on" exciting international work is often
contracted-out to consultants, contractors, nonprofit
organizations, and universities. United Nations work,
while well paid, is often boring and very political.

Competition for jobs and promotions tends to follow nationalistic lines since a certain percentage of jobs are reserved for particular nationals. Many jobs are simply boring—involve little work content, numerous unproductive meetings, and a great deal of bureaucratic routines. If you are interested in getting things done, seeing the results of your international labors, and productivity and responsiveness, these organizations may not be appropriate for you. Indeed, many employees with these organizations often wonder whatever happened to the really interesting international jobs and exciting lifestyles they expected when joining the organizations. Few recommend their jobs to their friends or relatives. Needless to say, there are many other more interesting and rewarding international jobs than those found with these high-profile organizations.

MYTH 25: **The international hiring process seems to take forever. It takes longer to find an international job than to land a job back home.**

REALITY: This also depends on the situation. Some organizations, especially government and the United Nations, may take an extraordinary amount of time to fill a vacancy because of the large number of candidates applying for a position, numerous decision-making levels, and the need for security clearances. Other organizations may take a long time because they are looking for someone with a highly specialized or technical skill that is difficult to find even with the hiring of an executive search firm. But other organizations may do just the opposite—hire in a very short period of time. Since many of the organizations have few legal restrictions on their hiring practices—especially time consuming affirmative action and equal opportunity requirements—they have a great deal of flexibility in determining how they will hire. In short, they will do what they want and need to do. As soon as an impending vacancy becomes apparent, for example, hiring officials will literally "spread the word" within their old boy/girl networks to identify candidates who have the proper mix of skills, experience, and motivation for the job. This network may be very efficient in identifying the three top candidates within a matter of hours without having to hire a firm to recruit someone or list the vacancy in some publication or data bank. If you make yourself known by plugging into these networks, you may discover finding an international job takes less time than landing a domestic job. Therefore, it's extremely important that you learn how to effectively network for international job information, advice, and referrals—an essential skill for continuing international job and career success.

MYTH 26:   **It's difficult to start one's own international business in today's economy.**

REALITY: Depending on what you want to do as well as your entrepreneurial skills, it's relatively easy to get started and operational within a short period of time. All you need is some basic information, a business plan, contacts, and the resources to finance the initial stages of your venture. In fact, the coming decade should be an unparalleled period for international entrepreneurship as "development" of countries increasingly becomes defined in terms of encouraging greater foreign investment, joint ventures, and import-export arrangements. Government agencies are becoming increasingly oriented toward encouraging and promoting private business involvement abroad, from large multinationals to small businesses and individual entrepreneurs. If you love to travel, and also want to have an international dimension to your career, starting your own business may be an ideal solution to the "international career" question.

MYTH 27: **The job search techniques that work for finding a domestic job also work well for finding an international job.**

REALITY: Some do but many don't because they are based upon a culturally-biased model of achieving career success in the American job market. They assume that job applicants are primarily motivated to get jobs they do well and enjoy doing and then make job moves that demonstrate career growth and advancement. Such skilled and motivated people are supposed to be oriented toward career success. However, many international job applicants could care less about such career success. Many of them are primarily oriented toward experiencing adventure and unique experiences as well as pursuing ideas, causes, challenges, and lifestyles. If an international career somehow develops from these experiences and pursuits, so be it. But success measured in terms of positions, money, and advancement up someone's organizational hierarchy is a cultural bias implicit in the standard career planning and job search models used by most career counselors.

MYTH 28: **It's best to learn about other cultures and adjust one's behavior to meet the local expectations. The more I act like the locals, the easier it will be for me and my job.**

REALITY: Yes, you should understand and be sensitive to other cultures. But it's not necessary to go to extremes by always behaving like the locals. Indeed, many people become overly sensitive to other cultures and engage in silly behaviors that are even embarrassing to the locals who aren't sure who such foreigners think they are! Other cultures have expectations for both foreigners and expatriates which are not the same as for the locals. As such, you are permitted to be different as long as you are not offensive. If you try to "go bush" you may not be respected as much as when you maintain your own identity. In addition, today's "global village" is changing rapidly and thus it's difficult to know exactly what the local expectations are for foreigners and expatriates. Furthermore, the international business, government and development cultures have increasingly become Americanized. Except for a few local cultural peculiarities, you should be able to adjust well to an international employment culture without having to "go native." Your identity should always be an asset when functioning in the international job market. Just don't become obnoxious and offensive.

The Job Search

And several other myths and realities directly relate to the job finding process. Taken together, they comprise a set of principles for conducting an effective job search. These myths illustrate important points for organizing and implementing your job search. These principles are outlined in several popular books on job finding strategies and techniques. The following 25 myths and realities should help you launch a successful search for a job involving travel:

MYTH 29:   **Anyone can find a job; all you need to know is how to find a job.**

REALITY: This "form versus substance" myth is often associated with career counselors who were raised on popular career planning exhortations of the 1970s and 1980s that stressed the importance of having positive attitudes and self-esteem, setting goals, dressing for success, and using interpersonal strategies for finding jobs. While such approaches may work well in an industrial society with low unemployment, they constitute myths in a post-industrial, high-tech society which requires employees to demonstrate both **intelligence and concrete work skills** as well as a **willingness to relocate** to new communities offering greater job opportunities. For example, many of today's unemployed are skilled in the old technology of the industrial society, and they live and own homes in economically depressed communities. These people lack the necessary **skills and mobility** required for getting jobs in high-tech, growth communities. Knowing job search skills alone will not help these people. Indeed, such advice and knowledge will most likely frustrate such highly motivated and immobile individuals who possess skills of the old technology.

MYTH 30: **The best way to find a job is to respond to classified ads, use employment agencies, and submit applications to personnel offices.**

REALITY: Except for certain types of organizations, such as government, these formal application procedures are not the most effective ways of finding jobs. Such approaches assume the presence of an organized, coherent, and centralized job market—but no such thing exists. The job market is highly decentralized, fragmented, and chaotic. Classified ads, employment agencies, and personnel offices tend to list low paying yet highly competitive jobs or high paying highly skilled positions that are hard to fill. Most of the best jobs—high level, excellent pay, least competitive—are neither listed nor advertised; they are most likely found through word-of-mouth. Your most fruitful strategy will be to conduct research and informational interviews on what career counselors call the "hidden job market."

MYTH 31: **Few jobs are available for me in today's competitive job market.**

REALITY: This may be true if you lack marketable skills and insist on applying for jobs listed in newspapers, employment agencies, or personnel offices. Competition in the advertised job market usually is high, especially for jobs requiring few skills. Numerous jobs with little competition are available on the hidden job market. Jobs requiring advanced technical skills often go begging. Little competition may occur during periods of high unemployment, because many people quit job hunting after a few disappointing weeks of concentrating job search efforts on working the advertised job market.

MYTH 32:   **I know how to find a job, but opportunities are not available for me.**

REALITY: Most people don't know the best way to find a job, or they lack marketable job skills. They continue to use ineffective job search methods. Opportunities are readily available for individuals who understand the structure and operation of the job market, have appropriate work-content skills, and use job search methods designed for the hidden job market.

MYTH 33:   **Employers are in the driver's seat; they have the upper-hand with applicants.**

REALITY: Most often no one is in the driver's seat. Not knowing what they want, many employers make poor hiring decisions. They frequently let applicants define their hiring needs. If you can define employers' needs as your skills, you might end up in the driver's seat!

MYTH 34:   **Employers hire the best qualified candidates. Without a great deal of experience and numerous qualifications, I don't have a chance.**

REALITY: Employers hire people for all kinds of reasons. Most rank experience and qualifications third or fourth in their pecking order of hiring criteria. Employers seldom hire the best qualified candidate, because "qualifications" are difficult to define and measure. Employers normally seek people with the following characteristics: competent, intelligent, honest, enthusiastic, and likable. "Likability" tends to be an overall concern of employers—will you "fit in" and get along well with your superiors, co-workers, and clients?

Employers want **value** for their money. Therefore, you must communicate to employers that you are such a person. You must overcome employers' objections to any lack of experience or qualifications. But never volunteer your weaknesses. The best qualified person is the one who knows how to get the job—convinces employers that he or she is the **most** desirable for the job.

MYTH 35: **It is best to go into a growing field where jobs are plentiful.**

REALITY: Be careful in following the masses to the "in" fields. First, many so-called growth fields can quickly become no-growth fields, such as aerospace engineering, nuclear energy, and defense contracting. Second, by the time you acquire the necessary skills, you may experience the "disappearing job" phenomenon: too many people did the same thing you did and consequently glut the job market. Third, since many people leave no-growth fields, new opportunities may arise for you. Fourth, if you go after a growth field, you will try to fit into a job rather than find a job fit for you. If you know what you do well and enjoy doing, and what additional training you may need, you should look for a job or career conducive to your particular mix of skills, interests, and motivations. In the long-run you will be much happier and more productive finding a job fit for you.

MYTH 36: **People over 40 have difficulty finding a good job.**

REALITY: Yes, if they apply for youth jobs. Age should be an insignificant barrier to employment if you conduct a well organized job search and are prepared to handle this potential negative with employers. Age should be a positive and must be communicated as such. After all, employers want experience, maturity, and stability. People over 40 generally possess these qualities. As the population ages and birth rates decline, older individuals should have a much easier time changing jobs and careers.

MYTH 37: **It's best to use an employment firm to find a job.**

REALITY: It depends on the firm and the nature of employment you are seeking. Employment firms that specialize in your skill area may be well worth contacting. For example, many law firms use employment firms to hire paralegals rather than directly recruit such personnel themselves. Many employers now use temporary employment firms to recruit both temporary and full-time employees at several different levels, from clerical to professional. Indeed, many temporary employment firms have temp-to-perm programs that link qualified candidates to employers who are looking for full-time employees. But make sure you are working with a legitimate employment firm. Legitimate firms get paid by employers or they collect placement fees from applicants only **after** the applicant has accepted a position. Beware of firms that want up-front fees for promised job placement assistance.

MYTH 38: **I must be aggressive in order to find a job.**

REALITY: Aggressive people tend to be offensive and obnoxious people. Try being purposeful, persistent, and pleasant in all job search activities. Such behavior is well received by potential employers!

MYTH 39: **I should not change jobs and careers more than once or twice. Job-changers are discriminated against in hiring.**

REALITY: While this may have been generally true 30 years ago, it is no longer true today. America is a skills-based society: individuals market their skills to organizations in exchange for money and position. Furthermore, since most organizations are small businesses with limited advancement opportunities, careers quickly plateau for most people. For them, the only way up is to get out and into another organization. Therefore, the best way to advance careers in a society of small businesses is to change jobs frequently. Job-changing is okay as long as such changes demonstrate career advancement and one isn't changing jobs every few months. Most individuals entering the job market today will undergo several career and job changes regardless of their initial desire for a one-job, one-career life plan.

MYTH 40: **People get ahead by working hard and putting in long hours.**

REALITY: Success patterns differ. Many people who are honest, work hard, and put in long hours also get fired, have ulcers, and die young. Some people get ahead even though they are dishonest and lazy. Others simply have good luck or a helpful patron. Moderation in both work and play will probably get you just as far as the extremes. There are other ways, as outlined near the end of this chapter, to become successful in addition to hard work and long hours.

MYTH 41: **I should not try to use contacts or connections to get a job. I should apply through the front door like everyone else. If I'm the best qualified, I'll get the job.**

REALITY: While you may wish to stand in line for tickets, bank deposits, and loans—because you have no clout—standing in line for a job is dumb. Every employer has a front door as well as a back door. Try using the back door if you can. It works in many cases. Networking strategies and techniques will help you develop your contacts, use connections, and enter **both** the front and back doors.

MYTH 42: **I need to get more education and training to qualify for today's jobs.**

REALITY: You may or may not need more education and training, depending on your present skill levels and the needs of employers. What many employers are looking for are individuals who are intelligent, communicate well, take initiative, and are trainable; they train their employees to respond to the needs of their organization. You first need to know what skills you already possess and if they appear appropriate for the types of jobs you are seeking.

MYTH 43: **Once I apply for a job, it's best to wait to hear from an employer.**

REALITY: Waiting is not a good job search strategy. If you want action on the part of the employer, you must first take action. The key to getting a job interview and offer is follow-up, follow-up, follow-up. You do this by making follow-up telephone calls as well as writing follow-up and thank you letters to employers.

MYTH 44: **A good resume is the key to getting a job.**

REALITY: While resumes play an important role in the job search process, they are often overrated. The purpose of a resume is to communicate your qualifications to employers who, in turn, invite you to job interviews. The key to getting a job is the job interview. No job interview, no job offer.

MYTH 45: **I should include my salary expectations on my resume or in my cover letter.**

REALITY: You should never include your salary expectations on your resume or in a cover letter, unless specifically requested to do so. Salary should be the very last thing you discuss with a prospective employer. You do so only after you have had a chance to assess the worth of the position and communicate your value to the employer. This usually comes at the end of your final job interview, just before or after being offered the job. If you prematurely raise the salary issue, you may devalue your worth.

MYTH 46: **My resume should emphasize my work history.**

REALITY: Employers are interested in hiring your future rather than your past. Therefore, your resume should emphasize the skills and abilities you will bring to the job as well as your interests and goals. Let employers know what you are likely to do for them in the future. When you present your work history, do so in terms of your major skills and accomplishments.

MYTH 47: **It's not necessary to write letters to employers— just send a resume or complete an application.**

REALITY: You should be prepared to write several types of job search letters—cover, approach, resume, thank you, follow-up, and acceptance. In addition to communicating your level of literacy, these job search letters enable you to express important values sought by employers—your tactfulness, thoughtfulness, likability, enthusiasm, and follow-up ability. Sending a resume without a cover letter devalues both your resume and your application.

MYTH 48: **Salaries are pre-determined by employers.**

REALITY: Most salaries are negotiable within certain ranges and limits. Before you ever apply or interview for a position, you should know what the salary range is for the type of position you seek. When you finally discuss the salary question—preferably at the end of the final job interview—do so with this range in mind. Assuming you have adequately demonstrated your value to the employer, try to negotiate the highest possible salary within the range.

MYTH 49: **It's best to relocate to an economically booming community.**

REALITY: Similar to the "disappearing job" phenomenon for college majors, today's economically booming communities may be tomorrow's busts. It's best to select a community that is conducive to your lifestyle preferences as well as has a sufficiently diversified economy to weather boom and bust economic cycles.

MYTH 50: **It's best to broadcast or "shotgun" my resume to as many employers as possible.**

REALITY: Broadcasting your resume to employers is a game of chance in which you usually waste your time and money. It's always best to target your resume on those employers who have vacancies or who might have openings in the near future. Your single best approach for uncovering job leads will be the process called networking.

MYTH 53: **Electronic resumes are the wave of the future. You must have one in order to get a good job.**

Electronic resumes are one of several types of resumes that are proliferating on today's new information highway. While over 90 percent of all resumes received by employers are conventional paper resumes, new electronic resumes are increasingly important for job seekers and employers alike. More and more employers use the latest resume scanning technology to quickly screen hundreds of resumes. Therefore, it also may be in your interest to write a "computer friendly" resume based on the principles of electronic resumes. These principles, along with examples, are outlined in two new books on this subject—Peter D. Weddle, *Electronic Resumes for the New Job Market: Resumes That Work for You 24 Hours a Day* (Impact Publications, 1995) and Joyce Lain Kennedy, *Electronic*

Resume Revolution (Wiley, 1994). These are very different resumes compared to conventional resumes. Structured around "keywords" or nouns which stress capabilities, electronic resumes may be excellent candidates for resume scanners but weak documents for human readers. Keep in mind that electronic resumes are primarily written for electronic scanners and high-tech distribution systems (job banks) rather than for human beings. Since human beings interview and hire, you should first create a high impact resume that follows the principles of human communication and intelligence. We also recommend developing a separate electronic resume designed for electronic scanners. At the same time, conventional and electronic resumes are not the only types of resumes being produced today. Some individuals now produce live action **video resumes**. Somewhat of a misnomer, video resumes are more on-screen interviews or summaries of qualifications rather than actual resumes. New electronic technology also has given rise to the **multimedia resume** which blends sound, graphics, animation, and text. Indeed, software is now available (Macromedia's *Director* and *Action!* and Apple's *HyperCard*) which enables you to produce the ultimate multimedia resume—a real plus for anyone in the field of graphics and design. Also, several online services, such as America Online and CompuServe and Internet's Online Career Center, permit users to submit multimedia resumes via electronic mail (for Internet's Online Career Center, E-mail your request to occ-info@occ.com or call 317/293-6499). What is common to many of these new types of resumes is that they can be transmitted via fax or a modem.

MYTH 54: **Individuals who join resume banks are more likely to get high paying jobs than those that don't.**

Electronic resume banks, such as Job Bank USA, SkillSearch, and University Pronet, offer alternative ways of distributing resumes to employers. Essentially a high-tech approach to broadcasting resumes, membership in one of these groups means your resume literally works 24 hours a day. Major employers increasingly use these resume banks for locating qualified candidates, especially for screening individuals with technical skills. And we know some individuals who join these resume banks do get jobs. However, not everyone belonging to these groups get interviews or jobs because of such membership. Nor is there evidence that membership results in higher paying jobs than nonmembership. The real advantage of such groups is this: they open new channels for contacting employers with whom you might not otherwise come into contact. Indeed, some employers only use these resume banks for locating certain types of candidates rather than use more traditional channels, such as newspapers and employment offices, for advertising positions and recruiting candidates. Therefore, it might be wise for you to join one of these groups. They could well open up new job leads you would not otherwise uncover.

MYTH 55:   **Telecommunication systems such as CompuServe, Prodigy, and America Online, with access to the Internet, are a great new way to find quality jobs.**

This job search method gets very mixed reviews. It's a new and relatively uncharted frontier run by a lot of high-tech cowboys and technicians who know little about the content of specialty communications, especially the art of job finding. There's a lot of hype and hoopla about conducting an electronic job search as well as using such information-saturated telecommunication systems. It's still uncertain whether many of these telecommunication systems are more information distractions and time-killers than truly useful and usable databases for most individuals, and especially for job seekers. Many of these systems approximate a game of chance, with slim odds of getting really useful information. Nonetheless, you may get lucky by trying your hand at venturing into this uncertain frontier. At present this job search channel is relatively unstructured, chaotic, and loaded with useless noise, questionable "authorities", and few quality job listings and employers. It's uncertain if many people get jobs by using this new technology and the so-called "information highway." Many advertised jobs on electronic bulletin boards are probably hard-to-fill positions—similar to positions found in classified job ads—or for individuals with high-tech skills. The most useful outcome of this telecommunication channel may be to get information and advice from individuals who are knowledgeable about your particular job field and interests. Information found in many job search books, usually in the form of excerpts, is now available through many of these services. Indeed, excerpts from several of our own books can be found on E-Span Job Search (800/682-2901), a free service on the Internet or through CompuServe, which includes nearly 150 employers and 3,500 job seekers who submit resumes through E-mail. But the quality and quantity of such information is unpredictable and short-lived. It depends on whom you encounter at any particular moment. But be careful. Do not become obsessed with this technology to the point where you spend a disproportionate amount of your job search time trying to telecommunicate for jobs. Use your phone and computer modem to plug into this information highway, but keep it in proper perspective. Our advice: don't spend more than 15 percent of your job search time on the computer. This new technology tends to disproportionately appeal to high-tech candidates and to individuals, especially men, who have a simplistic view of how to get a job—a quick and easy method at the tip of their fingers or with the lick of a postage stamp. The job search is much more complicated and requires a great deal of telephone, mail, and face-to-face work. In the meantime, it doesn't hurt to explore emerging opportunities on the new information highway, such as those found on Internet's Online Career Center, for job leads and vacancy announcements. We expect it will take at least five years before the electronic job search becomes a useful reality. And we expect services on the Internet will become the main players rather than America Online, CompuServe, or Prodigy which we see as transitional systems. Keep an eye on a newly formed service called CareerWeb which will be available on the Internet beginning in May 1995. CareerWeb is likely to become a long-term player in this highly competitive online career business. In the meantime, three useful books on this subject are Joyce Lain Kennedy's *Electronic Job Search Revolution* and *Hook Up, Get Hired* (Wiley) and James Gonyea's *The On-Line Job Search Companion* (McGraw-Hill).

You also should be aware of several other realities which will affect your job search or which you might find helpful in developing your plan of action for finding a job or changing a career:

- **You will find less competition for high-level jobs than for middle and low-level jobs.** If you aim high yet are realistic, you may be pleasantly surprised with the results.

- **Personnel offices seldom hire.** They primarily screen candidates for employers who are found in operating units of organizations. Knowing this, you should focus your job search efforts on those who do the actual hiring.

- **Politics are both ubiquitous and dangerous in many organizations.** If you think you are above politics, you may quickly become one of its victims. Unfortunately, you only learn about "local politics" **after** you accept a position and begin relating to the different players in the organization.

- **It is best to narrow or "rifle" your job search on particular organizations and individuals rather than broaden or "shotgun" it to many targets.** If you remain focused, you will be better able to accomplish your goals.

- **Employment firms and personnel agencies may not help you.** Most work for employers and themselves rather than for applicants. Few have your best interests at heart. Use them only after you have investigated their effectiveness. Avoid firms that require up-front money for a promise of performance.

- **Most people can make satisfying job and career changes.** They should minimize efforts in the advertised job market and concentrate instead on planning and implementing a well organized job search tailored to the realities of the hidden job market.

- **Jobs and careers tend to be fluid and changing.** Knowing this, you should concentrate on acquiring and marketing skills, talents, and abilities which can be transferred from one job to another.

- **Millions of job vacancies are available every day** because new jobs are created every day, and people resign, retire, get fired, or die.

- **Most people, regardless of their position or status, love to talk about their work and give advice** to both friends and strangers. You can learn the most about job opportunities and alternative careers by talking to such people.

As you conduct your job search, you will encounter many of these and other myths and realities about how you should relate to the job market. Several people will give you advice. While much of this advice will be useful, a great deal of it will be useless and misleading. You should be skeptical of well-meaning individuals who most likely

will reiterate the same job and career myths. You should be particularly leery of those who try to **sell** you their advice. Always remember
you are entering a relatively disorganized and chaotic job market
where you can find numerous job opportunities. Your task is to
organize the chaos around your skills and interests. You must
convince prospective employers that they will like you more than
other "qualified" candidates.

ADVANTAGES AND DISADVANTAGES

The preceding myths and realities provide a glimpse into some of the
perceived advantages and disadvantages that motivate individuals to
pursue jobs involving travel. They may raise important questions
about your own motivations and desire to pursue such jobs. The major
motivations most job seekers exhibit appear to be:

1. **Money:** Everybody wants it but only a few people really
   make big money in jobs and careers involving travel. The
   biggest money is usually made by people who manage other
   peoples' money—the investors, bankers, and venture
   capitalists who operate on percentages and at high risk
   levels. Many international jobs pay excellent salaries which
   may also be exempt from federal, state, and local taxes back
   home (first $70,000 is exempt from federal taxes if one
   lives abroad for at least 11 consecutive months). This tax
   break applies to private sector employees living and working
   abroad. Federal government employees working abroad are
   not exempt from federal taxes, and many private sector employees must pay taxes to their countries of residence. But
   given additional housing and living adjustment benefits, as
   well as lower costs of living in many countries, many
   individuals working abroad do well financially. Comparable
   jobs back home may pay less and have fewer benefits.

2. **Adventure:** Especially for young, restless, inexperienced,
   and single individuals, jobs involving travel can be very
   exciting, especially travel abroad. Working in Latin America, Africa, Europe, the Middle East, or Asia is for some
   people the last great frontier. New places and different
   cultures become extremely life enriching experiences.

3. **Curiosity:** Jobs involving travel are objects of curiosity for many people who always thought about having jobs involving a great deal of mobility. They may feel it is now time to do something different in their lives, so they decide to try a job involving travel to see what it's all about.

4. **Pursue a cause:** Several public causes can be pursued through international employment. Many individuals want to promote U.S. foreign policy, international peace, population planning, environmental control, and rural development. Numerous government agencies, private development organizations, religious groups, and nonprofit organizations are organized to pursue such causes.

5. **New challenges:** International work does offer new and unusual challenges, from basic living to getting a job done. Individuals often find such work challenges their basic assumptions about people as well as work itself.

6. **Lifestyle:** Many individuals are motivated to acquire jobs involving travel because of the seemingly attractive lifestyle. The work itself may bring them into contact with new and interesting cultures; the work may change constantly; and they are given an extraordinary amount of status and authority—the "big fish in a small pond" phenomenon—not commonly found with many jobs in the United States. Indeed, exaggerated status and bloated egos are widespread among many international workers.

7. **Travel:** Many people are hopelessly addicted to travel. Like clockwork, every three, six, or twelve months they have a burning desire to take to the road to discover new and exciting places. Many of these people believe it may be best to incorporate their travel addiction into a job or career that involves frequent travel.

8. **Escape and revitalization:** Some people wish to escape from their present jobs and careers which are basically boring, deadend, and unrewarding. Some are even unemployed individuals seeking jobs involving travel. They

believe such a job will be the antidote to revitalizing their careers and achieving renewed career success and personal happiness.

Those who work long-term in jobs involving travel often find the advantages outweigh the disadvantages in defining their motivations to continue pursuing such types of jobs and careers. In addition, many long-term international workers don't know what else they could or would do if they left this employment arena. Therefore, they see no other alternatives to their career and lifestyle.

BECOMING SUCCESSFUL ABROAD

Jobs involving travel abroad are not for everyone. Most organizations working in this arena identify a particular type of individual who is best suited for international work. These people tend to have the following characteristics:

1. **Adaptability and flexibility:** Willing to adapt to changing circumstances and adjust to the norms of the situation.

2. **Tolerance and empathy:** Listen to others, understand their behavior, accept different behaviors as legitimate, tolerate ambiguities, be open-minded, and respect others' beliefs.

3. **Sensitivity to cultural differences:** Adjust to cultural differences without going "native"; maintain one's own identity.

4. **Patience and perseverance:** Balance the American work ethics of punctuality, productivity, and getting things done now with work cultures that place higher value on maintaining and expanding power, developing harmonious interpersonal relations, avoiding face-to-face confrontations, and solving problems through consensus rather than through other rational decision-making techniques.

5. **Humor:** Maintain a sense of humor especially in situations which are sometimes frustrating; don't take oneself too

seriously. Many cultures respond well to people who always wear a friendly smile and an attitude of fun and humor.

6. **Curiosity:** Be open to new experiences, willing to learn, and accepting of new and unfamiliar patterns.

7. **Self-confidence and initiative:** Be willing to take initiative without being offensive or threatening the power of others. Entrepreneurs who are also sensitive to local decision-making practices are highly valued in the international arena.

8. **Facility in foreign languages:** Especially for individuals living and working in countries where the local language is important to day-to-day business, they should have some ability to learn a second or third language.

While these characteristics are common among many individuals who work in the international arena, there is also a negative side to them. Indeed, there is a fine line between being tolerant, sensitive, and patient, and being useless on the job. Some individuals adjust **too** well and thus accomplish little or nothing other than "enjoy" their international lifestyles. For many career-oriented professionals, international employment can take a serious toll on their professional development.

PREREQUISITES FOR SUCCESS

How successful you will be in landing a job involving travel as well as continuing in such employment depends on several factors that relate to you as an individual as well as the organizations offering job opportunities. Like any job, jobs involving travel have advantages and disadvantages, positives and negatives, ups and downs. Some people are fortunate enough to find jobs they really love. Many become obsessed with their work to the exclusion of all other interests and pursuits. Most people, however, find jobs that are okay but nothing particularly special or exciting. They are not unhappy with their jobs nor are they particularly happy with them. To many, a job is a job is a job; its advantages outweigh possible disadvantages of not having the job at all.

However, we do know what leads to job search success both at home and abroad. Success is determined by more than just a good plan getting implemented. It is not predetermined nor is it primarily achieved by intelligence, thinking big, time management, or luck. Based upon experience, theory, research, and common sense, we believe you will achieve career planning success by following many of these 20 principles:

1. **You should work hard at finding a job involving travel:** Make this a daily endeavor and involve your family. Spend the necessary time conducting research on employers offering on-the-job travel opportunities.

2. **You should not be discouraged with setbacks:** You are playing the odds, so expect disappointments and handle them in stride. You will get many *"no's"* before finding the one *"yes"* which is right for you. Expect to receive twice as many rejections for international jobs than for domestic jobs simply because of the more competitive nature of international jobs. This means you may have to work twice as hard in overcoming the rejections. If you are unable to deal with rejections as part of the game, you will be headed for trouble. Try to turn negatives into positives. Learn from them, leave them, but remember them as stepping stones to future acceptances.

3. **You should be patient and persevere:** Expect three to six months of hard work before you connect with a job involving travel that's right for you.

4. **You should be honest with yourself and others:** Honesty is always the best policy, but don't be naive and stupid by volunteering your negatives and shortcomings to others.

5. **You should develop a positive attitude toward yourself and others:** Nobody wants to employ guilt-ridden people with inferiority complexes. At the same time, neither do they want to hire self-centered individuals. Focus on your positive characteristics as well as the employer's needs.

6. **You should associate with positive and successful people:** Finding a job involving travel largely depends on how well you relate to others and how effectively you engage your networking skills. Avoid associating with negative and depressing people who complain and have a *"you-can't-do-it"* attitude. Run with winners who have a positive *"can-do"* outlook on life.

7. **You should set goals:** You should have a clear idea of what you want and where you are going. Without these, you will present a confusing and indecisive image to others. Clear goals help direct your job search into productive channels. Moreover, setting high goals will help make you work hard in getting what you want.

8. **You should plan:** Convert your goals into action steps that are organized as short, intermediate, and long-range plans.

9. **You should get organized:** Translate your plans into activities, targets, names, addresses, telephone numbers, and materials. Develop an efficient and effective filing system and use a large calendar for setting time targets and recording appointments and useful information.

10. **You should be a good communicator:** Take stock of your oral, written, and verbal and nonverbal communication skills. How well do you communicate? Since most aspects of your job search involve communicating with others, and communication skills are one of the most sought-after skills, always present yourself well both verbally and nonverbally.

11. **You should be energetic and enthusiastic:** Employers are attracted to positive people. They don't like negative and depressing people who toil at their work. Generate enthusiasm both verbally and nonverbally. Check on your telephone voice—it may be less enthusiastic than your voice in face-to-face situations.

12. **You should ask questions:** Your best information comes from asking questions. Learn to develop intelligent questions

that are non-aggressive, polite, and interesting to others. But don't ask too many questions.

13. **You should be a good listener:** Being a good listener is often more important than being a good questioner and talker. Learn to improve your face-to-face listening behavior (nonverbal cues) as well as remember and use information gained from others. Make others feel they enjoyed talking with you, because you are one of the few people who actually **listens** to what they say.

14. **You should be polite, courteous, and thoughtful:** Treat gatekeepers, especially receptionists and secretaries, like human beings. Avoid being aggressive or too assertive. Try to be polite, courteous, and gracious. Your social graces are being observed. Remember to send thank you letters—a very thoughtful thing to do in a job search. Even if rejected, thank employers for the "opportunity" given to you. After all, they may later remember you for additional opportunities.

15. **You should be tactful:** Watch what you say to others about other people and your background. Don't be a gossip, backstabber, or confessor.

16. **You should maintain a professional stance:** Be neat in what you do and wear, and speak with the confidence, authority, and maturity of a professional.

17. **You should demonstrate your intelligence and competence:** Present yourself as someone who gets things done and achieves results—a **producer**. Employers generally seek people who are bright, hard working, responsible, can communicate well, have positive personalities, maintain good interpersonal relations, are likeable, observe dress and social codes, take initiative, are talented, possess expertise in particular areas, use good judgment, are cooperative, trustworthy, and loyal, generate confidence and credibility, and are conventional. In other words, they like people who score in the "excellent" to "outstanding" categories of the annual performance evaluation. Many want God!

18. **You should not overdo your job search:** Don't engage in overkill and bore everyone with your "job search" stories. Achieve balance in everything you do. Occasionally take a few days off to do nothing related to your job search. Develop a system of incentives and rewards—such as two free days a week, if you accomplish targets A, B, C, and D.

19. **You should be open-minded and keep an eye open for "luck":** Too much planning can blind you to unexpected and fruitful opportunities. You should welcome serendipity. Learn to re-evaluate your goals and strategies. Seize new opportunities if they appear appropriate.

20. **You should evaluate your progress and adjust:** Take two hours once every two weeks and evaluate what you are doing and accomplishing. If necessary, tinker with your plans and reorganize your activities and priorities. Don't become too routinized and thereby kill creativity and innovation.

These principles should provide you with an initial orientation for starting your travel-related job search. As you become more experienced, you will develop your own set of operating principles that should work for you in particular employment situations.

TAKE TIME TO SAIL

Let's assume you have the necessary skills to open the doors to employers for the job you want. Your next step is to organize an effective job search. Organization, however, does not mean a detailed plan, blueprint, or road map for taking action. If you strictly adhere to such a plan, you will most likely be disappointed with the outcomes. Instead, your job search should approximate the art of sailing—you know where you want to go and the general direction for getting there. But the specific path, as well as the time of reaching your destination, will be determined by your environment, situation, and skills. Like the sailor dependent upon his or her sailing skills and environmental conditions, you tack back and forth, progressing within what is considered to be an acceptable time period for successful completion of the task.

While we recommend planning your job search, we hope you will avoid the excesses of too much planning. The plan should not become the **end**—it should be a flexible **means** for achieving your stated job and career goals. Planning makes sense, because it requires you to set goals and develop strategies for achieving the goals. However, too much planning can blind you to unexpected occurrences and opportunities, or that wonderful experience called **serendipity**.

---

*The plan should not become the end—
it should be a flexible means
for achieving your goals.*

We outline on page 65 a hypothetical plan for conducting an effective job search. This plan incorporates seven distinct but interrelated job search activities over a six month period. If you phase in the first four job search steps during the initial three to four weeks, and continue the final four steps in subsequent weeks and months, you should begin receiving job offers within two to three months after initiating your job search. Interviews and job offers can come at any time—often unexpectedly—during your job search. An average time is three months, but it can occur within a week or take as long as five months. During the recession of 1991-1993, international job seekers reported taking a longer time to complete their job searches than in the previous two-year period. Recessions can easily add two to three months to a job search.

While three months may seem a long time, you can shorten your job search time by increasing the frequency of each job search activity. If you are job hunting on a full-time basis, you may be able to cut your job search time in half. But don't expect to get a professional level job quickly. It requires time, hard work, and persistence.

This hypothetical time frame is generally applicable to most domestic jobs. The time frame for international jobs, however, may be longer given the logistics of recruiting and hiring. In some cases, the selection process will take a long time because the organization will need to narrow a large number of candidates in order to interview only

ORGANIZATION OF JOB SEARCH ACTIVITIES

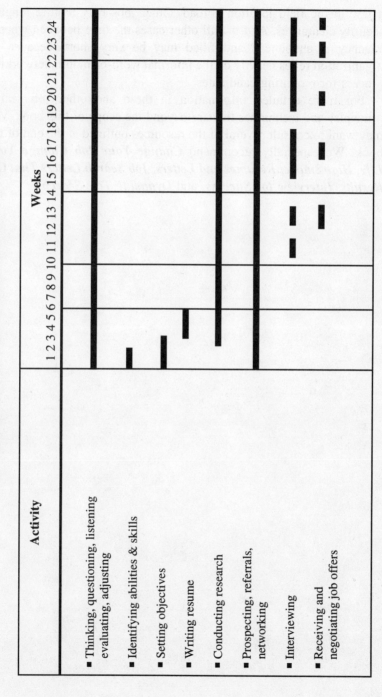

Activity	Weeks: 1 2 3 4 5 6 7 8 9 10 11 12 13 14 15 16 17 18 19 20 21 22 23 24
▪ Thinking, questioning, listening evaluating, adjusting	
▪ Identifying abilities & skills	
▪ Setting objectives	
▪ Writing resume	
▪ Conducting research	
▪ Prospecting, referrals, networking	
▪ Interviewing	
▪ Receiving and negotiating job offers	

a few in the field location abroad. Other jobs may require lengthy security clearances. And in still other cases the time between when a vacancy is announced and filled may be very short, because an organization relies heavily on the informal word-of-mouth networking process for recruiting candidates.

For more detailed information in these and other job search principles and techniques that are beyond the scope of this book, you may want to consult several of the resources outlined at the end of the book. We especially recommend *Change Your Job Change Your Life, High Impact Resumes and Letters, Job Search Letters That Get Results, Interview for Success,* and *Dynamite Tele-Search.*

4

TRAVEL AND HOSPITALITY INDUSTRY

*I*f you want a job involving travel, there's no better industry to direct your job search sights on than the travel industry. After all, the travel industry does exactly what you want to do—engages in a lot of travel. And you'll often travel free or receive major discounts on transportation to and accommodations at your favorite destinations. Your friends and acquaintances will most likely think you have a "really tough job" —probably the best around. They'll think you either receive some great job perks or you have a job that gives you terrific tax write-offs!

While many myths characterize working for the travel and hospitality industry, you will also discover some exciting realities that will both push and pull you into this industry. If you become a member of this industry, you'll join a group of very satisfied workers who belong to an extremely interesting work culture.

INTERNATIONAL JOB SEEKERS AND TRAVEL

Many individuals seek international jobs with business, government, international organizations, and nonprofit groups because they have had interesting and enjoyable international travel experiences. They now want to turn their pleasures into a full-time job or career involving international travel or residence abroad.

But working abroad is not the same as traveling abroad. Many successful international job seekers soon discover they would be much happier if they sought a job that enabled them to frequently travel rather than live abroad. Better still, they might really enjoy working in an industry that enables them to pursue their real passion—travel to exciting and exotic locations.

COMING GROWTH

Travel is one of the largest and fastest growing industries in the world. Gradually climbing out of the recession of 1989-1993, which saw major upheavals within the industry—especially amongst airlines, hotels, and tour operators—the travel industry is expected to be even bigger in the decade ahead; it should out-perform most other industries. Indeed, according to the U.S. Department of Labor, the hospitality industry will be the third fastest growing occupation (after health and education) between 1992 and 2005, growing by 2,241,000 new jobs. As economies improve, businesses expand, an affluent population ages, and more and more people travel, the travel industry will undergo major expansion in the decade ahead. It will offer some of the most exciting job and career opportunities for people who love to travel.

THE INDUSTRY AND ITS PLAYERS

The travel industry is much more than the stereotypical travel agent arranging tickets, tours, and hotels for tour groups and anxious tourists. This is a highly segmented industry consisting of a network of mutually dependent key players—airlines, hotels, resorts, cruise lines, restaurants, wholesalers, incentive groups, retail tour agents, car rental and catering firms, meeting planners, corporate travel divisions, educators, journalists, and travel writers. These as well as a host of related organizations, individuals, and jobs are focused on the business of moving and managing people from one location to another.

The travel industry is a challenging, exciting, and highly entrepreneurial industry. Its many players report a high degree of job satisfaction. Indeed, many claim to have found *"the best job in the world"*—and with all the perks to prove it! Public relations officers in major hotels, for example, continuously meet and entertain celebrities, work closely with the local business community, and participate in numerous community activities—a worklife many still can't believe they "fell into" in the travel industry.

While many of the businesses, such as major airlines and hotel chains, are huge corporations, most travel-related businesses appear big but are actually small and highly entrepreneurial. They appear big because they are connected to one another through efficient communication and marketing systems which places everyone within a mutually interdependent network of business transactions. It's the type of business where there is a high degree of competition as well as a high degree of mutual dependence, cooperation, and cooptation. Individuals working in this industry manage to advance their careers by moving from one player to another with relative ease.

It's much easier to break into this field than into many other international fields.

MOTIVATION AND SKILLS

If your major motivation for seeking a job is your desire to travel and see and experience new places, and if you seek challenges, like to do different things, and have a sense of entrepreneurship, you should seriously investigate the variety of job and career opportunities available in the travel industry. If you are especially interested in an international job, in contrast to many other international jobs that require a great deal of education, foreign language expertise, and international experience, the international travel business is more oriented to individuals demonstrating entrepreneurship and job performance skills relevant to the particular industry. In other words, it's much easier to break into this field than into many other international fields. Many individuals without college degrees are able to pursue successful careers in the travel industry.

POSITIVES AND NEGATIVES

Like any other industry, the travel industry has its positives and negatives. Depending on which segment of the industry you enter, you will find few high paying jobs. In fact, individuals in these industries make about 20 to 30 percent less than people in other industries, including government. However, they do get special travel benefits and perks not available in other industries, and members of this industry report a high degree of job satisfaction. Many people in the industry do not travel as much as they originally thought they would, or they travel too much to the point where traveling is no longer as exciting as it once was.

At the same time, given the highly segmented and interdependent nature of the industry, careers in travel may involve working for several segments within the industry. For example, you may start working on a cruise line and then later work for a hotel or resort chain and finally move into the incentive travel business or airlines. This mobility amongst segments within the industry leads to interesting and challenging career changes and work environments.

A HIGHLY SEGMENTED INDUSTRY

The travel industry is the ultimate example of a highly segmented yet integrated industry where entrepreneurship plays a key role in the continuing vitality and expansion of the industry as well as the career mobility of individuals within the industry. It's an industry organized to move about $300 billion spent on travel by Americans each year. It employs over 6 million people who work in over 500,000 businesses, from the small Mom and Pop corner travel agency to large corporate hotels and airlines. Huge franchised travel agencies such as Ask Mr. Foster, incentive travel groups such as Carlson-Wagonlit and Maritz, and the federal government dominated SatoTravel offer thousands of job opportunities in the travel industry. When linked to travel industries in other countries—including airlines, hotels, tour companies, ground operators, and incentive groups—this is a truly global industry characterized by a great deal of movement of employees among countries and segments of the industry.

The major segments or sub-industries and players within the travel industry include meeting planners, operators, suppliers, promoters, and supporters:

- travel agencies and operators
- corporate travel managers
- tour operators
- incentive travel companies
- convention and meeting planners
- airlines
- cruise lines
- rail services
- car rentals
- bus lines
- accommodations and lodging industry
- advertising agencies
- research and marketing groups
- travel writers and photographers
- publishing and journalism
- computer support services
- education and training
- public relations
- travel clubs
- tourist sites and attractions
- airport and aviation management groups
- government tourist promotion offices
- culture and arts promotion groups

Not surprising, the travel industry employs numerous types of workers from computer specialists to marketing researchers and artists. Many people also are able to freelance in this industry as wholesalers, travel agents, writers, and photographers.

While many people in this industry do little traveling, others may do a great deal of traveling as part of their day-to-day work. In addition, many people are involved in exciting international work environments.

BREAKING IN

There are no hard and fast rules on how to break into the travel industry. The bad news is that it is a highly competitive industry given its glamorous reputation and numerous job seekers who want to break in. The good news is that it is a rapidly expanding industry that offers many opportunities for individuals with the right combination of motivations, skills, abilities, interests, and drive. The good news also is that you don't need a great deal of education and training to make it in this industry. The skills you need are specific to each segment within the industry, and they are best acquired on the job. Therefore, what you need most of all is an entry-level job, an ability to learn, and entrepreneurial drive. With these you can acquire skills and contacts that will help you to later move within the larger industry.

While more than 200 colleges and universities offer travel programs and several travel schools offer courses of study that ostensibly lead to travel careers, the industry has yet to recognize such formal educational mechanisms as necessary prerequisites for entry into and advancement within the industry. Nonetheless, many of these programs and schools can assist you in specialized areas within the industry. They also can assist you in finding jobs through their network of contacts within the industry.

If you are interested in attending a travel school, many of which offer six month to one-year full-time courses of study, some of the best known and respected ones include: Ask Mr. Foster Travel Academy, Associated Schools, Wilma Boyd Career Schools, Colorado School of Travel, Conlin-Hallissey Travel School, Echols Travel School, Institute of Certified Travel Agents, Intensive Trainers, International Aviation and Travel Academy, International Travel Institute, International Travel Training Courses, Mundus Institute of Travel, The New York School of Travel, Southeastern Academy, Travel Career School of Minnesota, Travel Education Center, and Travel Trade School.

If you are interested in the hotel industry, Cornell University's School of Hotel Administration has a fine reputation. Other universities offering special degree programs in travel include: Adelphi University, Clemson University, Florida International University, George Washington University, Metropolitan State College (Denver), Michigan State University, National College (Rapid City), New School for Social Research, Parks College of St. Louis University, Quinsigamond Community College, Rochester Institute of Technology, Santa Ana College, University of Hawaii, University of Nevada, University of New Haven, University of New Orleans, and University of Notre Dame.

An excellent resource for identifying appropriate education and training programs is CHRIE's *A Guide to College Programs in Hospitality and Tourism* (New York: Wiley). This is a rich resource for locating programs that best relate to your interests.

You will also find several internship opportunities available with businesses in the travel industry. An internship can be an important way to acquire specialized experience and develop contacts within the industry. Three new internship books should help you in identify appropriate internship programs in the travel and hospitality industry:

America's Top 100 Internships (New York: Villard, 1994)

Arco's Internships (New York: Arco/Prentice-Hall, 1994)

Internships 1995 (Princeton, NJ: Peterson's, 1994)

While many of the formal education and training programs do have placement programs for graduates, your best strategy for breaking into the travel industry will be to network among individuals within the various segments of this industry. Make contacts, conduct informational interviews, and locate job vacancies that best fit your interests, skills, and abilities. Most entry-level positions will be based in the U.S. and hopefully provide opportunities to travel and work abroad.

TRAVEL AGENCIES AND OPERATORS

Travel agencies and operators primarily provide travel services for individuals, businesses, and government. Operating as the critical link between travel suppliers and the public, travel agencies and operators arrange airline tickets, cruises, hotels, and car rentals; offer packaged tours; and provide advice on the latest travel itineraries and costs.

The World of Agencies and Operators

The world of travel agencies and operators consists of nearly 100,000 firms, from small Mom and Pop travel agencies to a few large mega-firms such as American Express, Carlson-Wagonlit, and Rosenbluth, which have hundreds of offices nationwide and abroad. The trend within the industry is toward consolidation with larger firms offering a wide variety of travel services.

The travel agent is the most common position operating within this industry. Approximately 130,000 travel agent positions are found nationwide. By the year 2005 employment of travel agents is expected to increase by over 80 percent. More than 90 percent of travel agents work for travel agencies. Nearly 50 percent of travel agencies are located in suburban areas; 40 percent are found in large cities; and the remainder operate in small towns and rural areas. Many travel agents are self-employed.

However, despite such rosy growth projections, the travel agent may soon become an endangered occupation given three recent trends in the travel industry: airlines capping commissions to travel agencies; the ability of individuals to make direct reservations through online electronic commercial services; and ticketless airline reservations. Caps on agency commissions may force many travel agencies to cut back on personnel who normally handle ticketing arrangements. In fact, some industry analysts predict as many as 33,000 travel agencies may go out of business because of such caps. The rapid development of online electronic services with travel options, such as America Online, Prodigy, CompuServe, and GeNie, will allow individuals to make their own reservations directly with airlines and thereby bypass commissioned travel agents. As more and more airlines go to a ticketless reservation system, the need for travel agencies to make reservations and issue tickets will be further eliminated. Contrary to the rosy predictions of the U.S. Department of Labor for travel agents, we predict a restructuring of travel agencies due to today's electronic communication revolution that may result in an actual decline in the traditional travel agent.

The number and variety of job opportunities will vary depending upon the size of an agency. Small Mom and Pop agencies, with annual sales of $1-2 million a year, primarily have two or three travel agents whose main job is to make travel reservations for individuals and corporations. Linked to travel suppliers through computerized reservation systems, the ostensibly glamorous job of travel agent is often anything but glamorous. Travel agents often operate in a pressure cooker atmosphere; they are constantly on the telephone and computer terminal arranging travel itineraries for clients.

Larger agencies, those with annual sales of $25 million or more, offer numerous other travel services as well as additional job opportunities for customer service representatives, account executives, human resources specialists, trainers, accountants, meeting planners, product development managers, fare negotiators, public relations professionals, marketing managers, cruise specialists, and inventory control coordinators. The largest agencies tend to specialize more in corporate travel than on individual travelers. Many of the mega-agencies have more than 75 percent of their business tied to the lucrative corporate travel market. The larger agencies tend to be disproportionately found in major metropolitan areas.

Salaries, Benefits, and Opportunities

Salaries and career opportunities with large agencies are much better than amongst small travel agencies. Salaries for entry-level travel agents tend to be low, often starting at $13,000 a year or just over $6.00 per hour. Those with 10 or more years experience average more than $26,000 a year. Salaries of agency managers average about $27,000 a year. In larger agencies account executives earn around $37,000 a year; branch managers, $32,000 to $42,000; regional sales directors, $39,000; and senior meeting planners, $42,000.

For many individuals, the real benefit of working for travel agencies lies with the travel perks available for travel professionals. Travel suppliers, such as airlines, cruises, car rentals, hotels, and tour operators, routinely give travel agents discounts on their services. These discounts range from as little as 25% to as much as 50% or more. In some cases, travel agents receive free services, especially when familiarization or "fam" trips are offered to travel agencies in exchange for promoting new tour packages. In practice, however, only a few travel agents have the time or money to take advantage of such travel perks. In fact, many travel agents confine their "travel experience" to arranging itineraries and reservations for their clients and hearing about everyone else's travel experiences! Nonetheless, the travel benefits can be substantial for travel professionals who take advantage of the many opportunities available for discounted travel.

Breaking In

There are no hard and fast rules for breaking into travel agencies. Many people with high school educations and little work experience readily find entry-level jobs with small travel agencies. Those with good telephone and organizational skills, computer competence, ability to work under pressure, and a knowledge of geography tend to do well in these jobs. However, the trend amongst travel agencies is toward recruiting individuals with more specialized training. This hiring preference reflects the fact that few agencies are willing to give on-the-job training.

Many individuals now gain entry into travel agencies by first attending vocational schools, travel schools, or specialized training programs to acquire basic travel agency skills. Indeed, travel agencies more and more turn to these schools for recruiting trained personnel.

More than 1,200 travel schools operate a variety of programs for individuals interested in breaking into this field. These programs can vary widely in quality as well as breath and depth of skills training. Many vocational schools offer 3- to 12-week full-time programs as well as evening and weekend programs. Many adult education programs and community colleges and four-year colleges offer travel courses. A few colleges and universities offer bachelor's and master's degrees in travel and tourism.

If you are interested in surveying training opportunities, contact the following groups for copies of their directories of travel schools:

AMERICAN SOCIETY OF TRAVEL AGENTS (ASTA)
Fulfillment Department
1101 King Street
Alexandria, VA 22314
Tel. 703/739-2782 (Ask for recording on how to become a travel agent or start a travel agency—recording says to send a large self-addressed stamped envelope with 75¢ postage)

NATIONAL TOUR FOUNDATION
546 E. Main St.
Lexington, KY 40508
Tel. 606/226-4251 (Provides a listing of 500 schools and colleges offering tourism programs, from certificates to Ph.Ds. Free for the asking)

Some of the larger mega-agencies, such as American Express Travel and Carlson-Wagonlit Travel, operate their own schools and training programs from which they recruit their own personnel. For information on their programs and training opportunities, contact:

TRAVEL EDUCATION CENTER
100 Cambridge Park Drive
Cambridge, MA 02140
Tel. 617/547-7750 (Affiliated with, but independent of, American Express Travel. Has branch centers in Nashua, NH—603/880-7200—and Westchester, IL—708/531-8500)

CARLSON TRAVEL ACADEMY
Carlson-Wagonlit Travel
P.O. Box 59159
Minneapolis, MN 55489
Tel. 612/540-5000

One of the most widely recognized and respected educational programs in the industry is offered by the Institute of Certified Travel Agents (ICTA). Individuals completing their program become a Certified Travel Counselor (CTC). For information on programs offered by the ICTA, contact:

INSTITUTE OF CERTIFIED TRAVEL AGENTS
148 Linden St., P.O. Box 812059
Wellesley, MA 02181-0012
Tel. 617/237-0280

Travel agencies and operators are truly entrepreneurial operations. While these are very competitive businesses whose fortunes tend to fluctuate with general economic conditions and the overall state of the travel industry, the good news is that the travel industry will continue to expand in the coming decade. Expect more and more job opportunities to be available with travel agencies, and especially amongst the large and mega-agencies which continue to develop new and highly specialized service capabilities. The jobs increasingly require higher levels of education, training, and experience. Expect more and more agencies to turn to specialized training programs for meeting their recruitment and training needs.

For many people, this end of the travel business gets into their blood; they simply love the customer contacts and the planning and organizational challenges—with or without the accompanying travel perks. While much of their work will be confined to the office, telephone, and computer terminal, they can travel—and travel well—if they choose to do so.

AIRLINE INDUSTRY

Here's one of the most interesting industries in the travel business— it's basically bankrupt but everyone seems to love it. For those working in this industry, jet fuel seems to get in their blood!

A highly volatile industry, due to a combination of airline deregulation since 1978 and the recession of 1989-1993, the airline industry nonetheless offers excellent opportunities for individuals interested in travel. Today, over 130 carriers operate within the United States. Three major carriers—United, American, and Delta— control over 60 percent of the airline market as well as monopolize air travel in and out of its major hubs (Chicago, Atlanta, Dallas/Ft. Worth).

Over 500,000 individuals work for the airline industry. U.S. airlines with the largest number of employees include:

Airlines	Employees (est.)
American Airlines	95,800
Continental Airlines	40,000
Delta Airlines	73,533
Northwest Airlines	42,500
Southwest Airlines	15,175
Trans World Airlines	25,100
United Airlines	75,000
USAir	48,500

Like any big business, the airlines seek individuals with a variety of business and technical skills—accountants, salespeople, clerical workers, wordprocessors, computer programmers and technicians, managers, marketers, engineers, mechanics, security personnel, public relations specialists—as well as individuals with skills more specific to the industry—pilots, flight attendants, and ticketing and reservation clerks.

Future Growth and Hiring

The U.S. airline industry carries nearly 500 million passengers a year. A highly competitive industry which often experiences cut throat competition, periodic shake-outs, consolidation, and major financial losses, the industry is expected to experience steady growth in the decade ahead as more and more individuals continue to choose airlines for both business and pleasure travel.

On the other hand, hiring does not necessarily follow general growth and decline patterns. Airline personnel tend to be the highest paid individuals within the travel industry, and job satisfaction tends to be higher amongst airline personnel than with individuals in most other industries. An attractive employment arena for thousands of individuals, competition for airline jobs tends to be high and attrition low. Except for retirees, few people voluntarily leave their airline jobs for other employment opportunities. Competition for airline jobs is particularly intense during economic downturns which also tend to be periods of consolidation. In fact, more than 100,000 airline employees have been laid off since 1989. Many have seen their paychecks shrink.

Positions

Positions within the airline industry are generally divided into the following five areas:

1. **Flight Operations:** includes a variety of jobs essential for flight operations, from pilots and flight attendants to baggage handlers and meteorologists. The major such positions include:

   - Captain
   - Co-pilot
   - Second Officer/Flight Engineer
   - Flight Attendant
   - Operations Agent
   - Flight Dispatcher
   - Meteorologist

2. **Maintenance and Engineering:** Includes several major positions for ensuring the proper maintenance and mechani-

cal operations of aircraft:

- Maintenance Inspector
- Airframe and Power Plant (Engineer A&P) Mechanic
- Instrument Technicians
- Radio Technician
- Engineer

3. **Administration, Sales, and Marketing:** Includes numerous positions central for maintaining day-to-day operations and the competitive position of airlines. Good entry-level opportunities which tend to expand during periods of consolidation:

- Reservations Agent
- Ticket Agent
- Airport Operations Agent
- Passenger Service Agent
- Fleet Service Employee
- Sales Representative
- District Sales Manager
- District Operations Manager
- Freight Airport Operations Agent
- Freight Telephone Sales Representative
- Fleet Service Clerks

4. **Management/Special Positions:** Includes a variety of positions that may overlap with other positions and which may be particular to a specific airline. Among these are:

- Crew Scheduler
- Incentive Sales Representative
- Inspector
- Instructor
- Programmer/Analyst
- Purchasing Agent
- Supervisor
- Industrial Engineer
- Foreman
- Executive Secretary

- Passenger Service Manager
- Personnel Representative

Depending on the airline, numerous specialty areas offer a variety of job opportunities:

- Tour Operations
- Aircraft Purchase and Sales
- Charters
- Freight/Cargo
- Insurance
- Properties and Facilities
- Labor Relations
- Community and Environmental Affairs
- Purchasing

5. **Computer Reservations Systems:** The lifeblood of the airline industry is its reservation system. Several positions relate to the operations of the four major systems—Sabre (America), Apollo (United), Worldspan (Delta and TWA), and SystemOne:

- Computer Programmers
- Technicians
- Sales Representatives
- Marketing Personnel

6. **Food, Beverage, and Catering Services:** While most airlines contract for their food and beverage services, American Airlines operates its own meal service (Sky Chef). They hire for a variety of positions for handling their in-flight kitchen operations, from chefs to salad makers.

Benefits

Many positions with the airlines, especially pilots and flight attendants, involve extensive travel. Other positions may involve little or no on-the-job travel. Compensation with major airlines is generally good compared to jobs in other segments of the travel industry. In addition, airline personnel and their families receive excellent travel benefits—free or nearly free travel on a standby, space available basis as well as major discounts on confirmed reserved space.

Breaking In

Breaking into the airline industry depends on your particular skills and perseverance. Most jobs are highly competitive with some positions generating 1000 applicants for every vacancy. Many positions require specialized education and training. The best job opportunities that also offer good career advancement opportunities will be disproportionately found at the hubs of the three major airlines (Chicago, Atlanta, Dallas/Ft. Worth) that hire over 60 percent of airline personnel.

Don't forget the 150 regional airlines. Many offer excellent job opportunities and are easier to break into than the major airlines. Indeed, Dallas-based Southwest Airlines is considered by many informed observers of the airline industry to be the best place for airline professionals to work. It remains one of America's best managed organizations that also boasts extremely high employee morale and job satisfaction.

Small airlines headquartered abroad, many in Third World countries, offer opportunities for enterprising and highly skilled job seekers. While the pay may not be great and the equipment may be antiquated—pilots in Papua New Guinea, for example, may earn less than $30,000 a year, fly questionably maintained aircraft, and operate aircraft without a co-pilot—such airlines do offer opportunities to gain experience in the industry. And experience increasingly counts in this highly competitive global industry.

Resources

Several major trade publications provide useful information on developments within the airline industry as well as job information:

- *Air Transport*
- *Airport Journal*
- *Aviation News*
- *Aviation Weekly*
- *Commuter Air International*
- *Commuter/Regional Airline News*
- *Regional Aviation Weekly*

- *Travel Agent*
- *Travel Trade*
- *Travel Weekly*

The following books examine job and career opportunities within the airline industry:

Flying High in Travel, Karen Rubin (New York: John Wiley & Sons, 1992).

Opportunities in Airline Careers, Adrian A. Paradis (Lincolnwood, IL: National Textbook Co., 1987).

Opportunities in Travel Careers, Robert Scott Milne (Lincolnwood, IL: National Textbook Co., 1991).

Travel Agent, Wilma Boyd (New York: Arco/Prentice Hall Press, 1989).

FLIGHT ATTENDANT

Primarily responsible for the safety and comfort of passengers, flight attendants represent much of the airline industry to the traveling public. Altogether U.S. airlines employ approximately 100,000 flight attendants. They hire nearly 15,000 flight attendants each year. The following airlines employ the largest number of flight attendants:

Airlines	Flight Attendants (est.)
American Airlines	17,000
Continental Airlines	8,500
Delta Airlines	15,000
Northwest Airlines	11,000
Southwest Airlines	3,200
Trans World Airlines	7,200
United Airlines	18,000
USAir	9,900

The Work

Often viewed as working in a glamorous job, flight attendants do travel a great deal and have flexible work schedules. However, starting pay tends to be low ($13,000 a year) and the work can be very demanding and stressful. Flight attendants are responsible for ensuring the proper boarding and deplaning of passengers, preparing passengers for take offs and landings, providing safety briefings, serving food and beverages, and responding to passenger requests for information and additional services. Despite the low pay and stressful working conditions, many flight attendants simply love their work, especially their traveling lifestyle and being part of the airline culture.

Benefits

Few jobs offer so many opportunities to travel both on and off the job. Flight attendants by definition are constantly traveling on the job. They may work a four-day schedule during which time they might visit eight or ten cities. They may then have the next five or six days off before returning to work another four-day schedule. During off days and vacations they may choose to travel for pleasure.

One of the major benefits of being a flight attendant is free and discounted travel. Flight attendants can travel free—on a space available basis—with their airline. If their airline has reciprocal agreements with other airlines, they can travel on these other carriers with special deep discounted tickets. Hotels normally extend airline discounts to flight attendants—often 50 percent. These same travel benefits are usually extended to the flight attendant's family.

While starting pay is low, flight attendants with several years experience receive more adequate compensation. For example, flight attendants with six years of flying experience earn median annual incomes of just over $20,000. Senior flight attendants earn over $40,000 a year. In general, however, this is not a well paid profession. The real benefits lie in the lifestyle of this travel industry.

The combination of constant travel, flexible work schedules, and free and discounted travel makes this a very attractive job for many individuals. It is so attractive that competition for flight attendant positions is very keen. Indeed, some airlines receive 100 or more applications for each flight attendant position.

Breaking In

Flight attendants are required to meet certain age, education, height, and communication requirements and attend tuition-based training programs. Nearly 50 percent of all flight attendants have a four-year college degree; 70 percent have some college experience.

For application information with the major airlines, send a self-addressed stamped envelope—along with a cover letter requesting an application—to the following offices:

AMERICAN AIRLINES
Flight Attendant Recruitment
P.O. Box 619410, MD 4125
DFW Airport, TX 75261-9410

CONTINENTAL AIRLINES
Flight Attendant Recruitment
2929 Allen Parkway, P.O. Box 4607
Houston, TX 77210-4748

DELTA AIRLINES
System Employment Manager
P.O. Box 20530
Hartsfield Atlanta International Airport
Atlanta, GA 30320-2530

NORTHWEST AIRLINES
Department H 1470
5101 Northwest Drive
St. Paul, MN 55111-3034

SOUTHWEST AIRLINES
ATTN: Personnel
P.O. Box 36611
Dallas, TX 75235-1611

TRANS WORLD TRAVEL ACADEMY
Flight Attendant Recruitment
502 Earth City Expressway, Suite 204
St. Louis, MO 63045-1315

UNITED AIRLINES
Application Processing Center
Flight Attendant Employment
P.O. Box 6610
Chicago, IL 60666

USAIR
Application Distribution Center
Employment Services Department
Washington National Airport
Washington, DC 20001

Resources

For information on flight attendant opportunities, refer to the following books:

Come Fly With Me! Your '90s Guide to Becoming a Flight Attendant, Reginald Dunlop (Chicago: Maxamillian Publishing, 1993)

Flight Attendant, David Massey (New York: Arco/Prentice Hall Press, 1990).

A Guide to Becoming a Flight Attendant, Douglas K. Kinan (Holbrook, MA: Bob Adams, Inc., 1987).

PILOT

If you want a job that enables you to travel a lot, being a pilot is the ultimate job. Holding one of the most respected positions in the airline culture, you're in charge. Better still, you receive excellent salary and benefits for your travel passion!

Airline pilots hold one of the most prestigious and well paid jobs in the airline industry. They fly airplanes and helicopters in the process of hauling millions of passengers and tons of cargo and mail. They dust crops, reseed forests, take photographs, test aircraft, fight fires, assist with police and rescue work, and engage in logging, off shore natural resource exploration, and weather operations.

Approximately 90,000 civilian pilots are employed in the United States. Nearly 60 percent are employed with the airlines.

Requirements and Outlook

Licensed by the FAA, pilots must meet certain age (18-32), physical (excellent), and flight experience (3,000+ hours) requirements. Most have college educations, and the airlines prefer to hire college graduates.

Nearly 75 percent of all pilots received their training through the military. While the military continues to be a major source for recruiting new pilots, the recession in the early 1990s—coupled with the shakeout and consolidation of the airline industry and the drawdowns in the military—created a triple-whammy for budding commercial pilots seeking employment with the major commercial airlines. The job outlook for new pilots in the first half of the 1990s was very poor. Indeed, many pilots leaving the military in the early 1990s in the hopes of finding jobs as commercial pilots were disappointed with their poor job prospects; airlines were cutting back rather than hiring new pilots. Many of these highly motivated and skilled job seekers missed the small window of opportunity they must have (prime age and experience levels) when making the transition from military to civilian aviation. Civilian trained pilots faced an equally poor job market.

The job outlook for commercial pilots should improve in the latter half of the 1990s as the airline industry continues to expand. More and more pilots will be recruited from civilian training programs as the military produces fewer pilots. In fact, we expect a shortage of pilots in the second half of the 1990s as airlines expand, retirements increase, and fewer individuals receive pilot training.

Positions and Benefits

The major pilot positions include Captain, First Officer (Copilot), and Second Officer (Flight Engineer). Individuals in each of these positions must be certified by the Federal Aviation Administration as well as have a current medical certificate.

Airline pilots earn some of the highest salaries of any occupation. The average salary of airline pilots in 1995 was about $100,000.

Captains average about $125,000 a year; copilots $80,000; and flight engineers $55,000. Pilots working with jet aircraft and with the major airlines receive higher salaries than those working with nonjet aircraft and with regional airlines. Pilots working with noncommercial airlines receive lower salaries.

Airline pilots receive a host of excellent benefits, from life, health, and disability insurance to free or reduced fares on their own or other airlines.

Resources

If you are interested in becoming an airline pilot, contact the following organizations for information on training opportunities, requirements, salaries, and job opportunities:

AEROSPACE EDUCATION FOUNDATION
1501 Lee Highway
Arlington, VA 22209-1198
Tel. 703/247-5839

AIR LINE EMPLOYEES ASSOCIATION
5600 S. Central Avenue
Chicago, IL 60638
Tel. 312/767-3333

AIR TRANSPORT ASSOCIATION OF AMERICA
1301 Pennsylvania Avenue, NW
Washington, DC 20004
Tel. 202/626-4000

Pilot Information Program
Education Department
AIRLINE PILOTS ASSOCIATION
1625 Massachusetts Ave., NW
Washington, DC 20036
Tel. 202/797-4060

FEDERAL AVIATION ADMINISTRATION
Department of Transportation
Office of Training and Higher Education
400 7th Street, NW
Washington, DC 20590
Tel. 202/366-7503

FUTURE AVIATION PROFESSIONALS OF AMERICA
4959 Massachusetts Blvd.
Atlanta, GA 30331
Tel. 800/JET-JOBS (538-5627)

HELICOPTER ASSOCIATION INTERNATIONAL
1635 Prince Street
Alexandria, VA 22314
Tel. 703/683-4646

REGIONAL AIRLINE ASSOCIATION
1200 19th Street, NW
Suite 300
Washington, DC 20036
Tel. 202/857-1170

Several books also provide useful information for individuals interested in becoming an air pilot:

Airline Pilot, Future Aviation Professionals of America Staff (ed.) (New York: Arco Publishing Co., 1990).

Becoming an Airline Pilot, Jeff Griffin (Blue Ridge Summit, PA: TAB Books, 1990).

List of Certificated Pilot Schools (Superintendent of Documents, U.S. Government Printing Office, Washington, DC 20402).

World Aviation Directory (Aviation Week Group, McGraw-Hill, Inc., 1200 G St., NW, 9th Fl., Washington, DC 20005, Tel. 202/383-2484)

CRUISE LINES

Have you ever dreamed of working on the Love Boat? Put in exotic ports two or three times each week? Explore the Seven Seas, retracing the routes of some of the world's great explorers and writers? Eat great food, enjoy terrific entertainment, and party all day long? Do you want to combine your work and play in a truly hedonistic manner, travel free, and make great money at the same time?

These are stereotypical dreams of many individuals who see cruise ship work as the really glamorous end of the travel industry. Filled with numerous myths, but also involving many sobering realities, cruise ship jobs offer a very special worklife of hard work and play centered on a great deal of ocean travel. It is more a life than just another travel job. Work on a cruise ship and you will certainly travel a great deal. Best of all, you'll travel, eat, and sleep free while making a living at the same time!

Growing Industry

The cruise industry has experienced phenomenal growth during the past decade. And it is likely to continue experiencing major growth in the decade ahead. Each year cruise ships carry nearly 5 million North American passengers. The number of passengers is likely to triple over the coming decade as more and more people choose cruise ships as their favorite mode of vacation-resort travel. In response to this projected growth in passengers, approximately 50 new cruise ships will come on line by the year 2000. Even Disney will launch its own cruise ships soon as it continues to diversify its already substantial travel empire. Such growth translates into more and more jobs in this much sought-after industry.

Myths and Realities

There are many myths about cruise line jobs. The biggest myths are that these jobs are all fun and games, they pay well, and there are plenty of opportunities available on-board for Americans. The realities are that most cruise line jobs are hard work and do not pay well. And few Americans find jobs on-board. Cruise ship jobs involve long hours, a great deal of stress, a willingness to work with a diverse multinational team, an ability to please all types of passengers, and the willingness to give exceptional and exacting service. Above all, you must be people-oriented, tolerant, and flexible. You must have the disposition of a servant—the customer is always right, even though the passenger may be a jerk!

If you have a family, an on-board cruise ship job is likely to involve long separations. For many Americans, it's the type of job best enjoyed by young single individuals who see cruise ship jobs as short-term travel positions or entry-level positions for moving within the larger travel and hospitality industry. Many Americans will spend three to five years working with cruise lines—accumulating valuable travel and resort experience—before "settling down" to more stable family-oriented jobs on shore.

But our myths become important realities for individuals from many other nations that make up the diverse multinational crews of most cruise ships. With foreign ownership and registry, most cruise ships are operated with crews from Greece, Italy, Portugal, Indonesia, and the Philippines. These nationals tend to work for low wages with many primarily surviving on passenger tips. Few Americans work on board, and those that do tend to be found in a very limited number of "American" positions—entertainment, physical fitness, and sports. You won't find many Americans piloting ships, managing restaurants, serving tables, cooking food, or making beds. These positions tend to be dominated by other nationals. Most American involvement with the cruise ship industry tends to be on shore—in marketing, sales, and computer reservation systems.

The significance of such employment within a multinational context has different meanings for different nationals. For many nationals, cruise ship jobs are more than just short-term travel jobs; they are great job opportunities—well paid, secure, and prestigious compared to the limited job opportunities back home. While many foreign nationals—especially those from such Third World countries as the Philippines and Indonesia who occupy numerous low-paying positions in housekeeping and kitchen—make cruise ship jobs a long-term career, few Americans pursue such jobs as a career. Greeks and Italians tend to be in charge of food and beverage services and general ship operations. Given their limited job options back home, cruise ship jobs for such nationals are considered excellent paying, secure, and prestigious jobs. Americans don't last long in such crew environments.

Americans tend to be disproportionately found in the entertainment, physical fitness, public relations, and marketing and sales end of cruise ship jobs. Despite all the glamour, cruise ship pay and lifestyles simply are not sufficiently attractive for many Americans to continue long-term in this industry. Americans also are not noted for their talent in dispensing exceptional, exacting, and high level service that is the hallmark of many cruise lines. Many Americans most typically pursue cruise ship jobs in the hopes of moving on to other jobs within the travel and hospitality industry, especially with hotels, resorts, restaurants, and night clubs. A cruise ship job is often a short stop along the way to other more rewarding jobs and careers.

Positions and Benefits

Cruise ship jobs are highly competitive. Operating like large resorts whose main purpose is to pamper its guests during short three to 14-day cruises, most cruise ships maintain a high staff-per-passenger ratio. They hire for every type of department and position you would find in five-star resorts—housekeeping, kitchen, entertainment, health, fitness, tours, gaming, guest relations, engineering, maintenance, hair salon, and gift shop. They hire accountants, cooks, waiters, engineers, casino operators, pursers, photographers, massage therapists, cosmetologists, doctors, nurses, entertainers, youth counselors, water sports instructors, fitness instructors, and lecturers. However, they disproportionately hire crew members from Southern Europe and Asia.

For most Americans, cruise ship jobs seem to be low paying compared to jobs on shore in the United States. But for many Asians from Third World countries and Southern Europeans who make up the majority of the crews, these jobs seem well paying compared to limited opportunities back home; these individuals can save money to support their families back home.

While the pay may not be great for many Americans, cruise ship jobs offer numerous other benefits that can out-weigh the limited financial rewards. The major benefits are free travel, food, and accommodations—unusual benefits for any job! In addition, cruise ship jobs can provide valuable experience that can be transferred to numerous other jobs in the travel and hospitality industry, especially in hotel management, food and beverage service, and entertainment. Individuals working in this industry are well positioned to work in resort operations.

Breaking In

Breaking into the cruise industry can be difficult given the high competition for the limited number of positions that may interest you. However, numerous positions become vacant given the regular turnover of cruise line personnel.

A few training institutes now offer courses of study and internships leading to jobs and careers with the cruise industry. For more information on programs and requirements, contact:

CRUISE CAREER TRAINING INSTITUTE (CCTI)
1500 NW 49th Street
Ft. Lauderdale, FL 33309
Tel. 305/351-4045

INSTITUTE OF MARITIME HOTEL MANAGEMENT
Postfach 10
A-5061 Salzburg-Elsbethen
Austria
Tel. 43-662-853330

As you conduct a job search, you should be aware that many on-board positions are not controlled by the cruise lines. Gift shops, beauty salons, casinos, sports and recreation, and entertainment are often concessions operated by contractors. For example, dancers, musicians, singers, message therapists, cosmetologists, and medical doctors are often hired through firms that control these on-board concessions. If a position you desire relates to these concessions, you will need to make employment contacts with the appropriate concessionaire.

Your best approach is to become knowledgeable about particular cruise lines, make the right contacts with that cruise line or concessionaire, and offer these employers the right combination of desired skills and experience. It's always best to know someone working with a cruise line or concessionaire—a friend, for example, who already works on the cruise ship—who knows when vacancies occur and a ship needs to quickly hire. In many cases cruise lines place classified ads in magazines and newspapers to recruit needed personnel. Most require a resume and cover letter. Another approach is to send a copy of your resume along with an accompanying cover letter directly to the personnel office of a cruise line. Specify on the envelope whether you are applying for a "Shipside" or a "Shoreside" position, identify which department you wish to work for, and/or call ahead to get the name of the department or person you should address your correspondence to.

Cruise lines recruit individuals for both shore side and shipboard positions. Some of the major cruise lines you may want to direct your job search toward include:

CARNIVAL CRUISE LINES
3655 NW 87th Avenue
Miami, FL 33178-2428
Tel. 305/599-2600

CELEBRITY CRUISES
Personnel
5200 Blue Lagoon Dr.
Suite 1000
Miami, FL 33126
Tel. 305/262-6677

CRYSTAL CRUISES
Personnel
2121 Avenue of the Stars, Suite 200
Los Angeles, CA 90067
Tel. 310/785-9300

DOLPHIN AND MAJESTY CRUISE LINES
Marine Personnel
901 S. America Way
Miami, FL 33132
Tel. 305/358-5122

HOLLAND AMERICA LINE
Personnel
300 Elliot Ave. W.
Seattle, WA 98119
Tel. 206/281-3535

NORWEGIAN CRUISE LINE
c/o Worldwide Ship's Services
Pier 1
1265 S. America Way
Miami, FL 33132
Tel. 305/447-9660

PALM BEACH CRUISE LINE
Operations Department
157 E. Port Road
P.O. Box 10265
Riviera Beach, FL 33419
Tel. 407/845-7447

PRINCESS CRUISES
Human Resources
10100 Santa Monica Blvd., Suite 1800
Los Angeles, CA 90067
Tel. 310/553-1770

REGENCY CRUISES
Personnel
260 Madison Ave.
New York, NY 10016
Tel. 212/972-4774

ROYAL CARIBBEAN CRUISE LINE
Human Resources Department
1050 Caribbean Way
Miami, FL 33132
Tel. 305/539-6000

ROYAL CRUISE LINE
Personnel
One Maritime Plaza
Suite 1400
San Francisco, CA 94111
Tel. 415/956-7200

ROYAL VIKING LINE
Human Resources Department
c/o Kloster Cruise Limited
95 Merrick Way
Coral Gables, FL 33134

SEABOURN CRUISE LINE
55 Francisco St.
Suite 710
San Francisco, CA 94133
Tel. 415/391-7444

The following companies have concessions with several cruise lines. Depending on your area of interest and experience, you may want to contact these companies directly:

CASINO: CASINO ENTERTAINMENT, LTD.
                       Personnel
                       999 S. Bayshore Dr.
                       Tower 1, Suite 608
                       Miami, FL 33131
                       Tel. 305/372-2943

                       OM CONSULTANTS
                       1850 Eller Dr.
                       Suite 101
                       Ft. Lauderdale, FL 33316

                       TIBER ENTERTAINMENTS GROUP
                       Shoreside Consultants, Inc.
                       1177 S. America Way
                       Miami, FL 33132

CRUISE STAFF: GLOBAL SHIP SERVICES, INC.
                       141 NE 3rd Ave.
                       Suite 203
                       Miami, FL 33132
                       Tel. 305/374-8649

SHIP'S SERVICES INTL.
Personnel
370 West Camino Gardens Blvd.
Boca Raton, FL 33432
Tel. 407/391-5500

COSMETOLOGY/　COIFFURE TRANS OCEAN
MASSAGE　　　 Personnel
1007 N. America Way, 4th Fl.
Miami, FL 33132
Tel. 305/358-9002

THE GOLDEN DOOR SPA
P.O. Box 463077
Escondido, CA 92046-3077
Tel. 619/744-5777

ENTERTAINMENT:　CARIBBEAN CRUISE
　　　　　　　　　　MANAGEMENT
Personnel
80 SW 8th St., Suite 2640
Miami, FL 33130

JEAN ANN RYAN
　　　PRODUCTIONS
308 SE 14th St.
Ft. Lauderdale, FL 33316
Tel. 305/523-6414 (recorded message)

FOOD AND　　 APOLLO SHIPS CHANDLERS
BEVERAGE　　 1775 NW 70 Avenue
Miami, FL 33126
Tel. 305/592-8790

ZERBONE CATERING
100 S. Biscayne Blvd., Suite 700
Miami, FL 33131
Tel. 305/374-2491

GIFT SHOP	GREYHOUND LEISURE Personnel 8052 NW 14th St. Miami, FL 33126 Tel. 305/592-6460 ALLDERS INTERNATIONAL Personnel 1510 SE 17th St. Ft. Lauderdale, FL 33316 Tel. 305/763-8551
SPORTS AND **RECREATION**	RESORT AND COMMERCIAL RECREATION ASSOCIATION P.O. Box 1208 New Port Richey, FL 34656-1208 Tel. 813/845-7373 SPORTS CAREERS 2400 E. Arizona Biltmore Circle Bldg. 2, Suite 1270 Phoenix, AZ 85016 Tel. 602/954-8106

Resources

One of the best resources for surveying job opportunities in the cruise industry is Mary Fallon Miller's *How to Get a Job With a Cruise Line* (St. Petersburg, FL: Ticket to Adventure, 1992). The book is filled with useful tips on how to land a cruise job. It includes a comprehensive survey of the major cruise lines and concessionaires, descriptions of positions, information on training opportunities and special programs, insider's stories, tips on writing resumes and completing applications, and names, addresses, and phone numbers for contacting potential employers. Our forthcoming *Jobs for People Who Love Hotels, Resorts, and Cruise Ships* (Manassas Park, VA: Impact Publications, 1996) includes job information on the cruise industry.

    To keep abreast of developments in the cruise industry, as well as to learn more about particular cruise lines, we recommend reading such trade magazines as *Cruise Trade, Cruise Views, Tour and Travel News, The Travel Counselor, Travel Trade,* and *Travel Weekly.* You should also review the latest annual edition of the **CLIA Cruise Manual,** which is available through many travel agents or directly from the publisher (Cruise Lines International Association, 500 Fifth Avenue, Suite 1407, New York, NY 10110, Tel. 212/921-0066). This directory provides detailed information on 34 cruise lines that make up the membership of this important association.

RAIL SERVICES

Ever dream of hopping on a train and heading off into the sunset? It's a dream thousands of individuals realize each day as locomotive engineers, rail yard engineers, conductors, or brakeman on freight and passenger trains or as cooks, bartenders, waiters, waitresses, hosts, and hostesses on Amtrak passenger trains. Riding the rails is the ultimate travel high for many individuals pursuing jobs and careers in the travel industry. For many people, rail work is similar to airline or cruise line work—it literally gets into their blood. They become addicted to the work-travel lifestyle. Following a family tradition, members of their family often pursue careers in the rail industry.

Nearly 78 percent of all rail transportation jobs are with the railroads. In 1992 approximately 116,000 individuals worked in rail transportation. This included 35,000 brake operators, 29,000 conductors, 19,000 locomotive engineers, 8,900 rail yard engineers and dinkey operators, 22,000 subway and streetcar operators, and 1,700 in other jobs. The remaining jobs were with state and local governments and mining and manufacturing firms that operate their own railroad cars to carry freight.

Opportunities

Which end of the rail industry most appeals to you—freight or passenger service? If you are primarily interested in jobs involving travel on freight trains, you should focus on the positions of engineer, conductor, and brake, signal, and switch operator.

Passenger train service in the United States is operated by Amtrak, a quasi-government organization. Staffed by a workforce of nearly 25,000, Amtrak transports about 25 million passengers each year. Approximately 90 percent of Amtrak workers are union members; the remaining 10 percent are nonunionized management employees. While many positions with Amtrak, such as ticket agents and station personnel, involve little or no rail travel, those involving frequent travel relate to on-board services: porters, conductors, dining-car employees (chefs, waiters, waitresses), bartenders, and sleeping car personnel (hosts and hostesses). Other support personnel, such as inspectors and investigators, do not provide on-board services, but their work does involve frequent and interesting travel.

While job opportunities in rail transportation have steadily declined in recent years, opportunities for rail employees are expected to increase about as fast as average for all occupations in the decade ahead. However, this situation could change significantly depending on the future federal financing of Amtrak which is undergoing major changes. Amtrak has recently initiated major cutbacks, eliminating several routes and downsizing personnel. Intracity rail systems are expected to grow faster than average. Employment of subway operators will increase accordingly, and competition is expected to be high for what are relatively high-paying subway operator positions for jobs requiring limited educational requirements.

Benefits

Except for management personnel, most rail workers are unionized. As such, their salaries and benefits tend to be good to excellent with both freight and passenger rail services. In 1990 annual earnings of yard engineers was $42,000; locomotive engineers, both freight and passenger, earned an average of $55,000. Conductors with passenger service averaged $48,000 a year; those with freight service averaged $55,800. Brake operators averaged $46,000 in freight service and $36,000 in yard service.

As unionized workers, most railway employees receive good health and retirement benefits.

Breaking In

Most railway workers start out as trainees for either engineer or brake operator jobs. Applicants generally need a high school education, good health and eye sight, and demonstrate mechanical aptitude. Beginning engineers usually undergo a 6-month training program. Brake operators usually learn their job by working closely with experienced conductors and operators as well as participate in some classroom training. Conductors are usually hired from the ranks of experienced brake operators who have sufficient seniority to move into vacant conductor positions.

Applicants for subway operator positions normally need a high school education and must be in good health and use good judgment. They usually receive from a few weeks to six months of classroom and on-the-job training.

Numerous craft unions represent railway workers. However, most engineers belong to the Brotherhood of Locomotive Engineers; other railway workers tend to belong to the United Transportation Union. Most subway workers are represented by either the Amalgamated Transit Union or the Transport Workers Union of North America.

If you are interested in working for the railways, it's best to contact the employment offices of various railways or the appropriate craft unions for information on requirements and applications. For a list of addresses and telephone numbers of the major railroads, contact

ASSOCIATION OF AMERICAN RAILROADS
Communications Department
50 F Street, NW
Washington, DC 20021
Tel. 202/639-2563

For application and vacancy information relating to passenger service jobs, contact

AMTRAK
Human Resources
900 2nd Street, NE
Washington, DC 20002
Tel. 202/906-3287

Local offices of rail transit systems and State employment services also have information on job opportunities in rail transportation.

BUS LINES AND MOTORCOACH INDUSTRY

There's basically one position in the bus industry that involves extensive travel—busdriver. In 1992 busdrivers held 562,000 jobs and worked from nearly 4,000 companies. Most worked part time. Nearly 75 percent worked for school systems or companies providing school bus services to schools; 17 percent worked as local transit busdrivers. Only 4 percent worked as intercity busdrivers. The remaining 5 percent work as busdrivers for charter, tour, commuter service, package express, feeder service, and other types of private companies.

Opportunities

Employment opportunities for busdrivers in the decade ahead should grow faster than average. This is primarily due to the coming growth in elementary and secondary school enrollments and the consequent need for more buses and busdrivers. Opportunities for busdrivers with local transit and intercity bus systems will gradually grow as bus ridership increases. However, expect high competition for these jobs because many of these positions are well paid and come with excellent benefits for individuals with limited educational achievement. Opportunities also should be excellent for busdrivers with tour and charter companies—one of the fastest growing and most innovative segments of the industry.

Benefits

The nature of this business is such that busdrivers often work part-time and experience seasonal layoffs. Seniority tends to determine the extent of part-time and full-time employment for busdrivers. Salaries are often low but more than adequate in many communities.

Salaries of busdrivers vary greatly. In 1992 the median weekly earnings of full-time bus drivers was $400. Local transit busdrivers working in companies with over 1,000 employees and in communities of more than 2 million residents earned a top median hourly wage of $16.41 in 1993; busdrivers in communities with fewer than 50,000 people earned a median hourly wage of $10.64. During the 1991-1992 school year, the median wage for school busdrivers employed by public school systems was $10.04 an hour.

Earnings of intercity busdrivers largely depends on the number of miles they drive. In 1992, beginning intercity busdrivers working six months a year averaged $22,000; senior full-time busdrivers working year round earned more than $48,000 a year.

Fringe benefits also vary greatly from employer to employer. Most intercity and local transit busdrivers receive paid health and life insurance, sick leave, and free bus rides. Most full-time busdrivers annually receive four weeks vacation. Most intercity and many local transit busdrivers belong to the Amalgamated Transit Union. Local transit busdrivers in New York and many other large cities belong to the Transport Workers Union of America. Some drivers belong to the United Transportation Union and the International Brotherhood of Teamsters, Chauffeurs, Warehousemen and Helpers of America.

Resources

Information on employment opportunities for busdrivers is available by directly contacting local transit systems, intercity buslines, school systems, tour and charter companies, or the local offices of the State employment service. For information on school busdriving, contact:

NATIONAL SCHOOL TRANSPORTATION
   ASSOCIATION
P.O. Box 2639
Springfield, VA 22152
Tel. 703/644-0700

Information on local transit busdriving is available by writing to:

AMERICAN PUBLIC TRANSIT ASSOCIATION
1201 New York Ave. NW, Suite 400
Washington, DC 20005
Tel. 202/898-4000

For information on intercity and charter busdriver careers, write to:

AMERICAN BUS ASSOCIATION
1100 New York Ave., NW
Suite 1050
Washington, DC 20005-1645
Tel. 202/842-1645

For information on opportunities with the growing tour and charter bus companies, contact:

NATIONAL MOTORCOACH MARKETING NETWORK
10527 Braddock Road, Suite C
Fairfax, VA 22032
Tel. 703/250-7897

NATIONAL TOUR FOUNDATION
546 W. Main St.
Lexington, KY 40508
Tel. 606/226-4251

TOUR OPERATORS AND GUIDES

One of the most exciting ends of the travel industry are the numerous companies that organize and conduct tours. Highly specialized, entrepreneurial, and competitive, these companies are responsible for putting together packaged tours as well as providing both outbound and inbound tour services. Jobs involve everything from organizing packages, marketing tours, and selling services to making reservations, coordinating inbound ground services, and actually conducting tours.

Opportunities

During the past ten years the number of specialty tour operators has increased dramatically. Most are small two to seven-person operations which specialize in destinations (Europe, the Caribbean, Asia, Africa, Latin America); activities (ballooning, mountain climbing, white water rafting, safaris, bicycling, scuba diving); educational experiences (museums, archeological ruins, culture, university courses); lifestyle choices (environment, habitats, nudism); and markets (women, youth, retirees, teachers, singles, religion, disabled, grandparents, gays). Others are large well established firms, such as American Express, Travco, and Globus, which offer hundreds of different tour options to special destinations. The average firm is run by four full-time and two part-time employees and sells 80 different tours to 2,500 clients a year. In the larger scheme of things, these are small travel operations.

Tour managers—also known as tour guides or tour escorts—experience the greatest amount of on-the-job travel. The work is very demanding. Tour managers must be well-organized, responsible, and great diplomats that handle a host of daily demands. Given the seasonal nature of this business, most tour managers are freelancers who are hired by tour operators for specific itineraries. Many individuals prefer this lifestyle because it enables them to travel as well as have several months off each year to pursue other interests.

The specialty tour business should continue to expand in the decade ahead as more and more people choose to go beyond the standard destinations and sightseeing that has largely defined tour operations during the past 30 years. Job opportunities will continue to expand for individuals with expertise in specialty travel.

Benefits and Salaries

The major benefits for tour operators are the ability to travel free or at low cost to exciting destinations, participate in stimulating programs, and work with interesting people. Salaries of tour operators and tour guides are relatively low. However, many talented tour guides do very well on tips from satisfied clients. Most make $50,000 a year or more—with tips making up two-thirds of their earnings. Given the highly competitive nature of the industry and the pressure to offer good value to clients, profit margins for tour operators tend to be very narrow.

Most individuals working in this end of the travel business, including presidents and managers of tour firms, earn under $40,000 a year; many earn under $25,000 a year. This is type of industry many people enter because they primarily enjoy the non-monetary benefits of the business.

Resources

If you are interested in pursuing jobs with tour operators, you should refer to some of the following publications:

- *International Travel News*
- *Specialty Travel Index*
- *Tour & Travel News*
- *Tour Trade*
- *Tours!*
- *Travel Agent*
- *Travel Weekly*

For a good overview of the growing specialty travel business, read Arthur Frommer's *The New World of Travel* (New York: Prentice-Hall Press).

The following organizations can provide you with information on opportunities with tour operators:

AMERICAN SOCIETY OF TRAVEL AGENTS
1101 King St.
Alexandria, VA 22314
Tel. 703/739-2782

NATIONAL TOUR FOUNDATION
546 E. Main St.
Lexington, KY 40508
Tel. 606/226-4251

PROFESSIONAL GUIDES ASSOCIATION
    OF AMERICA
2416 S. Eads St.
Arlington, VA 22202-2532
Tel. 703/892-5757

TRAVEL INDUSTRY ASSOCIATION OF AMERICA
1100 New York Ave., NW
Suite 450
Washington, DC 20005
Tel. 202/408-8422

U.S. TOUR OPERATORS ASSOCIATION
211 E. 51st St., Suite 12B
New York, NY 10022
Tel. 212/944-5727

U.S. TRAVEL AND TOURISM ADMINISTRATION
U.S. Department of Commerce
14th and Constitution Ave. NW
Washington, DC 20230

CONVENTION AND MEETING PLANNERS

Do you like to party? What about organizing the largest party you've ever seen? And travel to great places at the same time? That's what meeting planners do—throw really big parties that can involve a great deal of travel to exciting places.

Who's in charge of putting on nearly 250,000 meetings, conferences, conventions, and workshops attended by over 40 million people spending over $50 billion each year? If you work for an association, incentive house, travel agency, hotel, conference center, convention bureau, or a consulting firm specializing in organizing meetings, you may have one of the most enjoyable and challenging jobs that also involves a great deal of travel. Indeed, as much as 75 percent of your time may involve travel.

Being a meeting planner is not the same as working in Hollywood. But you are in charge of putting on a major production that may last only one day or as long as one week. From start to finish, you want a flawless production in which everyone knows their part and plays it well. If not, you must be well prepared to deal with problems and crises.

Meeting planners are in charge of nearly every aspect of organizing and conducting professional meetings of groups as small as 50 or as large as 50,000. They select sites; plan programs; negotiate facilities; publicize events; block space; make hotel and airline reservations; organize food and beverages; set up registration; arrange equipment and security; organize shipping and exhibits; schedule speakers; and attend to 1001 other logistic details necessary for operating successful meetings.

Meeting planners must have excellent communication, organization, negotiating, planning, and management skills as well as exhibit a great deal of initiative, creativity, and attention to detail. They are constantly on the telephone planning and coordinating events. The nature of their jobs involves traveling a great deal to meeting sites. The larger the meeting, the more likely the meeting will be held in a large city that offers adequate facilities to accommodate attendees. Large associations, for example, can only be accommodated at large convention centers which are primarily found in New York City, Miami, Chicago, San Francisco, Los Angeles, Las Vegas, and Washington, DC.

Benefits

Salaries, travel, and excitement are the major benefits of the meeting business. Starting salaries are $20,000 or higher. Those with three or more years experience can earn $30,000 to $40,000. Senior meeting planners can earn $60,000 to $80,000 a year. The average salary of meeting planners in 1991 was just under $35,000.

Many people go into this business because of the travel benefits. Meeting planners are constantly traveling because of their need to examine sites, plan and negotiate facilities, and oversee the conduct of meetings. However, the travel benefits can become a negative for some individuals who discover they are traveling too much. The demands of the job are great—long hours and stress—and thus most appealing for certain types of individuals.

Breaking In

Given the seeming glamorous nature of these jobs as well as the extensive travel involved, competition for jobs in the meeting business is high. Many of the jobs are found with associations, which must plan annual conventions, while others are found with convention bureaus, incentive houses, travel agencies, hotels, and corporations.

Entry into this career field requires excellent communication and management skills. Most meeting planners have at least a Bachelor's degree, preferably in business administration. Many have attended degree programs in hotel/motel management as well as special training programs in meeting management.

The best way to break into this business is to learn as much as possible about employers and contact them directly. Some organizations, such as the American Society of Association Executives (Tel. 202/626-2723), Meeting Professionals International (Tel. 214/712-7700), and the Society of Corporate Meeting Planners (Tel. 408/649-6544), specialize in recruiting meeting planners. Some provide job and career information as well as sponsor job banks.

Resources

If you are interested in opportunities in the meeting business, you should consult several of the following trade publications:

- *Association Trends*
- *Business Travel News*
- *Corporate Travel*
- *Hotel and Resort Industry*
- *The Meeting Manager*
- *Meeting News*
- *Meetings and Conventions*
- *Successful Meetings*

The following organizations can provide you with information on opportunities for meeting planners:

INTERNATIONAL ASSOCIATION OF
    CONFERENCE CENTERS
243 N. Lindbergh Blvd., Suite 315
St. Louis, MO 63141
Tel. 314/993-8575

MEETING PROFESSIONALS INTERNATIONAL
1950 Stemmons Freeway, Suite 5018
Dallas, TX 75207-3109
Tel. 214/712-7700

SOCIETY OF CORPORATE MEETING PLANNERS
2107 Delmonte Avenue
Monterey, CA 93940
Tel. 408/649-6544

ACCOMMODATIONS AND LODGING INDUSTRY

One does not normally think of the accommodations and lodging industry offering travel opportunities. Jobs in this industry appear to be specific to individual properties. However, many jobs, especially with major international hotel chains, offer some wonderful opportunities that also involve frequent travel and residence abroad.

The lodging industry employs the largest number of people in the travel industry. Over 1.5 million people work in nearly 45,000 hotels, motels, and other accommodations in the United States. Many millions more work in hotels and resorts abroad.

One of the fastest growing segments of the travel industry, the accommodations industry in the United States is expected to experience major growth in the decade ahead—increasing employment by nearly 500,000 by the year 2,000.

Opportunities

The lodging or hospitality industry offers numerous job opportunities for people with a variety of skills, interests, educational backgrounds, and motivations. While desk clerks, housekeepers, and managers are most evident in small hotels and motels, large hotels and resorts hire numerous other individuals to staff their extensive operations and departments—food and beverage, restaurant, front office, accounting, engineering, public relations, convention and meeting rooms, tours, fitness center, business center, sales and marketing, security, laundry, purchasing, computer systems, maintenance, and operations.

Hotels with 800 rooms may operate with a staff of over 1,000. Positions with these properties are numerous: front-office manager, room clerk, reservation clerk, cashier, telephone operator, concierge bell captain, doorperson, controller, credit manager, purchasing agent, accounts payable supervisor, payroll supervisor, night auditor, catering manager, waiter/waitress, bartender, dietician, food/beverage manager, executive chef, fry cook, pastry chef, butcher, steward, executive housekeeper, room attendant, houseperson, marketing director, sales director, group sales coordinator, banquet manager, public relations manager, chief engineer, plumber, carpenter, and electrician.

Hotels and motels are not the only sources for jobs in this industry. Numerous parallel jobs also are available with firms managing condominiums, time-sharing facilities, and senior communities as well as with bed-and-breakfast operations, inns, and campgrounds.

Jobs should be plentiful throughout the 1990s for entry-level personnel in the lodging industry. Many of these jobs only require a high school education and little or no experience. Individuals receive on-the-job training, and many employees quickly move from entry-level positions to management positions—within five years and with significant increases in salary. Other jobs require extensive experience in the lodging and travel industries as well as high levels of education and training. Overall, however, this is one of the few industries where individuals with high school educations can enter and rapidly advance to positions of major responsibility within the industry.

Benefits

Salaries and benefits of those working in the lodging industry can vary greatly. Entry-level personnel receive relatively low wages, but mid- and upper-level management can earn above average salaries. In 1993, general managers averaged $59,100, ranging from $44,900 in hotels and motels with 150 or fewer rooms to $86,700 in large hotels with over 350 rooms. Front office managers averaged $26,500 a year. Many executive chefs earn more than $40,000 a year.

Working in the lodging industry has numerous benefits. Many employees simply love this industry because of the constantly changing nature of the work, the interesting guests they meet, the opportunities to frequently travel and relocate, and the fast-track career advancement they experience. Public relations managers in major international hotels, for example, feel they have one of the best jobs in the world—they work in a first-class environment and are constantly meeting and dining with celebrities and other VIPs. And they have opportunities to transfer to other properties within the hotel chain.

One of the major benefits for many individuals working in this industry is travel and relocation. After working three or four years with one hotel, one can move on to another hotel. Management personnel interested in international operations frequently relocate to hotels in different countries. Indeed, for many people, working in a major hotel or resort in Tahiti, Hong Kong, Bangkok, Singapore, Bali, Sydney, Rome, Madrid, Paris, London, Bermuda, or Anguilla is a dream come true. And to work in several of these exciting locations for a major hotel chain is the ultimate career high!

Breaking In

The lodging industry has a tradition of advancing individuals from entry-level positions to higher level management positions. Many of the major hotel chains, such as Hyatt, Marriot, Hilton, and Sheraton, offer excellent in-house training and career development programs and they transfer personnel to various properties. Getting a job with one of these companies can lead to an excellent career up the corporate ladder and within the larger travel industry. Indeed, it's not unusual to discover managers of major hotel chains began their careers as front desk clerks.

Employers in the accommodations industry look for candidates who demonstrate a willingness to work hard, the ability to learn, and enthusiasm in working with people. If you possess these traits, you may be a good candidate for the accommodations industry.

Entry into the lodging industry can be difficult, especially with major hotel chains where competition is very high. In fact, many hotels are inundated with resumes and applications for a limited number of positions.

The best way to break into this industry is to make direct application to individual hotels. If you don't have a personal contact, start by contacting the Personnel Office or Human Resources Department by telephone as well as send a copy of your resume for their files. You also should monitor classified job ads. Many hotels will advertise vacancies in local newspapers. Some employment firms specialize in recruiting hotel personnel.

If you follow this industry and individual hotels closely, you should be able to identify when and where new properties will open. A new 500-room hotel or resort, for example, may need to quickly staff itself with nearly 500 employees two or three months before its grand opening. You may want to include several of these properties in your job search.

While many hotels continue to hire individuals with little experience for entry-level positions, your chances of getting a job are better if you have some formal training in the industry. Nearly 1,000 schools, colleges, and universities offer a variety of programs for breaking into and advancing within the accommodations industry. Some of the best four-your programs in hotel and restaurant management are offered by Cornell University, Michigan State, Pennsylvania State University, University of Houston, University of Denver, Florida International, and Johnson and Wales.

Travel opportunities in the accommodations industry are best with large international hotel chains with 15 or more properties. Some of the largest or best international hotel chains include Hyatt, Sheraton, Regent, Mandarin Oriental, Holiday Inn, Intercontinental, Novotel, Shangri-La, Oberoi, Hilton, Amanresorts, Marriot, Ramada, Taj International, and Westin.

Resources

For more information on opportunities in the accommodations and lodging industry, contact:

AMERICAN HOTEL & MOTEL ASSOCIATION
1201 New York Ave., NW
Washington, DC 20005-3917
Tel. 202/289-3100

AMERICAN RESORT & RESIDENTIAL
    DEVELOPMENT ASSOCIATION
1220 L St., NW, 5th Floor
Washington, DC 20005
Tel. 202/371-6700

For information on colleges and universities offering programs and
courses relevant to this industry, contact the Council on Hotel,
Restaurant, and Institutional Education for a copy of *A Guide to
College Programs in Hospitality and Tourism*:

COUNCIL ON HOTEL, RESTAURANT,
    AND INSTITUTIONAL EDUCATION
1200 17th St., NW
Washington, DC 20036
Tel. 202/331-5990

The book also is available through the publisher, Wiley and Sons, or
Impact Publications.

TRAVEL WRITERS AND PHOTOGRAPHERS

Travel writers and photographers appear to have some of the most
glamorous jobs in the travel industry. Unlike others, they seem to have
the ultimate freedom to set their own schedules, choose their own
locations, and receive a variety of discounted and free travel benefits.
    Travel writers come in several forms. Many are freelance writers
who produce articles for magazines and newspapers and write travel
books. These individuals are usually paid for each article they write
or given royalties for books they produce. The pay is usually very
low—$25 for a short article or $150 for a two-page article is typical.
Other travel writers are salaried employees of major trade publications,
commercial magazines, and newspapers. Indeed, over 300 weekly and
monthly magazines employ travel editors. Over 400 newspapers have
full or part-time travel editors.

The Life

Do you want to travel free and do so in first-class style? You can if you become a travel writer.

Travel writing is as much a lifestyle as an occupation. Many people become travel writers because travel is in their blood and they love the wonderful benefits given to travel writers. Except for full-time travel editors who may combine their travel writing responsibilities with other editorial duties, most travel writers simply love to travel and write about it at the same time. Getting paid for it, however minimal, is even better.

The real benefits of a travel writer do not lie in direct compensation in the form of salaries, fees, or royalties. As most travel writers know, the real benefits come in the form of complementary air transportation and accommodations. Many airlines, hotels, restaurants, and travel wholesalers routinely give travel writers "freebies" in exchange for free publicity. An all-inclusive 10-day trip that might normally cost $5,000 may be given free to a travel writer in exchange for receiving major coverage in an article or travel book. Consequently, many if not most travel articles and books tend to be biased toward those airlines, hotels, travel wholesalers, and restaurants that provide the writer with freebies. Only a few travel writers claim to pay their own way and refuse to accept the perks that come with the occupation.

Opportunities

Freelance travel writers are basically travel entrepreneurs who become travel writers by getting travel articles published. Their major qualification is persuading editors to accept their work. They take trips, write about them, and submit their articles for publication in major magazines and newspapers. While this is the easiest way to break into travel writing—declare yourself a travel writer and get published—it can also be the most frustrating. Competition among freelance writers is great. Many publications prefer publishing pieces produced by their own staff rather than purchase freelance articles. Those that do publish outside articles usually rely on a core of established travel writers.

Given the nominal fees paid for freelance travel articles, it is extremely difficult to make a living as a freelance travel writer. As a result, many freelance travel writers do this type of work as a sideline to some other occupation. The real benefits for them lie in the free and discounted travel they receive rather than the income they generate from writing.

Numerous opportunities for travel writers are available with trade publications. Most professional travel associations publish newspapers and magazines. Their staffs report on developments within their respective associations. Major trade publications include:

- *Aviation Weekly*
- *ASTA Agency Management*
- *Business Travel News*
- *Corporate Travel*
- *Lodging*
- *Meetings & Conventions*
- *Meeting News*
- *Successful Meetings*
- *Tour & Travel News*
- *Travel Age (East, West, MidAmerica)*
- *Travel Agent*
- *Travel Management Daily*
- *Travel Trade*
- *Travel Weekly*
- *Travellife*

Numerous commercial magazines also hire travel writers as well as work with freelance travel writers. The three major travel magazines include:

- *Conde Nast's Traveler*
- *Travel & Leisure*
- *Travel/Holiday*

Others magazines which have travel sections and articles include:

- *Cosmopolitan*
- *Glamour*
- *Gourmet*
- *Seventeen*

- *Town and Country*
- *Vogue*

Over 400 newspapers either have a travel section or regularly include travel articles. The major position with these newspapers is Travel Editor. However, many individuals in these positions previously held other editorial responsibilities before being assigned to the travel desk. Few travel editors are hired directly from outside the newspaper. Newspapers normally buy freelance travel articles to supplement the writings of their travel editor and staff members. Newspapers with some of the most extensive and influential travel sections include:

- *New York Times*
- *Los Angeles Times*
- *Washington Post*
- *Chicago Tribune*

Travel guidebook writing tends to be dominated by a few publishing houses that offer major travel series which are published annually. The major travel series include:

- Birnbaum's
- Fielding's
- Fodor's
- Frommer's
- Insight Guides
- Lonely Planet
- Moon Guides

Most publishers of these series work with a core of writers who are assigned to complete specific travel volumes in a series. They normally pay their writers on a royalty basis (8-15 percent of net receipts).

Smaller publishers may offer less extensive and more specialized travel series, and some publish books submitted by freelance writers. However, most smaller publishers tend to specialize in particular travel areas and work with their own group of established writers.

It is very difficult to break into guidebook travel writing. The competition is extremely keen and the financial rewards are not particularly impressive except for a few bestselling books—mostly on Europe and the Caribbean—that appear in the major travel series.

Travel Photographers

Travel photographers face an even more competitive environment than travel writers. While magazines and newspapers use photographs, they often get them directly from the authors of articles, tourist offices, or photo bureaus. Rarely do editors give photo assignments to photographers. Consequently, most travel photographers tend to be freelance photographers who are constantly frustrated in trying to market their photos to travel publications. Many travel photographers find it easier to sell their photos to stock houses, such as New York-based Black Star, Freelance Photographers Guild, and Gamma/Liaison.

Resources

If you want to become a travel writer or photographer, you might begin by consulting the following books:

How to Make Money From Travel Writing, Casewit, Curtis (Chester, CT: The Globe Pequot Press, 1988).

Travel Photography: A Complete Guide to How to Shoot and Sell, Susan McCarthey (New York: Allsworth Press, 1991).

The Travel Writer's Guide, Gordon Burgitt (Rocklin, CA: Prima Publishing, 1990).

Travel Writer's Handbook, Louise Purwin Zobel (Chicago: Surrey Books, 1992).

Travel Writer's Markets, Elaine O'Gara (Boston: Harvard Common Press, 1989).

Travel Writing For Profit and Pleasure, Perry Garfinkel (New York: Plume/NAL-Dutton, 1989).

Writer's Market (Cincinnati: Writer's Digest, annual).

Several open universities (Learning Annex in New York and Washington, DC) offer intensive three to eight-hour courses on travel writing. Most are "how to" courses on how to travel free by becoming a travel writer. Most people attending these courses are probably more interested in learning how to travel free than becoming a legitimate travel writer.

Unfortunately, some travel writing books and short courses tend to abuse the hospitality of the travel industry as well as give travel writing a bad name—encourage individuals to rip off the travel industry for freebies. As a result, many sponsors of travel writers are understandably suspect of anyone claiming to be a travel writer. They usually want to see evidence of previous travel writing (clippings) as well as a letter from an editor confirming the fact that the writer is on a specific research/writing assignment. The days when anyone could just declare themselves a travel writer—perhaps print their own "Travel Writer" stationery and business cards—and expect to get travel freebies for ostensibly being "on assignment" are largely gone.

Many established travel writers belong to the Society of American Travel Writers (4101 Lake Boone Trail, Suite 201, Raleigh, NC 27607, Tel. 919/787-5181). Membership in this organization, however, is very restrictive, confined mainly to public relations directors with major airlines and travel editors and writers with years of experience. You must be sponsored by three members in order to be considered for membership in SATW. One of the major benefits of being a member of this organization is that most travel wholesalers, hotels, and airlines routinely offer free trips to members. Indeed, the SATW's monthly newsletter lists upcoming "fam" trips its members are encouraged to take advantage of. Many members of the travel industry prefer channeling such promotional efforts through the Society of American Travel Writers because members of this organization are considered legitimate travel writers who are constantly "on assignment." The chances of being ripped off by an enterprising and instant "Travel Writer" who may have just completed a "travel free" book or how-to course are much less by confining promotional efforts through the SATW.

USEFUL RESOURCES

You will find numerous resources available to assist you with a job search within the travel industry, from general job and career books to directories and publications of professional associations. In addition to the specific books mentioned throughout this chapter, you may want to refer to two books which give a good overview of opportunities in the travel industry:

Travel and Hospitality Career Directory, Bradley J. Morgan (ed.) (Detroit, MI: Visible Ink Press, 1992).

Flying High In Travel, Karen Rubin (New York: Wiley, 1992).

Each book has informative chapters on various segments of the travel industry. These two books are available through Impact Publications (see order form at the end of this book). You will also find a few other career books that deal with specific segments of the industry, such as careers as a travel agent, airline pilot, travel writer, or in hotel management and cruise lines. Many of these books should be available in your local library and a few bookstores.

You should also begin reading several of the trade publications and following developments within the professional travel associations. Magazines such as *Travel Digest, Travel Weekly, Hotel and Resort Industry, Meetings and Conventions, Successful Meetings,* and *Tour and Travel News* will keep you abreast of developments in the travel industry. Professional associations such as the Institute of Certified Travel Agents, International Association of Convention and Visitors Bureaus, Meeting Professionals International, and the Society of Incentive Travel Executives provide information on their organization and membership. Contact information on these and other travel industry publications, associations, and companies is provided in the *Travel and Hospitality Career Directory*.

5

FEDERAL, STATE, AND LOCAL GOVERNMENT

*F*ederal, state, and local governments offer numerous on-the-job opportunities to travel. Whether you are traveling or living abroad or inspecting projects, field offices, or products within the United States, government can be one of the best employers for travel.

INTERNATIONAL TRAVEL

The largest number of international job opportunities in the United States are found with various agencies of the federal government.

Approximately 140,000 federal civilian employees work overseas. Another 400,000 U.S. military work in overseas U.S. installations.

But these numbers represent less than half of all government employees working in international affairs. The majority of international-related government jobs are based in the United States. These jobs either provide support for agency field operations or they direct international operations from U.S.-based offices. Each agency has some international interest and staff themselves accordingly. At the same time, since many state and local governments are involved in international affairs, they too need international staff expertise.

While many of the federal government's international jobs are based in the United States and require occasional travel abroad, many other international jobs require residence in foreign countries and rotation from one field site to another as well as between field and headquarter offices. For example, the U.S. Information Agency (USIA) has nearly 7,800 employees of whom 3,400 work in the U.S. They provide support for field operations consisting of 4,000 foreign nationals hired by USIA.

For a detailed examination of overseas opportunities with federal agencies, see Will Cantrell's and Francine Modderno's 430-page guide, *How to Find an Overseas Job With the U.S. Government* (Oakton, VA: Worldwise Books, 1992). It is available directly from Impact Publications (see order form at the end of this book).

FEDERAL EXECUTIVE AGENCIES

The federal government hires all types of individuals for international positions, ranging from highly skilled intelligence specialists to clerk-typists. Most positions deal with international politics, economics, administrative, commercial, and information affairs as well as all support services required to perform numerous international activities.

The distinction between what is an international or a non-international job is not always clear. For example, one may be employed as a Department of State librarian in charge of maintaining an excellent international resource collection. While this position involves a great deal of knowledge and skill concerning international affairs, it does not involve overseas travel nor the use of foreign languages. Yet, the position could lead to other international positions requiring overseas travel and the use of foreign languages.

For our purposes, we consider any position which to some degree involves international affairs to be an international position. This broad definition includes Foreign Service Officers, Peace Corps volunteers and staff, U.S. Agency for International Development employees, members of intelligence and immigration agencies (CIA, DIA, FBI, DEA, INS) as well as thousands of individuals in other agencies promoting U.S. foreign, military, economic, and social goals in both policy and support staff positions at the federal, state, and local levels. Some agencies and positions are primarily oriented toward foreign policy whereas others are mainly concerned with promoting domestic policies, especially trade and economic development, through the use of international resources.

Executive Office of the President

The Executive Office of the President, while employing only 1,600 individuals, has a few international positions. The major offices with such positions include:

- Office of Economic Advisors
- National Security Council
- Office of Management and Budget
- Office of Science and Technology Policy
- Office of the U.S. Trade Representative
- White House Office

Executive Departments

Most international jobs in the federal government are found among the following executive departments:

- **Department of Agriculture**
  - Foreign Agricultural Service
  - Office of International Cooperation and Development
  - Economics and Statistics Service (International Economic Division)
  - Agricultural Market Service
  - Animal and Plant Health Inspection Service
  - Forest Service (International Forestry Staff)
  - Office of Transportation
  - Science and Education Administration

- World Food and Agricultural Outlook and Situation Board
- **Department of Commerce**
  - International Trade Administration
  - Foreign Commercial Service
  - Bureau of the Census
  - National Oceanic and Atmospheric Administration
  - Bureau of Economic Analysis
  - United States Travel Service
  - Maritime Administration
  - National Bureau of Standards
  - National Telecommunications and Information Administration
  - Office of Products Standards Policy
  - Patent and Trademark Office
- **Department of Defense and Related Agencies**
  - Office of the Assistant Secretary for International Security Affairs
  - Office of the Undersecretary of Defense for Research and Engineering
  - Army Materiel Development and Readiness Command
  - Planning and Policy Directorate of the Organization of the Joint Chiefs of Staff
  - Office of the Secretary of Defense
    NOTE: Department of Defense maintains a special service to assist individuals with overseas employment: Department of Defense Automated Overseas Employment Referral Program (DOD AOERP)
  - Defense Advanced Research Projects Agency
  - Defense Intelligence Agency
  - Defense Security Assistance Agency
  - Department of Defense Dependents Schools
  - National Security Agency/Central Security Service
- **Department of Education**
  - Office of International Education
  - Office of the Administrator of Education for Overseas Dependents
- **Department of Energy**
  - Office of International Energy Affairs
  - Assistant Secretary for Defense Programs
  - Assistant Secretary for Policy and Evaluation

- Economic Regulatory Administration
- Energy Information Administration
- Office of Energy Research
- **Department of Health and Human Services**
  - Office of International Health
  - Social Security Administration (Division of International Operations and Office of International Policy)
  - National Institutes of Health (Fogarty International Center)
  - National Center for Health Statistics
    —Alcohol, Drug Abuse, and Mental Health Administration
    —Center for Disease Control
- **Department of Interior**
  - Office of Territorial and International Affairs
  - Bureau of Mines
  - U.S.Geological Survey
  - Bureau of Land Management
  - Ocean Mining Administration
  - U.S. Fish and Wildlife Service
  - National Park Service
  - Water and Power Resources Service
- **Department of Justice and Related Agencies**
  - Department of Justice
    —Antitrust Division
    —Civil Division
    —Criminal Division
    —Office of the Deputy Attorney General
    —Office of Intelligence Policy Review
    —Foreign Claims Settlement Commission of the United States
  - Drug Enforcement Administration (DEA)
    —Office of Intelligence
  - Federal Bureau of Investigation (FBI)
  - Immigration and Naturalization Service (INS)
- **Department of Labor**
  - Bureau of International Labor Affairs
  - Bureau of Labor Statistics
- **Department of State**
  - U.S. Foreign Service
  - All other offices
- **Department of Transportation**
  - Office of International Policy and Programs

- Federal Aviation Administration (Office of International Aviation Affairs)
- Federal Highway Administration
- Saint Lawrence Seaway Development Corporation
- U.S. Coast Guard (Office of Public and International Affairs)
- **Department of Treasury**
  - Office of the Assistant Secretary for International Affairs
  - United States Customs Service
  - Office of International Tax Affairs
  - International Revenue Service (Office of International Operations; Foreign Tax Assistance Staff)
  - Office of the Comptroller of the Currency

Independent Agencies

Several independent agencies also are involved in international affairs. The major ones include:

- **Central Intelligence Agency**
- **Civil Aeronautics Board**
  - Bureau of International Affairs
- **Consumer Product Safety Commission**
  - Office of International Affairs
- **Environmental Protection Agency**
  - Office of International Activities
- **Export-Import Bank of the United States**
- **Federal Communications Commission**
  - Office of Science and Technology (International Staff)
  - Common Carrier Bureau (International Conference Staff)
  - International Facilities Office
- **Federal Maritime Commission**
- **Federal Reserve System**
  - Division of International Finance
  - Division of Banking Supervision and Regulation
  - Federal Open Market Committee
- **General Services Administration**
  - National Archives and Records Service
- **Inter-American Foundation**
- **National Aeronautics and Space Administration**
  - Office of International Affairs

- **National Science Foundation**
  - Division of International Programs
- **Nuclear Regulatory Commission**
  - Office of International Programs
- **Panama Canal Commission**
- **Peace Corps**
- **Securities and Exchange Commission**
  - Corporate Finance Division
  - Enforcement Division
  - Market Regulation Division
- **Smithsonian Institution**
  - Office of International Activities
  - Office of Fellowships and Grants
  - Office of Museum Programs
  - International Exchange Service
  - Traveling Exhibition Service
  - Woodrow Wilson International Center for Scholars
- **U.S. Institute of Peace**
- **U.S. Arms Control and Disarmament Agency**
- **U.S. Information Agency**
- **U.S. International Development Cooperation Agency**
  - Agency for International Development
  - Overseas Private Investment Corporation
- **U.S. International Trade Commission**
- **U.S. Postal Service**
  - Office of International Postal Affairs

Commissions, Committees, Advisory Groups

A final group of federal executive employers which hire international specialists are the various commissions, committees, and advisory groups established by the president or congress. Most of these groups are attached to particular departments or agencies. Some are permanent whereas others function for only one or two years. Examples of such groups include:

- Commission on the Ukraine Famine
- Committee for the Implementation of Textile Agreements
- Committee on Foreign Investment in the United States
  Japan-United States Friendship Commission

- National Advisory Council on International Monetary and Financial Policies
- U.S. National Commission for UNESCO (Department of State)

Your best strategy for getting a job with these groups is to monitor their formation through the *Congressional Record* and the *Federal Register*. As soon as you learn of the impending formation of a group, contact the individuals responsible for establishing the group. Schedule an appointment for an informational interview, and leave a copy of your resume with the individual you interviewed.

Overseas Staffs and Recruitment

Most executive agencies do not maintain overseas staffs. Agencies with overseas staffs sometimes recruit individuals locally, normally among staff spouses and talented expatriates, and through central personnel offices in Washington, DC. Overall, however, most recruitment for international jobs with federal agencies is done in the United States. Indeed, given the Washington bias of federal agencies, it is difficult to find employment with agencies if you are abroad, even though a vacancy is available for which you are highly qualified. Most agencies prefer recruiting individuals in the States and then transferring them to field sites.

The major agencies maintaining overseas staffs and conducting some in-country recruitment are:

- Department of Defense
- Department of State
- Peace Corps
- U.S. Agency for International Development
- U.S. Information Agency
- Central Intelligence Agency

Hiring Systems and Job Search Strategies

Hiring procedures and practices vary among executive agencies. Several agencies, for example, are exempted from the competitive service whereas others follow the Office of Personnel Management's (OPM) rules and regulations. Exempted services have their own hiring procedures. The **Department of State**, for example, follows the

European pattern of a career and rank personnel service. Responsible for promoting U.S. foreign policy, the Foreign Service employs over 9,000 people as Foreign Service Officers and Specialists. Special recruitment and selection procedures define entry into the Foreign Service. Each December approximately 12,000 individuals normally sit for the written Foreign Service examination to gain entry into the Department of State (Foreign Service Officers), the U.S. Information Agency (Foreign Service Information Officers), and Department of Commerce (Foreign Service Commercial Officers). However, occasionally this yearly exam is suspended when there is little or no demand for new officers.

Once selected, most Foreign Service Officers spend the rest of their career in the Foreign Service. Their "tour" involves being transferred to several of the 230 embassies and consulates the U.S. maintains throughout the world as well as moves from one type of position to another. Rather than being hired as specialists for a particular position, they are hired as international specialists who move through the ranks. The "ranks" consist of many positions requiring different types of skills and knowledge.

For information on employment opportunities in the Department of State and information on whether or not the annual Foreign Service examination is being given this year, contact:

> Recruitment Division
> U.S. DEPARTMENT OF STATE
> Box 9317
> Arlington, VA 22209
> Tel. 703/875-7490 or
>   1-800/JOB-OVER

The **U.S. Agency For International Development** (USAID) is structured similarly to the Foreign Service. In fact, the majority of USAID positions are designated as Foreign Service positions. At the same time, nearly 40 percent of USAID positions are civilian (GS positions and thus follow OPM procedures). USAID maintains two personnel offices—a civilian office and a Foreign Service office—which are located in Rosslyn, Virginia. If you want to work for USAID, you must decide which personnel system you want to enter. If your choice is Foreign Service, then your career will take a different pattern from that of the civilian-based civil service.

For information on employment opportunities with the Agency for International Development, contact:

U.S. AGENCY FOR INTERNATIONAL
    DEVELOPMENT
320 21st St., NW
Washington, DC 20523
Tel. 202/647-1850

The **Peace Corps** is a good example of another type of personnel system. Peace Corps is one of the most unique agencies created in the federal government. In many respects its volunteers are the "real" international workers. They learn local languages and work in the field with foreign counterparts. No other federal employees work to the same extent at the field level and literally get their hands dirty in international development work. However, entry into the Peace Corps is extremely competitive today. Each year Peace Corps receives more than 13,500 applications for fewer than 3,500 volunteer positions. Once selected, the typical Peace Corps tour is two years; some volunteers extend an additional year. Altogether, there are approximately 6,000 volunteers working in 62 countries throughout the Third World.

Most Peace Corps staff positions are largely limited to individuals with Peace Corps volunteer experience. In addition, staff positions have a built-in time limit. To discourage the growth of a traditional, conservative, and entrenched bureaucracy, Congress placed a statutory time limit on employment with Peace Corps: staff members cannot work more than five consecutive years with the Agency. Consequently, Peace Corps members are hired for two and one-half year tours, which may be extended to a second tour for a total of five years of service. After the second tour, they must leave the Agency. Many staff members look for employment with other federal agencies doing international development work. Indeed, the Department of State alone has 1,000 former Peace Corps volunteers and staff members on its staff. USAID has become one of the major recruiters and employers of former Peace Corps employees.

For information on employment opportunities with the Peace Corps, contact:

PEACE CORPS
1990 K Street, NW
Washington, DC 20526
Tel. 202/606-3886
      1-800/424-8580 x 2225

Applications and Procedures

While some executive agencies may follow other recruitment patterns, most executive departments adhere to the competitive civil service system associated with the Office of Personnel Management. Positions are classified and announced, and candidates must submit one of three optional formal applications—the Standard Form 171 (SF-171), OF-612, or a federal-style resume—and supporting documents to agency personnel offices.

While you may use your conventional resume in networking with agencies, the SF-171, OF-612, or federal-style resume are the critical documents for opening the doors of agencies. Similar to writing a resume, the SF-171, OF-612, or federal-style resume need to be written so they clearly communicate your qualifications to agency personnel. Writing an outstanding SF-171, OF-612, or federal-style resume is an art which follows certain principles of effective writing for federal agencies.

Employment with offices in the Executive Office of the President, independent agencies, committees, and commissions follow more independent hiring patterns. Most of these agencies and offices have their own internal hiring procedures. Therefore, it is best to directly contact their personnel offices to learn about vacancy announcements and the best procedures for applying for particular positions.

Knowing which federal agencies perform international functions and hire international specialists is only the first of many steps involved in getting a federal job with such agencies. You must go far beyond just names, addresses, and phone numbers. Above all, you will need a particular set of job search skills adapted to the federal hiring process.

Keep in mind that both formal and informal hiring systems operate in the case of most federal agencies. The formal system involves vacancy announcements and the submission of applications for specific positions. The informal system involves networking for information, advice, and referrals that hopefully lead to uncovering job vacancies as well as possibly being "sponsored" for positions or having positions "wired" around your qualifications. Your research and networking activities will provide you with the necessary knowledge and contacts to gain entry into these agencies.

Useful Resources

You will find numerous resources available to help you navigate through what is often a confusing federal government hiring process. These range from general job search books and manuals for completing the SF-171, OF-612, or federal-style resumes to directories of agencies and biweekly listings of job vacancy announcements which include international jobs.

While most hiring decisions are decentralized to agencies, you still must follow the formal federal hiring procedures outlined by OPM. Given major application changes initiated by OPM in January 1995, most books on federal employment published before 1995 are now obsolete. The new application system, which includes the use of optional SF-171, OF-612, and federal-style resumes, as well as informal job search strategies appropriate for federal agencies, are outlined in three of our public employment books:

Find a Federal Job Fast!, Ron and Caryl Krannich (Manassas Park, VA: Impact Publications, 1995)

Directory of Federal Jobs and Employers, Ron and Caryl Krannich (Manassas Park, VA: Impact Publications, 1995)

The Complete Guide to Public Employment, Ron and Caryl Krannich (Manassas Park, VA: Impact Publications, 1995)

For detailed information on how to create an effective SF-171, OF-612, or federal-style resume, consult the following workbooks:

Federal Applications That Get Results: From SF-171s to Federal-Style Resumes, Russ Smith (Manassas Park, VA: Impact Publications, 1995)

Using Today's Reinvented Vacancy Announcement (Vienna, VA: Federal Research Service, 1995)

Reinvented Federal Job Application Forms Kit (Vienna, VA: Federal Research Service, 1995)

When you get to the stage of actually producing an SF-171, OF-612, or a federal-style resume, we highly recommend purchasing a copy of the following computer software program which is designed for Windows:

Quick and Easy Federal Application Kit (Harrisburg, PA: DataTech, 1995).

Approved by the U.S. Office of Personnel Management, this program enables you to customize your SF-171, OF-612, or federal-style resume around the specific qualifications of agencies. You can easily expand sections and print the actual form without having to squeeze information onto a preprinted form or cutting and pasting a homemade form. Easy to use and complete with excellent technical support, *Quick and Easy Federal Application Kit* also permits you to print out on a laser, jet ink, or dot matrix printer your completed application.

While many of these resources are difficult to find in bookstores and libraries, most are available through Impact Publications. Order information is available at the end of this book.

Your best sources of information for conducting research on federal agencies with international positions will be several international job books and directories that primarily describe different types of federal agencies. The key international job books include:

The Almanac of International Jobs and Careers, Ron and Caryl Krannich (Manassas Park, VA: Impact Publications, 1994)

Guide to Careers in World Affairs, Foreign Policy Association (Manassas Park, VA: Impact Publications, 1993)

How to Find an Overseas Job With the U.S. Government, Will Cantrell and Francine Modderno (Oakton, VA: Worldwise Books, 1992)

International Jobs, Eric Kocher (Reading, MA: Addison-Wesley, 1993)

Several annual and biannual directories are also available for researching different federal agencies:

The United States Government Manual (Washington, DC: U.S. Government Printing Office, annual)

Federal Yellow Book (Washington, DC: Monitor Publishing Co., annual)

Washington Information Directory (Washington, DC: Congressional Quarterly, Inc., annual)

Federal Executive Directory (Washington, DC: Carroll Publishing Co., annual)

Federal Personnel Office Directory (Washington, DC: Federal Reports, annual)

Government Directory of Addresses and Telephone Numbers (Detroit, MI: Omnigraphics, annual)

Each of these books and directories provides names, addresses, and telephone numbers for locating the right offices and individuals you should contact for employment information.

One useful guide also provides information on where to find job vacancy resources, such as newspapers, magazines, newsletters, and job listing services: *The Government Job Finder*, Daniel Lauber (River Forest, IL: Planning/Communications, 1994).

If you are interested in job vacancy announcements with the federal government, two private firms publish biweekly listings of such announcements. Many of their listings include international jobs:

Federal Career Opportunities (Vienna, VA: Federal Research Service)

Federal Jobs Digest (Scarborough, NY: Break Through Publications)

Most of these resources are available through Impact Publications (see the "Career Resources" section at the end of this book).

CONGRESS

Both Congress and legislative agencies hire a variety of international specialists who have numerous opportunities to travel. Within Congress, international positions are found with congressional committee staffs and personal staffs of senators and representatives.

Committee Staffs

International positions on committee staffs are limited in number and are primarily found on the two most important committees dealing with international issues:

- Senate Foreign Relations Committee
- House Foreign Affairs Committee

Other committees and subcommittees in the House of Representatives also deal with international matters and thus hire individuals with some international background. The relevant committees include:

- Agriculture Committee
- Appropriations Committee
- Armed Services Committee
- Banking, Finance, and Urban Affairs Committee
- Energy and Commerce Committee
- Government Operations Committee
- Science and Technology Committee
- Ways and Means Committee

On the Senate side, several committees deal with similar international issues:

- Agriculture and Forestry Committee
- Appropriations Committee
- Armed Services Committee
- Banking, Housing, and Urban Affairs Committee
- Commerce Committee
- Finance Committee
- Government Affairs Committee

Both the House and Senate have various joint committees which also offer international employment opportunities. The major such committees include the Joint Economic Committee and the Joint Committee on Taxation.

Personal Staffs

Not all Senators and Representatives hire international specialists on their personal staffs. Those that do usually have major responsibilities on assigned committees and subcommittees which deal with international issues. Therefore, you need to first identify who sits on which international committee, and then contact their staffs for information on international positions. Most of these staff positions will involve conducting research, writing reports, and drafting legislation on committee-related matters.

Contact information on the various congressional committees and personal staffs can be found in *Congressional Yellow Book*, *Congressional Directory*, *Congressional Staffing Directory*, and *The American Almanac of Politics*. Follow the same strategies for finding an international job on these staffs as you would for finding any type of staff position in Congress. These strategies are detailed in our books on public employment, *Find a Federal Job Fast!* and *The Complete Guide to Public Employment*.

Legislative Agencies

Most legislative agencies also have international interests and thus hire international specialists. The major agencies and offices include:

- **Congressional Budget Office**
  - National Security and International Affairs Division
- **General Accounting Office**
  - International Division
- **Library of Congress**
  - Congressional Research Service
  - Office of Research Services (Office of the Director for Area Studies)
- **Office of Technology Assessment**

The *Directory of Federal Executives* provides the names and telephone numbers of key individuals to contact in each of these legislative agencies and offices.

STATE AND LOCAL GOVERNMENTS

International opportunities with state and local governments are both relatively unknown and widely overlooked among most international specialists. This is in part due to the expectation that only the federal government engages in foreign policy and international affairs.

During the past two decades, state and city governments have increasingly become involved in international affairs. Many have their own foreign policies involving:

- Trade promotion
- Tourism
- Local economic development
- Immigration
- International shipping

Florida, for example, maintains a state tourism agency which attempts to promote travel to Florida among European tourists. Virginia Beach maintains sister city relationships and promotes foreign industrial investment in the city through their Department of Economic Development. In certain areas, regional economic development authorities, tourism boards, and port authorities perform international functions for several units of government.

State and local governments offer unique international opportunities. They combine local economic issues with international development activities. For individuals who want to be involved in international affairs but wish to avoid many of the negative aspects of international careers—such as living abroad and transfers—these positions may be ideal.

Finding an international job with state and local governments requires a great deal of research and initiative on your part. Except for a section (Chapter Eight) in the Foreign Policy Association's *Guide to Careers in World Affairs* (Manassas Park, VA: Impact Publications, 1993) on international job opportunities with state governments, no directories or books outline state and local agencies with opportunities in international affairs. Hence, your best approach will be to identify which city or state governments you would like to work with and then research the organizations to find the offices involved in international affairs. Both the national and local branches of the World Affairs Council may be helpful in uncovering international positions with these governmental units.

DOMESTIC OPPORTUNITIES

Government also offers numerous opportunities to travel within the United States. Most agencies within the federal government, for example, have extensive field operations. Indeed, only 12 percent of federal government employees work in the Washington, DC metropolitan area. A nearly equal number of federal employees—300,000—reside in California.

Many federal government jobs involve frequent travel between headquarters offices in Washington, DC and field offices spread throughout the continental United States, Alaska, Hawaii, Puerto Rico, and other U.S. territories. Individuals in positions involving inspections, audits, and extension work tend to travel most frequently between field and headquarter offices.

Federal employees that travel the most frequently are U.S. postal workers who have local delivery routes or move the mail by truck between cities and regions each day. If you want a government job that constantly lets you travel, though perhaps not far from home, set your sights on your local post office. For information on how to get a job with the U.S. Postal service, we recommend Veltisezar Bautista's *The Book of U.S. Postal Exams* which is available through Impact Publications.

Many federal jobs relating to law enforcement involve frequent travel. Federal agencies such as the Federal Bureau of Investigation (FBI), Central Intelligence Agency (CIA), Environmental Protection Agency (EPA), Immigration and Naturalization Service (INS), INTER-POL, National Security Agency, Bureau of Alcohol, Tobacco and Firearms (ATF), Customs Service, and the Secret Service, have numerous investigative positions involving travel. For information on how to land a job with these agencies, see John W. Warner, Jr.'s *Federal Jobs in Law Enforcement* (New York: Arco/Prentice-Hall, 1992) and Russ Smith's *Federal Jobs in Law Enforcement* and *Federal Jobs in Secret Operations* (Manassas Park, VA: Impact Publications, 1995).

Many state and local government positions also involve frequent travel. State agencies with field offices or operations, especially in law enforcement, agriculture, and transportation, will have many positions that permit you to regularly travel. At the local level, police officers, building and health inspectors, and maintenance workers are constantly traveling on the job. For information on jobs at the state and local level, we recommend Daniel Lauber's *Government Job Finder* (River Forest, IL: Planning/Communications, 1994).

6

INTERNATIONAL EDUCATION, INTERNSHIPS, & VOLUNTEERISM

*F*or many people, education is synonymous with travel. Indeed, numerous people got their first taste for travel because of a particularly inspiring teacher or an educational program they participated in during their undergraduate or graduate years. Many students have an opportunity to participate in exchange programs, attend semester or summer abroad programs, acquire international internships, or become involved in off-campus field research. For them, combining education with travel is an exciting experience.

Whatever the particular experience, for many individuals it is their key years in education that often convinced them to pursue educational careers in specialties that also permit them to engage in frequent travel at home and abroad. Many literally become travel junkies within education, spending two or more months a year traveling "on assignment" for professional development purposes—be it teaching, research, attending conferences, or acquiring new subject matter or administrative skills. Some even become involved in sponsoring travel abroad programs for students, faculty, and alumni.

TRAVEL AS EDUCATION

Whether you are teaching, conducting research, or administering education programs in the United States or abroad, education offers numerous travel opportunities. Teachers and education administrators regularly attend professional meetings, participate in special programs and seminars, study for higher degrees, and deliver educational services in many different locations. While most teachers working in the traditional classroom, housed in a single school building, travel very little on a daily basis, others who provide outreach, tutorial, adult, and special education services travel daily from one location to another.

Higher education researchers in biology, ecology, geology, geography, oceanography, anthropology, and international relations may spend weeks and months conducting research in remote and exotic locations both at home and abroad. Studying on-site environmental problems along the Amazon River, the family structure of tribal groups in Papua New Guinea, volcanic eruptions in Hawaii and the Philippines, or the latest political developments in Moscow and Beijing can be some of the most exhilarating moments in the lives of educators. This type of travel, rather than classroom teaching or administration, is what draws and keeps many educators in education. For them, one of the major benefits of a job in education is the ability to frequently travel to the "field." Best of all, they often travel free—transportation and per diem expenses—because their projects are frequently funded through grants, contracts, research awards, and seed money provided by foundations, corporations, government, or their educational institution.

INTERNATIONAL EDUCATION

Educational institutions have always been a major avenue for acquiring international experience as well as for pursuing education-related jobs and careers. One of the best ways to break into the international arena is through an educational program. Numerous colleges and universities offer area studies programs as well as internships and semester abroad programs which enable students to acquire first hand experience in living and studying abroad. Some programs even involve working abroad as part of an internship experience.

INTERNSHIPS

Internships both in the United States and abroad provide excellent entry into the international job market. With an internship you may gain valuable international work experience as well as develop important contacts for gaining full-time international employment. Many internships also provide unique opportunities to study and travel while working abroad. Sponsoring internship organizations normally arrange all the details for placement, travel, and accommodations. Upon completing the internship, participants can expect the sponsoring organization to arrange for letters of recommendation from the interns' employers.

International internships come in several forms. Ideally, most people would like to find paid internships with organizations overseas that might lead to being hired on a full-time basis. Some internships come in this form, especially those for business, engineering, and science majors sponsored by the International Association of Students in Economics and Business Management (AIESEC) and the International Association for the Exchange of Students of Technical Experience (IAESTE). These are the two premier international internship organizations that offer paid internships with major international companies.

Most internships, however, tend to be nonpaid, volunteer positions sponsored by colleges and universities or nonprofit organizations. Many of these internships require enrollment, tuition, or program fees to participate in the program. Some of these internship experiences are basically study abroad programs which include a short work experience. Most such programs are designed for students in foreign languages, social sciences, and the humanities. If sponsored by a college or university, students can usually earn academic credits while participating in the internship program. A three to twelve-month internship program may cost participants between $3,000 and $6,000, including international transportation, insurance, visas, and room and board. Like many volunteer positions, these internships may involve basic living and working conditions, such as participating in home-stays and workcamps.

Other international internships are based in the United States with nonprofit public interest, education, and research organizations. While these groups give interns an opportunity to work with important international organizations and issues, they involve little or no international travel. Many of these internships will involve basic research, copyediting, and clerical tasks, but they also offer opportunities to attend seminars, conferences, and make important international contacts.

Many internships are for two to three-month periods while others run for six to twelve-months or coincide with regular or summer college semester programs. Others may be flexible, depending on the individual interns interests and skills. Many internships can lead to full-time employment with the sponsoring organization.

Most international internship programs tend to be centered in Washington, DC, the center for hundreds of government, nonprofit, and consulting organizations involved in international affairs.

Most internship programs have application deadlines and several charge fees for processing applications. Some require an application package consisting of a resume, transcript, writing sample, recommendations, and a letter of availability and interest. Be sure to call, fax, or write the organization for current application details.

If you are interested in an internship or volunteer position with an organization involved in the international arena, do not restrict your search efforts only to the organizations included in this chapter. You should be creative, aggressive, and persistent. Many of the organizations and employers listed in previous chapters, especially nonprofit organizations and consultants, are open to enterprising individuals who approach them with a proposal for an internship. In other words, you can create your own internship by directly approaching an organization with a detailed proposal. Do your homework on the organization. Identify what knowledge and skills you can bring to such a position as well as the experience you hope to acquire from such an experience. You'll be surprised how many employers will be interested in your proposal. In the process you will gain invaluable international work experience specifically tailored to your needs and long-term international career goals.

Major Internship Organizations and Programs

The following businesses, government agencies, nonprofit organizations, and educational institutions offer a variety of internship experiences throughout the world. Many of the internships are based in the United States while others involve working overseas.

ACCESS: A Security Information Service
1730 M Street, NW, 605
Washington, DC 20046
Tel. 202/785-6630

A computerized database clearinghouse that assists educators, researchers, journalists, and other interested groups in acquiring information on international affairs. Has three internship positions which pay $50 per week: inquiry/speakers referral intern; outreach intern; and publications intern. Positions require good communication, research, marketing, and coordination skills and a strong background in international affairs. Contact the Internship Coordinator.

ACCION International
130 Prospect Street
Cambridge, MA 02139
(no phone calls please)

A nonprofit group operating in Central and Latin America for the purpose or reducing poverty and improving the employability of the poor. Offers two types of internships: Latin American operations intern and resource development intern. These are unpaid, volunteer internships open to college undergraduates, graduates, graduate students, and those with work experience. Positions require good organization and communication skills. Contact the Communications Specialist.

AIESEC-United States, Inc.
841 Broadway, Suite 608
New York, NY 10003
Tel. 212/757-3774

One of the premier international internship organizations managed by students for students majoring in economics and business. Operates with local chapters on 73 member campuses throughout the U.S. Focuses on international management. Approximately 300 internships available each year with such companies as AT&T, IBM, and Unisysm. These are paid internships ($200-$400 a week). Most internships are for 2-18 month periods. Applicants must apply through campus chapters. Most applicants are college juniors or seniors who have completed at least two years of basic business and language courses.

American Institute for Foreign Study, College Division
102 Greenwich Avenue
Greenwich, CT 06830
Tel. 800/727-AIFS, Ext. 6097
Fax 203/869-9615

This organization arranges the international exchange of high school and college students and adults. Its field of operations encompasses 14 campuses in Mexico, Europe, Asia, and Australia. It offers about 40 internships each year for a duration of 12 to 15 weeks each. Participants combine academic classes with work experience. These are unpaid, voluntary internships for college juniors, seniors, and graduate students. Requires a $35 applicant processing fee.

The American-Scandinavian Foundation
725 Park Avenue
New York, NY 10021
Tel. 212-879-9779
Fax 212/249-3444

This nonprofit organization promotes educational and cultural exchanges between the United States and Denmark, Finland, Norway, and Sweden. Designed for college juniors and seniors, this program offers 50-100 summer internships for engineers, computer specialists, agriculturalists, and horticulturalists. These are paid internships in which participants receive a stipend. Participants are expected to pay from $120 and $385 each month for housing. Application deadline is December 15. Requires a $50 applicant processing fee and a resume.

American Slavic Student Internship
1841 Broadway, Suite 607
New York, NY 10023
Tel. 212/262-3862

This nonprofit organization arranges internships in Russia in the fields of education, business, publishing, media, tourism, and sports. Participants receive a monthly stipend. Duration of internships is from one month to two years. Requires program fees ranging from $1,500 to $4,500, depending on the destination, duration of program, and type of accommodations provided.

Africa News Service
Internship Program
Box 3851
Durham, NC 27702
Tel. 919/286-0747

Offers 10 internships for students of journalism and African affairs. Work involves research, writing, and clerical duties. These are unpaid internships, but the Africa News Agency will assist in finding inexpensive living accommodations in Durham, NC. Applicants must submit an approach letter, letters of recommendations, transcripts, and a writing sample.

Amnesty International USA, Washington Office
304 Pennsylvania Avenue, SE
Washington, DC 20003
Tel. 202/544-0200
Fax 202/546-7142

This global nonprofit organization focuses on the release of prisoners of conscience. It lobbies international organizations and governments as well as focuses media attention on the release of political prisoners and the end of torture and executions. It offers 10 unpaid internships each year for a minimum of 10 weeks each. Applicants must be high school graduates.

The Arms Control Association
11 Dupont Circle, Suite 250
Washington, DC 20036
Tel. 202/797-4626
Fax 202/797-4611

This nonprofit research organization focusing on educating the public about arms control and related issues. Offers 12 unpaid internships each year involving research, writing, proofreading, editing, layout, and general clerical work. Open to college sophomores, juniors, seniors, college graduates, and graduate students. Application deadline is May 15. Contact the Intern Coordinator for information and application details.

ASHOKA: Innovators for the Public
1700 North Moore St., Suite 1920
Arlington, VA 22209
Tel. 703/527-8300
Fax 703/527-8300

This nonprofit organization awards fellowships for innovation ideas related to social change in Africa, Asia, and Latin America. Offers 15 unpaid internships each year related to publications, press relations, publicity, fundraising, and fellowship relations. Duration of internships varies. Contact the Intern Coordinator for information and application procedures.

Association to Unite the Democracies
1506 Pennsylvania Avenue, SE
Washington, DC 20003
Tel. 202/544-5150
Fax 202/544-3742

This association promotes world order and democracy through educational programs, publications, and conferences. It offers paid internships ($250 per month) for periods of 4-6 months each. Candidates should have an interest in international relations, demonstrate a good command of English, and have good computer and foreign language skills. Applicants must submit a resume, writing sample, transcript, recommendation, and a letter explaining their interest in working for AUD. Application deadline is January 1 for spring, May 1 for summer, and August 1 for fall.

The Atlantic Council of the United States
1616 H Street, NW
Washington, DC 20006
Tel. 202/347-9353
Fax 202/737-5163

This nonprofit, nonpartisan organization formulates policy recommendations for the developed democracies of the European and Asian communities. Offers several 8-12 week nonpaid internships. Most internships involve program development, policy research and recommendations, special projects, fundraising, and publication support. Open to college juniors, seniors, graduates, and graduate students. Contact the Internship Coordinator for further information.

Beaver College Center for Education Abroad
Beaver College
Glenside, PA 19038
Tel. 800/767-0029

Beaver College arranges junior-senior year study abroad programs for numerous colleges and universities. It offers 60 unpaid internships each year. Internships run for one semester. Candidates must be currently enrolled in an accredited American college or university with a GPA of 3.0 and at least a 3.3 in three courses in the internship discipline. Interns receive academic credit for courses taken during the internship period. Open to college juniors and seniors. Requires a $35 application fee. Application deadlines are October 15 for spring and April 20 for fall. Contact the Program Coordinator for further information.

Brethren Volunteer Service
1451 Dundee Avenue
Elgin, IL 60120
Tel. 708/742-6103
Fax 708/742-6103

Sponsored by the Church of the Brethren, this organization promotes peace, justice, and human and environmental welfare through numerous programs in 20 countries. Offers over 100 domestic and overseas internships. Domestic internships run for 1 year. Overseas internships require a 2-year minimum commitment and involve working in one of 34 projects in such countries as China, El Salvador, France, Germany, Israel, the Netherlands, Nicaragua, Nigeria, Northern Ireland, and Poland. Internships pay $45-$65 per month and include free room and board. Candidates for overseas internships should be college graduates, Christians, at least 21 years of age, and in good health. Candidates for domestic internships should be high school graduates, Christians, and at least 18 years of age. Application deadlines are July 1 for fall, January 1 for spring, and May 1 for summer. Contact the Recruiter for further information.

CDS International, Inc.
330 7th Avenue
New York, NY 10001
Tel. 212/760-1400
Fax 212/268-1288

CDS combines language training and work experience for Americans interested in Germany and Germans interested in the U.S. Offers different types of 3, 6, 12, and 18 month paid internships. Requires an in-person interview. Open to college juniors, seniors, and graduates. Favors individuals with majors in a business, technical, or agricultural field. Application deadline is five months prior to starting the internship. Contact the Program Officer for detailed information on different internship programs.

Center for the Study of Conflict
5842 Bellona Avenue
Baltimore, MD 21212
Tel. 301/323-7656

This is a research and education organization dedicated to the study and application of conflict resolution methods. Offers two unpaid internships each year. Length of internship is flexible. Interns perform research, copyediting, and general office work. Open to high school seniors, high school graduates, college students, college graduates, graduate students, and others. Contact the Director.

Committee for National Security
1601 Connecticut Avenue
Washington, DC 20009
Tel. 202/745-2450
Fax 202/387-6298

This nonprofit educational research group focuses on the study of arms control, defense budgets, and chemical and biological weaponry. It offers three unpaid research and legislative tracking internships lasting 3-4 months each. Each semester one internship is awarded to an minority student who also receives a $500 stipend. Open to college sophomores, juniors, seniors, and graduate students. Apply to the Program Coordinator with a letter, resume, transcripts, and recommendations. Final selection requires an in-person interview. Application deadlines are May 1 for summer, August 1 for fall, and December 1 for spring.

Delegation of the Commission of the European Communities
2100 M Street, NW
Suite 707
Washington, DC 20037
Tel. 202/862-9544
Fax 202/429-1766

This organization promotes better communication and understanding between the United States and the European Community. It offers 10-12 internships in academic affairs, public inquiries, speakers' bureau, and the Europe Magazine. Individuals perform research, information dissemination, and clerical duties. Each internship is unpaid and lasts five months. Open to college juniors, seniors, graduates, and graduate students. Contact the Assistant for Academic Affairs for more information.

Educational Programs Abroad
540 Giordano Drive
Yorktown Heights, NY 10598
Tel. 914/245-6882

This nonprofit organization provides 80-100 internships in Europe (Bonn, Cologne, London, Madrid, Paris, and Strasbourg) for a variety of fields—advertising, business, law, education, health care, politics, social science, theater, and urban planning. During the academic year internships run for one semester; summer internships last 10 weeks. These are unpaid internships in which participants are expected to pay a program fee ranging from $1,780 to $6,300 which includes room and board. Open to college juniors, seniors, and graduate students. Foreign language competence a necessity for interns in Bonn, Paris, and Madrid. Requires an application fee of $25. Applicants should send a transcript, two letters of recommendation, and an essay on their career goals.

Export-Import Bank of the United States (Eximbank)

811 Vermont Avenue, NW
Washington, DC 20571
Tel. 202/566-8834

This independent government agency promotes the export financing of U.S. goods and services. It sponsors 15-20 summer and semester interns each year in the areas of accounting, economics, financial analysis, and computer work. Open to undergraduate and graduate students. Favors majors in business administration, computer science, economics, finance, and marketing. Applicants must summit a federal application and college transcripts. Application deadline is March 31.

General Electric Company

Recruiting and University Development
1285 Boston Avenue, Building 23CE
Bridgeport, CT 06601
Tel. 203/382-2000

General Electric Company hires numerous undergraduate and graduate interns for offices around the world: aerospace, aircraft engines, National Broadcasting Company (NBC), electrical distribution and control communications and services, motors, financial services, industrial and power systems, lighting, transportation systems, appliance, medical systems, and plastics. These are paid internships. Applicants should send a resume and cover letter indicating their desired position.

Independent University

3001 Veazey Terrace, NW
Washington, DC 20008
Tel. 202/362-7855; Fax 202/364-0200

Promoting better relations between the United States and the Commonwealth of Independent States, this organization primarily holds conferences, seminars, and education programs for students and leaders in business, politics, and academia in these countries. It offers two unpaid program coordinator internships for a period of 4 months. Applicants should be proficient in WordPerfect and dBase software. Open to college juniors, seniors, graduates, and graduate students. Contact the president for more information.

INET For Women

P.O. Box 6178
McLean, VA 22106
Tel. 703/873-8541
Fax 703/241-0090

This international trade and business organization promotes more effective strategies for cross-border transitions. It offers several unpaid internships lasting from 1½-6 months in information systems, public relations, advertising, marketing, membership administration, and events planning. Open to college juniors, seniors, graduates, and individuals re-entering the work force. Requires a $10 registration and processing fee. Contact the President for more information.

Institute for Central American Studies (ICAS)

Apartado 300
1002 San Jose, Costa Rica

ICAS promotes the peace, justice, and well-being of people in Central America through research and information dissemination. It offers 12-18 internships each year for journalism and area studies majors. Internships last six months and can commence at any time. Applicants pay a $200 administrative fee. Open to recent college graduates as well as some undergraduate and graduate students. Must have a working knowledge of Spanish.

The International Center

731 8th Street, SE
Washington, DC 20003
Tel. 202/547-3800
Fax 202/546-4783

The International Center focuses on U.S. foreign policy in Asia and Russia for the purpose of promoting democratic movements and the resolution of regional conflicts. It offers 10 internships. The internships involve research, writing, and general clerical duties centering on projects relating to Asia and Russia as well as the New Forests Project (promotes reforestations and economic development in developing countries). These are unpaid internships lasting for a period of 10 weeks. Open to college juniors, seniors, graduates, and graduate students. Application deadlines are June 30 for the fall, November 30 for the spring, and March 31 for the summer.

International Visitors Information Service (IVIS)

1623 Belmont Street, NW
Washington, DC 20009
Tel. 202/939-5566
Fax 202/232-9783

Affiliated with the Meridian International Center, IVIS sponsors programs and provides services to international visitors in Washington, DC. Offers one paid ($5.85 per hour) internship involving general office work. Duration of internship is one semester. Candidates should have foreign language skills. Contact the Executive Director for more information.

Legacy International
128 North Fayette Street
Alexandria, VA 22314
(no phone calls please)

Primarily focusing on Russia, this organization sponsors research, programs, and projects for promoting environmentally sound development, resolution of ethnic and religious conflicts, education, and experiential leadership training. Offers unpaid internships involving research, administration, and clerical support. Preferred candidates should have a background in international politics, Russian area studies, environmental studies, and intercultural education. Open to college graduates. Requires an in-person interview. Contact the Administrator.

Marymount Study Abroad Program
Marymount College
Terrytown, NY 10591-3796
Tel. 914/332-8222
Fax 914/631-8586

This unique study abroad program is designed for undergraduates who attend universities and polytechnics in central London. The program provides unpaid internships in a variety of fields, such as fashion design, merchandising, public relations, publishing, museums, journalism, communications, hotel management, and international business. Open to college juniors and seniors. Contact the Director, Study Abroad Program for more information.

The Ohio International Agricultural Intern Program
Ohio State University
2120 Fyffe Road
Columbus, OH 43210-1099
(no phone calls please)

This program provides both American and foreign agricultural students with opportunities to learn about agricultural/horticulture and veterinary medicine in different national and cultural settings. About 50 American internships are available each year for 3 month periods. These are paid ($4.25-$8.00 an hour) internships. Applicants should have backgrounds in agriculture/horticulture, veterinary, or medicine and the ability to speak a foreign language. Open to 19-26 year old college students and college graduates. Requires a $120 fee for administration and visas. Contact the program manager for more information.

People to People International
501 East Armour Boulevard
Kansas City, MO 64109-2200
Tel. 816/531-4701
Fax 816/561-7502

This nonprofit educational and cultural exchange organization administers exchange programs for high school, college, and adult/professional groups in over 30 countries. Offers unpaid internships for 2-3 month periods. Interns are responsible for matching individuals to the various exchange programs. Candidates should have overseas experience. Open to college seniors, graduates, and graduate students, and career changers. Contact the Vice President for Programs. Application deadline is April 15 for summer; some fall and spring placements.

Radio Free Europe/Radio Liberty Fund, Inc.
Training Department Personnel Division
Box 86 Oettingenstrasse 67, D-8000
Munich 22 Germany

This independent news and broadcasting corporation promotes better communication with the peoples of Eastern Europe and the Commonwealth of Independent States. It hires more than 10 research and electrical engineering interns for 8-12 week periods. Interns are paid $48 a day. Research interns travel to Munich and should be fluent in a language of Eastern Europe or the Commonwealth of Independent States. Electrical engineering interns should be fluent in German, Portuguese, or Spanish. Open to highly qualified undergraduates and graduate students. Application deadline in mid-February. For more information, including an application, contact: Summer Internship Program, RFE/FL, Inc., 1201 Connecticut Avenue, NW, Washington, DC 20036.

Robert Bosch Foundation Fellowship Program, CDS International, Inc.
330 Seventh Avenue
New York, NY 10001
Tel. 212/760-1400

This program takes place in Germany and is for Americans with degrees in business, economics, journalism, law, mass communications, political science, and public affairs. It provides 15 paid ($2200-$2500 per month) executive level internships in the German government and private sector for 9 month periods (September to May). Open to graduate students and individuals with graduate or law degrees. Application deadline is October 15. Contact the program officer for more information.

Sister Cities International
1210 South Payne Street
Alexandria, VA 22314-2939
Fax 703/836-4815 (no phone calls please)

This nonprofit association assists U.S. communities in developing formal linkages with other cities throughout the world for the purposes of increasing international understanding and promoting exchanges. Offers one unpaid internship for a minimum of 6 weeks. Candidates should have some international and community service background and be computer literate. Open to college juniors, seniors, graduates, graduate students, and career changers. For more information, contact the Personnel Office.

United Nations Association of the USA
485 Fifth Avenue
New York, NY 10017
Tel. 212/697-3232

The purpose of this nonprofit organization is to strengthen the United Nations system and promote U.S. participation in the organization. It offers several unpaid internships of variable duration. Most internships involve research, proofreading, writing, and general office responsibilities. Open to college juniors, seniors, graduates, graduate students, and career changers. Application deadlines are April 1 for summer, August 19 for fall, and January 15 for spring. Contact the Intern Coordinator for more information.

The U.S. Chamber of Commerce
Personnel Department, Internship Coordinator
1615 H Street, NW
Washington, DC 20062
Tel. 202/659-6000

This organization promotes business, trade, and professional associations. Hiring 85 interns each year, it offers unpaid semester-long international internships for college juniors and seniors. Interns conduct research, write articles, attend congressional hearings, and follow legislation.

U.S. and Foreign Commercial Service (U.S.& FCS)
Work-Study Internship Program
Office of Foreign Service Personnel
P.O. Box 688
Ben Franklin Station
Washington, DC 20044-0688

This U.S. Department of Commerce organization promotes U.S. exports and business. It sponsors a summer work-study intern program for 10 to 12 week periods. Open to college juniors, seniors, and graduate students. It offers several unpaid internships involving research, writing, and marketing/promotion. Interns work abroad and are responsible for financing all of their travel, living, and other expenses. Applicants must submit a federal application, transcripts, two letters of reference, and a 500 to 700-word essay on their career goals. Deadlines for applications are November 1.

Visions in Action
3637 Fulton Street, NW
Washington, DC 20007
Tel. 202/625-7402
Fax 202/625-2553

This nonprofit organization offers 10-15 unpaid internships each year in urban areas of Kenya, South Africa, Uganda, and Zimbabwe. Visions in Action focuses on urban development and includes such issues as refugee relief, famine relief, women, agriculture, family planning, appropriate technology, and youth work. Interns work on urban development, public relations, administrative support, and fundraising. Open to college students, graduates, graduate students, and career changers. For more information, contact the U.S. Director.

World Federalists
418 7th Street, SE
Washington, DC 20003
Tel. 202/546-3950
Fax 202/546-3749

This organization promotes the work of the United Nations in the areas of environmentalism, human rights, and conflict resolution. It offers four paid ($100) internships for one semester each. Interns get experience in conducting policy research, coordinating conferences, writing, editing, public relations, and lobbying. Open to college students, graduates, and graduate students. Applicants should submit a resume and cover letter to the Director of Student Programs.

WorldTeach
Harvard Institute for International Development
One Eliot Street
Cambridge, MA 02138
Tel. 617/495-5527; Fax 617/495-1239

Each year WorldTeach places nearly 200 teaching interns in Africa, Asia, Latin America, and Europe. Most interns teach English as a foreign language but some also teach science and mathematics. Individuals must pay a fee of $3,000 to participate in the program, a fee which covers their insurance, training, and international transportation. The program provides housing and a small monthly stipend. It also offers 8 unpaid summer teaching positions in China and an unpaid sports coaching position in Black South African townships for 6 month periods. Candidates for teaching English should have an undergraduate degree from any accredited college or university as well as 25 credit hours of TEFL (Teaching English as a Foreign Language). Contact the Internship Coordinator for more information.

Youth for Understanding
International Exchange
3501 Newark Street, NW
Washington, DC 20016-3167
Tel. 202/966-6808
Fax 202/895-1104

This nonprofit, educational organization seeks to promote greater world peace and understanding through exchange programs for high school students. It offers several unpaid internships in consumer services, public relations, finance, school relations, sales and marketing, sports, and promotion. Open to college students, graduates, graduate students, and career changers. For more information, contact the Assistant Director Volunteer Services.

Other Internship Opportunities

Numerous other organizations—from government agencies to private companies and nonprofit firms—offer internship opportunities. You may want to contact some of the following:

Africare
Director of International Development
440 R Street, NW
Washington, DC 20001
Tel. 202/462-3614

Agency for International Development
ATTN: Student Programs Coordinator
Office of Human Resources Development
   and Management
2401 E Street, NW
Washington, DC 20523-0105

The Aires Group, Ltd.
Vice President, Projects
1745 Jefferson Davis Highway, Suite 404
Arlington, VA 22202
Tel. 703/802-9123

American Association of Overseas Studies
Summer Internship Coordinator
158 West 81st Street, Suite 112
New York, NY 10024
Tel. 800/338-2748

American Bar Association
International Legal Exchange Program
Executive Director
1700 Pennsylvania Ave., NW, Suite 620
Washington, DC 20006
Tel. 202/393-7122

American Friends Service Committee
Personnel Department
1501 Cherry Street
Philadelphia, PA 19102
Tel. 215/241-7295

American Jewish Congress
Office of the Washington Representative
Internship Coordinator
2027 Massachusetts Ave., NW
Washington, DC 20036
Tel. 202/332-4001

American Society of Travel Agents
Education Department
1101 King Street
Alexandria, VA 22314
Tel. 703/739-2782, Ext. 608

American Security Council (ASC)
Executive Director
916 Pennsylvania Avenue, SE
Washington, DC 20003
Tel. 202/484-1676

Americas Society
Director of Personnel and Administration
680 Park Avenue
New York, NY 10021
Tel. 202/628-3200

Amigos De Las Americas
Recruiting
5618 Star Lane
Houston, TX 77057
Tel. 800/231-77796

Army JAGC Professional Recruiting Office
(Summer Intern)
Building 1834, Franklin Road
Fort Belvoir, VA 22060-5818
Tel. 800/336-3315
in Virginia 703/355-3323 collect

The Asia Foundation
Personnel Officer
P.O. Box 193223
San Francisco, CA 94119-3223
Tel. 415/982-4640
Fax 415/392-8863

The Atlantic Council of the United States
Internship Coordinator
1616 H Street, NW
Washington, DC 20076

Beijing-Washington, Inc.
4340 East West Highway, Suite 200
Bethesda, MD 20814
Tel. 301/656-4801

The Brookings Institution
Governmental Studies Program
1775 Massachusetts Avenue, NW
Washington, DC 20036
Tel. 202/797-6052

CARE
660 First Avenue
New York, NY 10016
Tel. 212/686-3110

Carnegie Endowment for International Peace
Intern Coordinator
2400 N Street, NW
Washington, DC 20037
Tel. 202/862-7900

Caribbean Conservation Corp.
RA/Internship Program
P.O. Box 2866
Gainesville, FL 32602

The Catholic University of America
Parliamentary Internship Program
Department of Politics
Washington, DC 20064
Tel. 202/635-5000

Center for Strategic and International Studies (CSIS)
CSIS Intern Coordinator
1800 K Street, NW
Washington, DC 20006
Tel. 202/887-0200

Central Intelligence Agency
Student Programs Office
P.O. Box 1255
Department IEH
Pittsburgh, PA 15230

Commission on Security and Cooperation in Europe (CSCE)
237 Ford House Office Building
Washington, DC 23515
Tel. 202/225-1901

Council on Hemispheric Affairs
Secretary of Internships
724 9th Street, NW
Suite 401
Washington, DC 20009
Tel. 202/393-3322
Fax 202/393-3424

Council for Inter-American Security (CIS)
Director of Research
122 C Street NW
Suite 710
Washington, DC 20001
Tel. 202/393-6622

Department of State, PER/CSP
Intern Coordinator
P.O. Box 18657
Washington, DC 20036

The Ford Foundation
Manager Employment & Training
320 East 43rd Street
New York, NY 10017
Tel. 212/573-4794

Freedom House, Inc.
Intern Coordinator
120 Wall Street
26th Floor
New York, NY 10005
Tel. 212/514-8040

Georgetown University
Center for Immigration Policy and Refugee Assistance
Director of Internship Programs
P.O. Box 2298
Washington, DC 20057-1011
Tel. 202/298-0229 or 202/298-0214

Global Exchange
2141 Mission Street
Room 202
San Francisco, CA 94110
Tel. 415/255-7298
Fax 415/255-7498

Grassroots International
P.O. Box 312
Cambridge, MA 02139
Tel. 617/497-9180
Fax 617/497-4397

Habitat for Humanity International
ATTN: Personnel Department
Habitat and Church Streets
Americus, GA 31709-3498
Tel. 912/924-6935

**Human Rights Watch/Everett Public
Service Internships**
Intern Coordinator
486 Fifth Avenue
New York, NY 10017

Institute of International Education
Educational Counseling Center
P.O. Box 3087
Laredo, TX 78044
Tel. 525/211-0042, ext. 3500

International Atomic Energy Agency
Personnel Office (Internships)
Wagramerstrasse 5
P.O. Box 100
A-1400 Vienna
Austria

International Finance Corporation
Summer Employment Program
1818 H Street, NW
Room I-2001
Washington, DC 20433

International Labor Office
Personnel Office (Internships)
1828 L Street, NW
Suite 801
Washington, DC 20036

International Monetary Fund
Summer Internship Program
Recruitment Division
Room 6-525
700 19th Street, NW
Washington, DC 20431

Interns for Peace
270 West 89th St.
New York, NY 10024
Tel. 212/580-0540
Fax 212/580-0693

Joint Baltic American National Committee
Director of Public Relations
400 Hurley Avenue
P.O. Box 4578
Rockville, MD 20849
Tel. 301/340-1954

MAP International
RDIF Coordinator
2200 Glynco Parkway
P.O. Box 50
Brunswick, GA 31521

Meridian International Center
Director of Personnel
1630 Crescent Place, NW
Washington, DC 20009
Tel. 202/667-6800

The Middle East Institute
Internship Coordinator
1761 N Street, NW
Washington, DC 20036
Tel. 202/785-1141

Minnesota Studies in International Development (MSID)
Program Associate
106 Nicholson Hall
University of Minnesota
Minneapolis, MN 55455
Tel. 612/625-3379

National Resources Defense Council (NRDC)
Intern Coordinator
1350 New York Avenue, NW, Suite 300
Washington, DC 20005
Tel. 202/783-7800

Organization of American States
OAS Internship Coordinator
1889 F St., NW, Seventh Floor
Washington, DC 20006
Tel. 202/458-3519

Overseas Private Investment Corporation
Intern Program Coordinator
1615 M Street, NW
Washington, DC 20527
Tel. 202/457-7094

Overseas Schools Assistance Corporation
International Schools Internship Program
445 R West Center Street, P.O. Box 103
West Bridgewater, MA 02379
Tel. 508/588-0477

Pan American Development Foundation
ATTN: Internship Coordinator, Personnel
1889 F St., NW
Washington, DC 20006
Tel. 202/458-3969
Fax 202/458-6316

The Partnership for Service-Learning
Director
815 Second Avenue
Suite 315
New York, NY 10017
Tel. 212/986-0989

Population Institute
Director of Future Leaders Program
107 2nd Street, NE
Washington, DC 20002
Tel. 202/544-3300

Society for International Development
Executive Director
1401 New York Avenue, NW
Suite 1100
Washington, DC 20005
Tel. 202/347-1800

TransAfrica
Administrative Director
545 Eighth Street, SE
Washington, DC 20003
Tel. 202/547-2550

UNICEF
The Internship Coordinator
Three United Nations Plaza
New York, NY 10017

The United National Ad Hoc Internship Program
Internship Coordinator, United Nations
Recruitment Programs Section, Room 2475
Office of Personnel Services
New York, NY 10017

United Nations
Recruitment Programmes Section
Room 2500
Office of Personnel Services
New York, NY 10017

United Nations
Coordinator of the DPI Graduate
Student Intern Programme
Room S-1037G
Department of Public Information
New York, NY 10017

**United Nations Development Program
(UNDP) Summer Internship Program**
Chief, Recruitment Section
Summer Internship Program
Division of Personnel
UNDP, One United Nations Plaza
New York, NY 10017

United Nations Fund for Population Activities
Chief, Recruitment Section (Internships)
One United Nations Plaza
New York, NY 10017

The United Nations Headquarters Internship Program
Coordinator, Internship Program
Room S-2500E, United Nations
New York, NY 10017
Tel. 212/963-1223

United Nations Industrial Development Organization (UNIDO)
Personnel Services Division
UNIDO, Room E0554
Vienna International Centre
P.O. Box 300
A-1400 Vienna, Austria
Tel. 43-1-211 31

United Nations Institute for Training and Research (UNITAR) Internship Program
Executive Director of UNITAR
801 United Nations Plaza
New York, NY 10017

United Nations Office at Geneva
Information Service
Palais des Nations
CH-122 Geneva 10
Switzerland

U.S. Department of State
Intern Coordinator
P.O. Box 9317
Arlington, VA 22219

Voice of America
VOA Internship Program
Room 3521, HHS-N
330 Independence Avenue, SW
Washington, DC 20547

The Washington Center for Internships and Academic Seminars
514 Tenth Street, NW
Suite 600
Washington, DC 20004
Tel. 202/624-8000

The Washington International Studies Center
214 Massachusetts Avenue, NE
Suite 450
Washington, DC 20002
Tel. 202/547-3275

Washington Office of Africa (WOA)
Executive Assistant
110 Washington Avenue, NE
Suite 112
Washington, DC 20002
Tel. 202/546-1545

Washington Office on Latin America (WOLA)
Intern Coordinator
110 Maryland Office, NE
Washington, DC 20002-5695
Tel. 202/544-8045
Fax 202/546-5288

The Wilson Center
Smithsonian Institution Building
Washington, DC 20560
Tel. 202/357-2567

**Women's International League for
Peace and Freedom (WILPF)**
1213 Race Street
Philadelphia, PA 19107-1691
Tel. 215/563-7110

The World Bank
Summer Employment Program
Room O-5079
1818 H St., NW
Washington, DC 20433
Tel. 202/477-1234

YMCA of Metropolitan Washington
Director, Intern Abroad Program
1711 Rhode Island Avenue, NW
Washington, DC 20036
Tel. 202/862-9622

Zero Population Growth (ZPG)
Internship Program
1400 16th Street, NW
Suite 320
Washington, DC 20036
Tel. 202/332-2200

Additional Resources

The organizations listed above for internship opportunities are only a few of many offering such opportunities. For more information on these and other international internship programs, please consult the following books and directories:

Development Opportunities Catalog: A Guide to Internships, Research, and Employment With Development Organizations (San Francisco: Overseas Development Network, 1990).

Directory of International Internships: A World of Opportunities, Thomas D. Luten, Charles A. Gliozzo, and Timothy J. Aldinger eds. (East Lansing, MI: Michigan State University, Career Development and Placement Services, 1990).

The Imaginative Soul's Guide to Foreign Internships, Laura Hitchcock (Greenville, NY: Ivy House, 1992).

International Directory of Youth Internships, Cynthia Morehouse (Croton-on-Hudson, NY: Apex Press, 1993).

International Internships and Volunteer Programs, Will Cantrell and Francine Modderno (Oakton, VA: WorldWise Books, 1992).

International Schools Internship Program (West Bridgewater, MA: Overseas Schools Assistance Corporation).

Internships: 1995 (Princeton, NJ: Peterson's, 1995).

Internships and Careers in International Affairs, James Muldoon, Jr., ed. (New York: United National Association of the U.S., 1989).

Internships in Foreign and Defense Policy: A Complete Guide for Women (and Men), Women in International Security (Arlington, VA: Seven Locks Press, 1990).

If you are interested in volunteer or study abroad programs, we recommend consulting the following directories:

Academic Year Abroad, Sarah J. Steen, ed. (New York: Institute of International Education, 1993-1994).

Alternatives to the Peace Corps: A Directory of Third World and U.S. Volunteer Opportunities (San Francisco: Food First Books, 1993).

Fellowships, Scholarships, and Related Opportunities in International Education, James Gehihar, ed. (Knoxville, TN: University of Tennessee, 1994).

Going Places: The High School Student's Guide to Study, Travel, and Adventure Abroad (New York: St. Martin's Press, 1995).

Guide to International Education in the United States, David S. Hoopes and Kathleen R. Hoopes (Detroit, MI: Gale Research, 1990).

International Directory of Volunteer Work, David Woodworth, ed. (Oxford, England: Vacation Work, 1995).

International Scholarship Book, Daniel J. Cassidy, ed. (Hawthorne, NJ: Career Press, 1993).

International Workcamp Directory (Belmont, VT: Volunteers for Peace, 1993).

Kibbutz Volunteer, John Bedford (Oxford, England: Vacation Work, 1993).

Smart Vacations: The Traveler's Guide to Learning Adventures Abroad, Priscilla Tovey, ed. (New York: St. Martin's Press, 1995).

Study Abroad (Princeton, NJ: Peterson's, 1995).

Study Abroad, 1992-1994 (New York: UNESCO, 1991).

Study Abroad: The Astute Student's Guide, David Judkins (Charlotte, VT: Williamson Publishing, 1989).

Time Out: Taking a Break from School to Travel, Work, and Study in the U.S. and Abroad, Robert Gilpin with Caroline Fitzgibbons (New York: Simon and Schuster, 1992).

Vacation Study Abroad, Sarah J. Steen, ed. (New York: Institute of International Education, 1993-94).

Volunteer-Sending Organizations for Eastern Europe (Washington, DC: Citizens Democracy Corps, 1993).

Volunteer Vacations, Bill McMillon (Chicago: Chicago Review Press, 1993).

Volunteer Work (London: Central Bureau, 1993).

Work, Study, Travel Abroad: The Whole World Handbook, CIEE (New York: St. Martin's Press, 1995).

The World of Learning (Bristol, PA: International Publications Service, 1994).

For arranging your own short-term paid work abroad, review these useful resources:

The Au Pair and Nanny's Guide to Working Abroad, Susan Griffith and Sharon Legg (Oxford, England: Vacation Work, 1993).

Directory of Overseas Summer Jobs, David Woodworth, ed. (Oxford, England: Vacation Work, 1993).

Summer Jobs Britain, Emily Hatchwell, ed., 1993 (Oxford, England: Vacation Work, 1993).

Work Your Way Around the World, Susan Griffith, ed. (Oxford, England: Vacation Work, 1993).

Working Holidays 1993 (London: Central Bureau, 1993).

Working in Ski Resorts—Europe, Victoria Pybus and Charles James, ed. (Oxford, England: Vacation Work, 1993).

TEACHING ENGLISH ABROAD

Some of the most appealing and popular ways to travel are found in teaching English abroad. Indeed, each year thousands of college educated individuals yearn to explore the world by landing a teaching job abroad.

Teaching abroad is probably the easiest way for someone with limited international skills and experience to break into the international employment arena. Numerous teaching opportunities exist in schools throughout the world. Many of these jobs are for certified teachers who teach in the U.S. Department of State schools, U.S. Department of Defense schools, or international schools. Teaching jobs with these schools include all subject matters as well as administrative positions. These teaching positions pay comparable to teaching positions in the United States. Moving from one country to another every three to six years, many teachers make a career of teaching in these overseas schools.

However, the largest number of overseas teaching positions are for teachers of English who work in local schools, institutes, or universities on either a short- or long-term basis. While few of these positions require teaching experience or teacher certification, some type of teacher training will be helpful for landing such teaching positions. Several universities in the United States, for example, offer special training as well as overseas placements for individuals interested in teaching English as a foreign language. Earnings for these types of teaching positions vary greatly. Most such positions are low paying or volunteer positions, but earnings can be very good in such countries as Japan, Korea, or Taiwan.

Teaching English as a Foreign Language

If you are willing to teach English as a foreign language, you can easily find a job abroad. Indeed, the worldwide demand for English language teachers remains high and the jobs are plentiful. Most recently, the demand for English teachers has increased substantially in Eastern Europe, Russia, and the former Soviet republics.

The first thing you need to do is to understand the language of this occupational group. Teachers of English language usually refer to themselves and their training programs in the following abbreviated forms:

TEFL or TFL: teaching English as a foreign language
TESL or TSL: teaching English as a second language
TESOL: teaching English to speakers of other languages

Several universities in the United States and abroad provide degree programs in TEFL or TESOL, and many others offer teacher training courses in TEFL or TESOL. You are well advised to participate in such a program. After all, teaching English as a foreign language involves specific methodologies you should be familiar with before venturing into this field. Fortunately you can participate in several short intensive TEFL or TESOL training programs which will get you up and running quickly for English language teaching.

You basically have two approaches to landing an English language teaching position abroad—either apply through a U.S.-based organization specializing in the training and placement of English language teachers or apply directly to an overseas school, institute, or university. It is probably easiest to work through a U.S.-based organization since most handle placements and arrange other details such as visas, work permits, housing, and transportation. A third option is to become a freelance teacher of English, offering your services to individuals and groups at an hourly rate.

During the past 30 years the U.S. Peace Corps has trained thousands of volunteers to teach English in many Third and Fourth World countries throughout the world. While today's Peace Corps places volunteers in many technical and business fields, it still recruits volunteers to teach English and other subjects in nearly 100 countries, including most recently the Peoples' Republic of China. In fact, nearly 40 percent of the 6,529 volunteers serving in 1994 were in the field of education; most were English teachers. Volunteer assignments are for two years. For more information, contact:

PEACE CORPS
Box 941
Washington, DC 20526
Tel. 800/424-8580, Ext. 2293

Several private, nonprofit, and educational organizations also recruit, train, and place college graduates who are interested in teaching English and other subjects abroad. Many are volunteer positions similar to internships while others are salaried positions. Contact the following organizations for information on their placement programs:

AEON
9301 Wilshire Blvd., #202, Beverly Hills, CA 90210, Tel. 310/550-0940 or 2 Mid-America Plaza, Suite 800, Oakbrook Terrace, IL 60181, Tel. 718/954-2323. This is a private language school which places English teachers in 190 schools in Japan. Applicants need a bachelor's degree and are required to pay one-way airfare. Teachers earn around 250,000 yen ($2,300) per month.

AMITY TWO PROGRAM
Amity Institute, P.O. Box 118, Del Mar, CA 92014, Tel. 619/755-3582. Places TEFL teachers in K-12 schools in Latin America and Martinique. Room and board provided, but participants are responsible for their own living expenses. Applications should be submitted six to nine months prior to anticipated starting date.

AASSA
The Association of American Schools in South America Teacher Service (AASSA), 14750 NW 77th St., Suite 210, Miami Lakes, FL 33016, Tel. 305/821-0345 or Fax 305/821-4244. Contact the Placement Coordinator. Sponsors a yearly job fair in Orlando, Florida during the last week of November or the first week of December. At present there is a $40 registration fee to attend this job fair. Call or write for details, including an application/job fair package.

BRETHREN VOLUNTEER SERVICES
1451 Dundee Ave., Elgin, IL 60120, Tel. 708/742-5100. Fields English teachers for two-year assignments in the Czech and Slovak Republics, Poland, Israel, Nigeria, South Korean, and the People's Republic of China. Provides expenses.

CHARTER 77 FOUNDATION
Masaryk Fellowship Program, 1270 Avenue of the Americas, Suite 609, New York, NY 10020, Tel. 212/332-2890. Places TEFL-trained English teachers in the Czech and Slovak Republics for one month during the summer as well as offers one-year teaching positions for TEFL professionals. Provides homestay and stipend. Application deadline is March.

ELS INTERNATIONAL INC.
5761 Buckingham Parkway, Culver City, CA 90230-6583, Tel. 213/642-0982 or Fax 213/410-4688. This private firm operates a network of 40 language schools in Asia, Latin America, and Europe. They recruit individuals with bachelor's degrees and 1-2 years of ESL/EFL experience.

EDUCATION FOR DEMOCRACY
P.O. Box 40514, Mobile, AL 36640-0514, Tel. 205/434-3889. Places TEFL trained teachers in the Czech and Slovak Republics for periods of five months to one year. Provides accommodations and stipend. Requires a $50 processing fee.

FANDANGO OVERSEAS PLACEMENT
1613 Escalero Road, Santa Rose, CA 95409, phone or fax 707/539-2722. Arranges teacher placements in client schools of the Czech Republic, Hungary, France, Baltic States, Russia, Poland, and Japan. Charges a $375 placement fee for graduates of Transworld Teachers, Inc. (San Francisco) or $450 for graduates of a comparable 100-hour teacher training program.

GEORGETOWN UNIVERSITY
Internship Program, CIPRA-AIR, P.O. Box 2298, Washington, DC 20057-1011, Tel. 202/298-0200. Students earn six academic credit hours for completing a two-week TEFL training course and teaching abroad for one-year. Current placements are in the Czech and Slovak Republics, Bulgaria, Poland, Hungary, Russia, Lithuania, Estonia, Vietnam, Indonesia, and the People's Republic of China. Participants pay a $1,500 tuition fee as well as receive room, board, and a small stipend while in-country. Application deadline is March 1.

GLOBAL ROUTES
5554 Broadway, Oakland, CA 94618, Tel. 510/655-0321 or Fax 510/655-0371. Offers volunteer English teaching internships for 10-week periods. Interns are assigned to village schools in Ecuador, Kenya, and Thailand. Requires a program fee of $3,200 for the summer and $3,400 for the spring and fall semesters. Airfare is extra.

INTERCRISTO
P.O. Box 33487, 19303 Fremont Ave. N., Seattle, WA 98133, Tel. 206/546-7330. This is a Christian ministry group which operates a computerized job network and placement service for nonprofit Christian organizations.

INTERNATIONAL SCHOOLS INTERNSHIPS PROGRAM
P.O. Box 103, W. Bridgewater, MA 02379, Tel. 508/580-1880. Places interns in the network the international schools found throughout the world. K-12 certification is not required. Application deadline is December. Requires two $75 application fees.

INTERNATIONAL SCHOOLS SERVICES
P.O. Box 5910, 15 Roszel Road, Princeton, NJ 08543, Tel. 609/452-0990. The New Perspectives program places teachers without previous teaching experience but who have teacher certification. Places over 500 teachers and administrators in international and American schools around the world each year. Requires as $50 application fee. Its regular staffing program places teachers in international schools for a placement fee of $600. Individuals must have two years of current teaching experience (no

certification required). Math and science teachers with certification but no experience are eligible for consideration. Holds recruitment meetings in February and June.

JET PROGRAM
Embassy of Japan, 2520 Massachusetts Ave., NW, Washington, DC 20008, Tel. 202/939-6700. This Japanese government-sponsored program places English teachers in Japanese schools for one-year assignments. Application deadline is December 15.

KOREA SERVICES GROUP
147-7 Bum Jeon Dong Jin-Ku, Pusan 614-064, Korea, Tel. 011-82-51-817-3611 or Fax 011-82-51-817-3612. Provides native speaking instructors for more than 50 Korean foreign language institutes. Hires a large number of foreign instructors each year. Some hirees can expect to start within 60 days. Recruits extensively amongst former U.S. Peace Corps Volunteers. Expects to place over 150 American instructors in 1994.

OHIO STATE UNIVERSITY JOB FAIR
Educational Career Services, 110 Arps Hall, 19435 N. High St., Columbus, OH 43201-1172, Tel. 614/292-2741. In February of each year this program sponsors a job placement fair for international elementary and secondary teachers.

OVERSEAS PLACEMENT SERVICE FOR EDUCATORS
University of Northern Iowa, Student Services Center #19, Cedar Falls, IA 50614-0390, Tel. 319/273-2061 or Fax 319/273-6998. Conducts an annual recruiting fair and publishes a newsletter with teaching vacancies.

PRINCETON-IN-ASIA
224 Palmer Hall, Princeton, NJ 08544, Tel. 609/458-3657. Operates one- and two-year teaching programs in the People's Republic of China, Taiwan, Korea, Hong Kong, Japan, Thailand, Singapore, and Indonesia. Application deadline is December 15. Requires a $30 application fee and a $250 participant fee.

QUEEN'S UNIVERSITY
Overseas Recruiting Fair Placement Office, Faculty of Education, Kingston, Ontario K7L1 3N6, Tel. 613/545-6222. Hosts an annual overseas teaching job fair.

SEARCH ASSOCIATES
P.O. Box 100, Mountaintop, PA 18707, Tel. 717/474-0370 or Fax 717/474-0380. Recruits experienced elementary and secondary teachers for schools throughout the world. Holds recruiting fairs in Massachusetts, California, Indonesia, and New Zealand. Charges a $600 placement fee.

TEACHERS OVERSEAS RECRUITMENT CENTER
National Teacher Placement Bureau, P.O. Box 609027, Cleveland, OH 44109, Tel. 216/741-3771. Sponsors a job fair for international teachers.

TESOL INC.
Teachers of English to Speakers of Other Languages, 1600 Cameron St., Suite 300, Alexandria, VA 22314, Tel. 703/836-0774. This 23,000 member nonprofit organization includes a placement service for its members. Membership dues are $69 for regular members or $48.50 for students. A basic membership also is available for $38. The placement service costs an additional $20 in North American and $30 abroad.

UNIVERSITY OF NORTHERN IOWA JOB FAIR
Overseas Placement Services for Educators, Cedar Falls, IA 50614-0390, Tel. 319/273-2311 or Fax 319/273-6998. Sponsors an annual job fair for international teachers and administrators attended by more than 60 overseas schools.

YMCA OVERSEAS SERVICE CORPS
909 4th Avenue, Seattle, WA 98104, Tel. 206/382-5008. Sponsors teaching programs in Taiwan and Japan for one- and two-year assignments respectively. Application deadlines are February and September for fall and spring placements. Requires a $25 application fee.

WORLDTEACH
Harvard Institute for International Development, One Eliot Street, Cambridge, MA 02138-5705, Tel. 617/495-5527 or Fax 617/495-1239. Each year places nearly 200 volunteer teachers in the local schools of Costa Rica, Ecuador, Namibia, Poland, Thailand, Russia, and South Africa. Positions are for one year. Participants pay a fee of $3,300-$4,300 which covers the cost of airfare, insurance, training, and administration. Local employers provide room and board and provide a small stipend.

Training Programs to Get
You Up and Running

The best qualified candidates possess teacher certification and are skilled in teaching English as a foreign language. Ideally, you should have a bachelor's or master's degree in TEFL or in a substantive academic field. If you lack such qualifications, don't worry. You can easily establish your teaching credentials and land an overseas teaching job by enrolling in a TEFL program that also has a good placement record. In fact, we do not recommend looking for an English language teaching position unless you have completed a TEFL program. You will quickly discover these programs have several advantages. Many use the highly respected RSA/University of Cambridge and Trinity College London teaching methods for qualifying participants.

In the United States most TEFL programs are integrated into

regular university academic programs which are usually part of an undergraduate or graduate Applied Linguistics program. A few universities and private institutes now offer intensive four-week TEFL programs modelled after the British 100-hour intensive TEFL teacher certification programs. These intensive four-week programs quickly prepare you for overseas teaching positions and thus save you time and money in the process of getting ready for an overseas job. Many of these programs also provide job assistance through their employment contacts with schools, institutes, and universities abroad.

Within the United States, the following public and private organizations provide training for teachers of English as a foreign language. While most are traditional university-based applied linguistics degree programs requiring two to four years preparation, many are private institutes offering certification through intensive four- to eight-week training programs. We've assigned asterisks (*) to quickly identify the intensive four to six-week programs. Others are degree programs.

BALL STATE UNIVERSITY
Director of Graduate Programs, Department of English, Muncie, IN 47306-0460, Tel. 317/285-8415 or Fax 317/285-3766. Offers an M.A. in TESOL. Out-of-state tuition is $2,488 per semester.

BRIGHAM YOUNG UNIVERSITY—Hawaii Campus
Director, TESOL Studies, LLC Division, Laie, HI 96762. Offers a bachelor's degree in TESOL. Tuition is $1,335 per semester for non-LDS church members or $890 per semester for LDS members.

*CENTER FOR ENGLISH STUDIES
330 Seventh Avenue, New York, NY 10001, Tel. 212/620-0760 or Fax 212/594-7415. Offers a four-week intensive TEFL course four times a year, from June to September. Costs $1,475.

*COAST LANGUAGE ACADEMY
20720 Ventura Blvd., Suite 300, Woodland Hills, CA 91364, Tel. 818/346-5113 or Fax 818/346-6619. Offers an intensive four-week or a part time eight-week, TEFL course four times a year. Cost $1,675. Homestay accommodations available for $500 a month.

*ENGLISH INTERNATIONAL
655 Sutter St., Suite 500, San Francisco, CA 94102, Tel. 415/749-5633 or Fax 415/749-5629. Excepting December, each month this organization offers an intensive four-week TEFL course. Participants become RSA/University of Cambridge certified TEFL teachers. Tuition is $1785.00.

FAIRLEIGH DICKINSON UNIVERSITY
Director of M.A.T., School of Education, 1000 River Rd., Bancroft Hall

Rm. 208, Teaneck, NJ 07666, Tel. 201/692-2838. Offers a Multilingual M.A. and a M.A.T. in ESL which takes from one and one-half to five years to complete. Requires 36-credit hours which cost $400 per credit.

*GEORGETOWN UNIVERSITY
Center for Language Education and Development, 3607 O Street, NW, Washington, DC 20007, Tel. 202/687-4400 or Fax 202/337-1559. Offers an intensive 150-hour RSA/Cambridge Certificate in Teaching English as a Foreign Language to Adults (CTEFLA) course. Successful participants receive the RSA/CTEFLA and a Georgetown certificate. Tuition is $3,000 for this five-week course.

HAWAII PACIFIC UNIVERSITY
TESL Coordinator, 1188 Fort St. Mall, Honolulu, HI 96813. Offers a four-year B.A. and a one-year post-bachelor's certificate in TESL. Tuition costs $7,030 per academic year.

PORTLAND STATE UNIVERSITY
Chair, Department of Applied Linguistics, P.O. Box 751, Portland, OR 97207-0751, Tel. 503/725-4088. Offers a post-bachelor's TESL Certificate and an M.A. in TESOL. Costs $2,641 per term for post-bachelor program and $2,204 per term for graduate program.

***THE SCHOOL OF TEACHING ENGLISH
AS A SECOND LANGUAGE**
2601 NW 56th, Seattle, WA 98107, Tel. 206/781-8607 or Fax 206/781-8922. Offers an intensive four-week ESL/EFL teacher training program. Participants can earn 12 academic credits (graduate or post-baccalaureate) and a Certificate in TESL from the Seattle University School of Education. Costs $145 per credit or $1,740 for the intensive 12-credit program.

*ST. GILES LANGUAGE TEACHING CENTER
One Hallidie Plaza, Suite 350, San Francisco, CA 94102, Tel. 415/788-3552. Offers a four-week intensive RSA/University of Cambridge teacher training certificate course. Requires a $35 application fee. Tuition is $1,690.

*TRANSWORLD TEACHERS, INC.
683 Sutter Street, San Francisco, CA 94102, Tel. 800/241-8071. Offers a one-month intensive or three-month part time TEFL Certificate Course involving 100+ hours of instruction. Tuition is $1,675. Guest house accommodations cost $460 per month.

*UNIVERSITY OF CALIFORNIA
P.O. Box 6050, Irvine, CA 92716-6050, Tel. 714/856-2033. Offers an accelerated certificate program in TEFL. Costs $3,900 (includes tuition, materials, accommodations, and student services).

UNIVERSITY OF DELAWARE
ESL/Bilingual Coordinator, Department of Educational Studies, Newark,

DE 19716. Offers an M.S. with a specialization in TESOL. Tuition for in-state students is $3,500 per year; out-of-state students pay $9,500 per year.

UNIVERSITY OF ILLINOIS

Division of English as an International Language, 3070 FLB, 707 S. Mathews Ave., Urbana, IL 61801. Offers an M.A. in the Teaching of English as a Second Language. Costs $2,023 per semester for in-state students and $4,219 for out-of-state students.

UNIVERSITY OF NEW HAMPSHIRE

Graduate Director, Department of Education, Durham, NH 03824. Offers an M.A. in English Language and Linguistics with a specialization in ESL. Costs $2,142.50 per semester for in-state students and $5,967.50 for out-of-state students.

UNIVERSITY OF GEORGIA

Graduate Coordinator, Language Education Department, 125 Aderhold Hall, Athens, GA 30602-7123. Offers M.Ed. and Ph.D. programs in TESOL. Costs $1,980 per quarter (out-of-state).

WRIGHT STATE UNIVERSITY

Department of English Language and Literatures, 441 Millett Hall, Dayton, OH 45435. Offers undergraduate and graduate certificates (22 quarter hours) and an M.A. (50-52 quarter hours) in TESOL. Costs $122 per credit hour for in-state students and $218 per credit hour for out-of-state students.

Numerous other teacher training programs are offered by universities and private institutes in Canada, England, Ireland, France, Germany, Greece, Hong Kong, Malaysia, Spain, Turkey, and Australia. The oldest, largest, and most highly respected TEFL training program awarding the RSA/University of Cambridge Certificate is in England. For detailed information on their programs, contact:

INTERNATIONAL HOUSE TEACHER TRAINING
International House, 106 Piccadilly, London W1V 9FL,
Tel. 44 71 491 2598 or Fax 44 71 499 0174.

This four-week (110 hour) program costs about $2,000. International House offers courses at Teacher Training Centers in its affiliated schools in Barcelona, Budapest, Cairo, Krakow, Lisbon, Madrid, New York, Paris, Poznan, Rome, San Sebastian, and Vienna. It also recruits nearly 200 teachers each year for its network of over 100 schools in 23 countries. If you want premier training in TEFL, enroll in this well established program. For more information on TEFL training programs in these and other countries, consult Susan Griffith's latest edition of *Teaching English Abroad*.

Job Listing Services for Teachers

Several organizations offer current job vacancy listings for teachers interested in overseas positions. The most popular such publications include:

Bulletin of Overseas Teaching Opportunities: 72 Franklin Avenue, Ocean Grove, NJ 07756, $38 per year.

Instant Alert: Education Information Service, 15 Orchard St., Wellesley Hills, MA 02181, Tel. 617/237-0887 or 4523 Andes Drive, Fairfax, VA 22030. Every six weeks this organization publishes a listing of nearly 150 vacancies in international and American schools.

International Education Placement Hotline: World Learning, Box 676, Kipling Road, Brattleboro, VT 05302-0676, Tel. 802/258-3397 or Fax 802/258-3248; $15 for 6 months of $25 for 1 year. Publishes a monthly newsletter which includes job vacancies for international education administrators and teachers of TESOL.

International Educator: International Educator's Institute, P.O. Box 513, Cummaquid, MA 02637, Tel. 508/362-1414. $25. Published quarterly. July issue includes a "Jobs Only" supplement.

Options Newsletter: 20533 Biscayne Boulevard, Suite 4/467, Miami, FL 33180.

Overseas Academic Opportunities: 949 E. 29th Street, Brooklyn, NY 11210. $38 per year.

TESOL Placement Bulletin: TESOL Inc., 1600 Cameron St., Suite 300, Alexandria, VA 22314, Tel. 703/836-0774. Must be a member of TESOL Inc. ($38-$60) in order to subscribe to this publication. $20 per year if mailed to addresses in the U.S., Canada, Mexico; $30 per year for all other countries.

Several enterprising companies sell country-by-country listings of schools for $10 to $20 per country. One of the most popular such publications is *Overseas Teaching Opportunities* which is available through Friends of World Teaching (P.O. Box 1049, San Diego, CA 92112-1049 or 619/275-4066, $20 for first three countries and $4 for additional countries). This publication includes over 1,000 schools in 100+ countries of interest to Americans and Canadians. However, much of this same information is readily available through several other less expensive resources such as Susan Griffith's *Teaching English Abroad*, Transition Abroad's *Teaching English Abroad, The*

ISS Directory of Overseas Schools, and the free directories available through the U.S. Department of Defense and the State Department. Consult these directories before purchasing similar lists.

Other Teaching Opportunities

If you teach at the university level, you may find opportunities to teach and conduct research abroad through your present institution, through a regional international consortium or through special programs such as the Fulbright Program (Council for International Exchange of Scholars). You should also monitor the job vacancy announcements appearing in The *Chronicle of Higher Education* as well as in professional journals and newsletters of your academic discipline. Occasionally overseas university vacancy announcements appear in *The New York Times, Washington Post, Wall Street Journal, National Business Employment Weekly,* and a few other major newspapers. Major international magazines, such as *The Far Eastern Economic Review* and *The Economist,* regularly list university vacancy announcements.

Enterprising job seekers don't limit their search to established teaching programs, training institutes, and placement and job listing services. Numerous other teaching opportunities are available by directly applying to local schools in each country without the assistance of a U.S.-based organization or with a U.S.-sponsored school. While salaries may appear low in many of these schools, such teaching positions often come with free housing and they do offer an opportunity to gain experience in living and working abroad. They enable you to work in a truly international environment where you get to know faculty members and become a member of the local community—important international experiences which are sometimes best acquired by living off the local economy at the level of fellow faculty members.

Take, for example, one of our favorite colleges abroad in which we have been personally involved for years. If you are interested in teaching English in Thailand, you might consider applying directly to Yonok College in Northern Thailand. We know this college very well since we have been closely involved with its evolution since 1973. One of Thailand's newest and most rapidly expanding and beautiful private colleges located in a delightful provincial town near the famous city of Chiengmai, Yonok College offers an excellent English language program for its nearly 2,000 students who are studying for bachelor's degrees in business, arts, and the sciences. Actively promoting a diverse international faculty, Yonok College has an ongoing exchange program with the faculty and students of Baylor University in Waco, Texas as well as welcomes applicants from other education institutions around the world. Numerous Americans have taught English here for periods of one to five years, and they love their work.

If you are interested in working at Yonok College, contact the president directly. Send him a cover letter and a copy of your resume:

> Dr. Nirund Jivasantikarn, President
> YONOK COLLEGE
> Lampang-Denchai Road
> Lampang 52000, Thailand

Indicate in your letter what you would like to do and when you are available. Yonok College also welcomes resumes and applications from individuals who have experience in educational administration at the university level.

Key Resources on Teaching

The following books and directories provide useful information on teaching abroad:

Directory of English Schools in Spain. Robert Kloer, 3 Sunset Avenue, Suncook, NH 03275. $9.95 plus $2.50 postage ($5 overseas). 1991.

ERIC Digest. Center for Applied Linguistics, 1118 22nd St., NW, Washington, DC 20037. A free leaflet on opportunities for TEFL teachers.

How to Get a Job and Teach in Japan. Bonnie Kuroaka, 3595 S.E. First St., Gresham, OR 97030. $9 (postpaid). 1991. Provides useful information on living and working in Japan. Complete with contact information.

The ISS Directory of Overseas Schools. International Schools Service, P.O. Box 5910, Princeton, NJ 08543, Tel. 609/452-0990, $29.95 plus $3.00 shipping. Also available through Peterson's and Impact Publications. Organized by country, this guide provides detailed information on overseas schools attended by American and international students in expatriate communities in 133 countries.

Jobs in Japan. John Wharton. Global Press, 697 College Parkway, Rockville, MD 20850, Tel. 202/466-1663. $16.95 (postpaid). This periodically revised book only focuses on teaching jobs in Japan. Includes names and addresses of schools as well as information on living and working in Japan.

Schools Abroad of Interest to Americans. Porter Sargent Publishers, 11 Beacon St., Suite 1400, Boston, MA 02108, $35 plus $1.98 postage. Includes 800 elementary and secondary schools in 130 countries with American and English-speaking students.

Teach Abroad. 1993. The Central Bureau, Seymour Mews House, Seymour Mews, London, W1H 9PE. $18.95 plus $3.50 postage. Also available in the United States through Seven Hill Book Distributors (49 Central Ave., Cincinnati, OH 45202, Tel. 800/545-2005). Includes volunteer and paid teaching opportunities.

Teaching EFL Outside the U.S.. TESOL, 1600 Cameron St., Suite 300, Alexandria, VA 22314-2751, Tel. 703/836-0774. $22 plus $2.50 postage. Outlines both public and private teaching opportunities and employment conditions. Includes a listing of institutions offering TEFL courses.

Teaching English Abroad. Transitions Abroad, 18 Hulst Rd., P.O. Box 1300, Amherst, MA 01004-1300. $9.95 postpaid. Newly revised booklet describes country-by-country teaching opportunities for both experienced and inexperienced English language teachers. Includes job directories, training centers, agencies and organizations, and resource books.

Teaching English Abroad. Susan Griffith, Vacation Work, 9 Park End St., Oxford OX1 1HJ, England. $15.95 (from Peterson's or Impact Publications). This classic annual directory includes thousands of short- and long-term teaching positions for both certified and uncertified teachers. Organized by country. Includes useful information on training and job search.

Teaching English in Eastern Europe. Citizens Democracy Corps, 2021 K St., NW, Suite 215, Washington, DC 20006, Tel. 800/394-1945. Free upon request. Lists organizations placing volunteer teachers in Eastern Europe, the Baltics, and Russia.

Teaching Opportunities in the Middle East and North Africa. 1987. AMIDEAST, 1100 17th St., NW, Suite 30, Washington, DC 20036. $18. Includes information on more than 140 schools in the region.

Teaching Overseas: The Caribbean and Latin American Area. Carton H. Bowyer. 1989. Inter-Regional Center for Curriculum and Materials Development, Foundations of Education, College of Education, Memphis State University, Memphis, TN 38152. Provides information on teaching opportunities in 30 U.S.-sponsored schools in the Caribbean and Latin America.

The U.S. government publishes useful information on teaching opportunities with the Department of Defense Dependents Schools, State Department schools, and the Fulbright Exchange Program:

Opportunities Abroad for Educators: U.S. Information Agency, Office of Academic Programs, Fulbright Teacher Exchange Branch, 301 4th St., SW, Washington, DC 20547. Free. Provides information and application form for K-12 educators interested in classroom exchanges in 34 countries.

Overseas Employment Opportunities for Teachers: Office of Overseas Schools, U.S. Department of State, Rm. 245, SA-29, Washington, DC 20522-2902, Tel. 703/235-9600. Free. Includes over 100 international schools.

Overseas Employment Opportunities for Educators: Department of Defense Dependent Schools, Teacher Recruitment Section, 2461 Eisenhower Ave., Alexandria, VA 22331, Tel. 703/325-0885 or 703/746-7864. Free. Includes information on employment opportunities in the more than 200 military base schools administered by the U.S. Department of Defense.

CHOOSING TRAVEL-RELEVANT EDUCATIONAL FIELDS

If you are interested in traveling in education, what are the best fields that will enable you to pursue your passion for travel? Agriculture is still one of the major fields involving travel both at home and abroad. Within the sciences, biology, ecology, oceanography, and geology are naturals. Individuals conducting research in these fields must frequently make trips to field research sites. Many educators in their fields also teach special courses or conduct summer programs in the field. Indeed, many U.S.-based universities offer semester and summer courses that take students to the Caribbean islands, the Amazon, the South Pacific, and Antarctica to study local flora, fauna, oceans, geology, and ecology.

Anthropologists and archaeologists have traditionally engaged in some of the most exotic travel in their pursuit of information on primitive and traditional societies. However, with the increasing disappearance of these population groups, anthropologists now engage in all types of research, from rural development to urban anthropology. While their subjects have changed, anthropologists still travel a great deal to interesting and exotic locations. Practicing archaeologists must constantly travel to field research sites where they literally get their hands dirty. Anthropologists and archaeologists are not noted for traveling in comfort. They seldom see the inside of a four or five-star hotel and they frequently must put up with the inconveniences of life, from battling mosquitos, heat, and humidity to handling the logistics of food, transportation, and accommodations in poor underdeveloped Third and Fourth World countries. Tents and basic village accommodations, with the absence of electricity, running water, and modern toilet facilities, most often characterize the style of travel anthropologists and archaeologists must become accustomed to. If you prefer "creature comforts" when traveling, then these may not be good career options for you to pursue.

Any international field, be it in economics, business, agriculture, foreign language, sociology, political science, international relations, history, geography, or education, will offer both study and research opportunities for travel. Many universities offer special interdisciplinary area studies programs and international programs that focus on particular countries or regions of the world. If you are interested in specializing on Japan, China, India, Africa, the Middle East, Russia, or France, you will find several universities offering programs on these countries and regions. You will normally pursue a degree in a particular field as well as take several related courses outside your major as part of an interdisciplinary area studies or international program.

MORE THAN A JOB

Whatever your course of study, numerous fields in education offer excellent opportunities for frequent travel. While the pay may not be great compared to many other jobs and careers, educators are probably more than adequately compensated given their flexible work hours, lengthy vacation periods, and their level of work output; for the actual hours worked, most are anything but underpaid. In fact, many individuals in higher education work fewer than eight months a year.

Indeed, few careers outside education offer as much flexibility to pursue travel and career interests simultaneously as teaching. One of the best kept secrets amongst teachers is that they receive anywhere from two to four months vacation each year, and they can often manipulate their work schedules to create on-the-job travel opportunities. When their semester or term is over, their work is finished and they can go on to something else—a new semester or term, travel, or relaxation. While some teachers use that time to study and conduct research for career development purposes, other educators, especially many tenured faculty, use that time to pursue their own travel interests. It's not unusual for many teachers to take one major trip abroad each year. Some manage to take such trips two or more times a year, depending on how they manage their teaching schedules and research time.

What many educators most wish is that their jobs paid more so they could engage in more and higher quality travel! In fact, many people go into education precisely because they love to travel. Few would leave their profession for higher paying opportunities because they feel they would lose their flexibility to travel each year, and they would have to work much longer and harder. Teaching is one of the few fields that offers them the flexibility to pursue their travel passions. Today, as you read this book, thousands of educators throughout the United States and abroad are planning their next trip for December, April, or June through August! Many love teaching because their job enables them to engage in frequent travel—much of which is subsidized by their educational institution or by other education-related groups.

7

JOBS AND CAREERS ABROAD

*M*any people who love to travel are primarily interested in pursuing international jobs that enable them to either live abroad for lengthy periods of time or make frequent trips abroad. While many of these jobs are found in government, education, and business (Chapters 5, 6, and 8), many other jobs are found with three types of organizations:

- International organizations
- Contracting and consulting firms
- Nonprofit organizations

183

Jobs with these types of organizations often lead to long-term careers. Working for the United Nations, for example, becomes a career for many individuals who thrive on receiving excellent salary, benefits, advancement opportunities, and job security. Individuals working for international consulting and contracting firms often make careers of their work, even though they may change jobs many times over a 25 to 40 year period, moving from one firm to another or starting their own firm. And individuals working for nonprofit organizations often remain committed to an international career by working with several types of PVO's (private voluntary organizations) or NGO's (nongovernmental organizations) throughout their worklife.

INTERNATIONAL ORGANIZATIONS

Numerous international organizations offer job opportunities for talented individuals. Most of these organizations are either directly tied to the United Nations or function as regional military, political, economic, and social organizations. In most cases the United States is involved as a major bilateral or multilateral partner.

Since historically the United States has played a major role in developing international organizations and continues as a major funding source, many Americans have been employed with these groups. Yet, American participation in the day-to-day administration of international organizations is normally limited by specific hiring quotas imposed on all member nations related to population and financial contribution criteria. As a result, only certain positions requiring specific expertise will be open to American job seekers. In this sense, employment with many international organizations is very political in terms of both hiring for a position and retaining a job in competition with eager job seekers from the United States and other countries.

Future job opportunities with international organizations is difficult to predict given the ending of the Cold War. The whole structure of multilateral and bilateral international organizations is under review in this new post-Cold War period. While the United Nations should logically play a more important role during this period, at the same time, the United Nations frequently functions like a classic Third World bureaucracy—highly politicized, unresponsive, inefficient, ineffective, and often inept. It often functions in the interests of its bureaucrats, who are intent on keeping and advancing their jobs, rather than in response to specific international missions. Consequently, its future direction is at best in question. Nonprofit organizations (PVO's and NGO's) may play a much greater role in this post-Cold War period than the United Nations and other bilateral and multilateral international organizations.

In this section we provide a brief overview of employment alternatives with numerous international organizations. Each organization has its own hiring system which you must understand in order to be effective in landing a job. Most important of all, each organization has a particular political environment which may or may not meet your criteria for a rewarding job or career involving travel.

The United Nations

The United Nations is the largest single employer of international specialists. Its bureaucracy consists of nearly 50,000 individuals who work in over 600 duty stations throughout the world. Less than 10 percent of the UN civil servants are Americans.

The United Nations consists of a central organization and a loose collection of relatively autonomous specialized agencies and organizations. Given both the centralized and decentralized nature of the United Nations, all specialized agencies and related organizations recruit their own personnel. The United Nations, in effect, consists of more than 25 different hiring systems.

Organizations

The United Nations consists of six major organizational units and numerous specialized and autonomous agencies, standing committees, commissions, and other subsidiary bodies. The six principal organs are the:

- General Assembly
- Security Council
- Economic and Social Council
- Trusteeship Council
- International Court of Justice
- Secretariat

While job opportunities are available with all of these organs, the most numerous jobs are found with the Economic and Social Council and the UN Secretariat.

The **Economic and Social Council** is under the General Assembly. It coordinates the economic and social work of the United Nations and numerous specialized agencies, standing committees, commissions, and related organizations. The work of the Council involves international development, world trade, industrialization, natural resources, human rights, status of women, population, social welfare, science and technology, crime prevention, and other social and economic issues.

The Economic and Social Council is divided into a headquarters staff in New York City and five regional economic commissions:

- Economic Commission for Africa (Addis Ababa)
- Economic and Social Commission for Asia and the Pacific (Bangkok)
- Economic Commission for Europe (Geneva)
- Economic Commission for Latin America and the Caribbean (Santiago)
- Economic Commission for Western Asia (Beirut)

Each Commission maintains a large staff of specialists. Furthermore, they promote the work of several standing committees and commissions which also have their own staffs.

Specialized or intergovernmental agencies are autonomous organizations linked to the United Nations by special intergovernmental agreements. In addition, they have their own membership, budgets, personnel systems, legislative and executive bodies, and secretariats. The Food and Agriculture Organization (FAO), for example, consists of a staff drawn from 160 member nations. It is administered by a professional staff of nearly 3,200 which is headquartered in Rome; some employees work in FAO regional offices located in Ghana, Thailand, Chile, New York City, and Washington, DC. Each year the FAO hires nearly 500 staff members; 60 to 65 of these new hirees are U.S. citizens.

The Economic and Social Council coordinates the work of these organizations with the United Nations as well as with each other. Altogether, there are 12 specialized agencies:

- Food and Agriculture Organization (FAO)
- International Civil Aviation Organization (ICAO)
- International Fund for Agricultural Development (IFAD)
- International Labour Organization (ILO)
- International Maritime Organization (IMO)
- International Monetary Fund (IMF)
- International Telecommunication Union (ITU)
- United Nations Educational, Scientific and Cultural Organization (UNESCO)
- United Nations Industrial Development Organization
- Universal Postal Union (UPU)
- World Health Organization (WHO)
- World Intellectual Property Organization (WIPO)
- World Meteorological Organization (WMO)

These organizations are variously headquartered in Geneva, Vienna, Paris, Rome, London, Montreal, and New York City.

Several other major organizations also are attached to the Economic and Social Council as well as the Secretariat. These consist of:

- General Agreement on Tariffs and Trade (GATT)
- International Sea-Bed Authority
- International Atomic Energy Agency (IAEA)
- International Bank for Reconstruction and Development (IBRD or World Bank)
- Office of the United Nations Disaster Relief Co-Ordinator
- United Nations Centre for Human Settlements (HABITAT)
- United Nations Children's Fund (UNICEF)
- United Nations Development Programme (UNDP)
- United Nations Environment Programme (UNEP)
- United Nations Fund for Population (UNFPA)
- United Nations High Commissioner for Refugees (UNHCR)
- United Nations Industrial Development Organization (UNIDO)
- United Nations Institute for Training and Research (UNITAR)
- United Nations Observer Mission and Peacekeeping Forces in the Middle East
- United Nations Relief and Works Agency for Palestine Refugees in the Near East (UNRWA)
- World Food Council (WFC)
- World Food Programme (WFP)

The UN Secretariat employs nearly 14,000 international civil servants from 160 countries. Most are stationed at the UN headquarters in New York City. The Secretariat is the central "bureaucracy" in charge of carrying out the day-to-day work of the UN

The largest UN agencies—those employing at least 1,500 individuals—consist of the following:

- Food and Agriculture Organization
- World Health Organization
- United Nations Development Programme
- World Bank
- UNESCO
- International Labor Organization
- UNICEF
- International Monetary Fund

The United States is especially involved in the following United Nations organizations which are headquartered in various cities throughout the world:

- Food and Agricultural Organization (Rome)
- International Atomic Energy Agency (Vienna)
- International Bank for Reconstruction and Development or World Bank (Washington, DC)
- International Civil Aviation Organization (Montreal)
- International Finance Corporation (Washington, DC)
- International Monetary Fund (Washington, DC)
- International Telecommunication Union (Geneva)
- Universal Postal Union (Bern, Switzerland)
- World Health Organization (Geneva)

Consequently, U.S. citizens may have a higher probability of landing jobs with these UN agencies than with other agencies.

Employment Alternatives

The United Nations and related specialized agencies and organizations hire all types of professionals and general service staff as full-time, permanent staff, technical assistance experts, and consultants. Major positions include engineers, accountants, doctors, lawyers, researchers, translators, interpreters, demographers, guides, and typists. The UN also hires technical assistance experts who are then loaned to Third World governments. Except for general service staff positions, most UN jobs require highly educated and experienced professionals.

Many United Nations jobs are exciting. They involve traveling to interesting places, working with highly intelligent and competent professionals, and dealing with important international problems and issues. At the same time, many UN offices have acquired characteristics of Third World and Byzantine bureaucracies. They spend much of their time in meetings, which produce little or nothing except for a great deal of memos and reports requiring further meetings. Bureaucratic intrigue, power struggles, and maneuvers to take over others' positions characterize the daily work of some UN offices.

Competition for UN positions is keen for several reasons. UN jobs pay extremely well compared to comparable jobs in the U.S. federal government or in any national government. Indeed, competition is most keen and the personnel process is most political among professionals from Third World countries—especially those from India, Pakistan, and Bangladesh—who cannot find comparable professions and pay elsewhere. For many of them, working for the United Nations, specialized agencies, or related organizations is extremely important to financing their lifestyles which frequently include plush homes, servants, private schools, and one or two Mercedes.

Qualifications and Positions

The United Nations describes its "typical recruit" as a 36-year old economist who has an advanced degree and is fluent in two of the official languages of the UN—Arabic, Chinese, English, French, Russian, or Spanish. For professional and technical positions, the United Nations places special emphasis on formal educational qualifications—the higher your degree the better—international experience, and language competency. Without these three in combination, you may be wasting your time applying for many UN positions. Translators or interpreters, of course, must demonstrate their competency by taking a qualifying examination.

The United Nations hires individuals for all types of positions. The major categories include the following positions: Administrative, Public Information, Social Welfare, Demography and Population, Information Systems and Computers, Legal, Teachers, Political

Affairs, Telecommunications, Economics, and Translators and Interpreters. The UN also offers several other types of positions for individuals interested in gaining some experience with the international organization: Summer Employment, UN Guides, Intern Programs, and UN Volunteers. Clerical and secretarial personnel are normally recruited from local residents where particular UN offices are located. Since the United States withdrew support from UNESCO, there are few job opportunities for Americans, especially teachers, in this agency.

Hiring Practices

The United Nations hires individuals for positions within the secretariats as well as its technical assistance programs. While many positions are full-time professional positions complete with generous salaries and retirement benefits, many other positions are short-term technical assistance positions that require the expertise of experts and consultants. The bias again is for individuals with post-graduate degrees, extensive international experience, and appropriate language competency. The United Nations in general hires few inexperienced people for entry-level positions, although politics within the United Nations is not adverse to hiring well connected individuals who appear to lack many of the so-called "prerequisite" educational, technical, experience, and language qualifications.

The hiring process is largely decentralized within the United Nations and among the specialized agencies and related organizations. Therefore, you must directly contact each agency for job vacancy information as well as network with your resume by conducting informational interviews. If, for example, you are interested in working for the UN Secretariat in New York City, contact the following office for information on job vacancies:

> Recruitment Programs Section
> Office of Personnel Services
> United Nations
> New York, NY 10017

Most agencies and organizations will have a personnel office which issues job vacancy announcements. Bulletin boards outside personnel offices or cafeterias often include the latest vacancy announcements.

For technical assistance positions, you should contact the following office for information:

> Technical Assistance Recruitment Service
> Department of Technical Cooperation
> United Nations
> New York, NY 10017

The U.S. Department of State provides a recruitment and job referral service for individuals interested in working for the UN, specialized agencies, and related organizations. The Office of UN Employment Information and Assistance identifies qualified Americans who are then referred for UN assignments. Most candidates should have specialized and advanced academic degrees and several years of recent international experience. The categories of positions covered include: public information personnel; computer programmers; military personnel; administrative posts; legal posts; translators; interpreters; summer employment; clerical personnel; UN guides; intern programs; political affairs posts; telecommunication posts; economists; and UN volunteers. The Bureau maintains a computerized roster of qualified professional candidates whose backgrounds are matched against the qualifications specified in UN vacancy announcements. To get on this roster and be referred, send a detailed resume to:

> Staffing Management Officer
> Office of UN Employment Information and Assistance
> Bureau of International Organization Affairs
> IO/S/EA, Rm. 4808, NW
> Department of State
> Washington, DC 20520-6319
> Tel. 202/736-4824

You can write or call this office for information on the UN and the referral system. Ask for their "Fact Sheet" on employment with international organizations and "United Nations People." The "Fact Sheet" includes names and addresses of various UN agencies to which you can apply directly for vacancies. It also includes a useful list of U.S. counterpart agencies that work with the United Nations. These include:

UN Agency	U.S. counterpart agency
Food and Agriculture Organization (FAO)	Foreign Agriculture Service Department of Agriculture
International Atomic Energy Agency (IAEA)	Office of International Affairs, Department of Energy
International Civil Aviation Organization (ICAO)	Office of International Organization Aviation Affairs, Federal Aviation Administration
Universal Postal Union	International Postal Affairs, U.S. Postal Service
World Health Organization (WHO)	Office of International Health, Public Health Service, Department of Health and Human Services
World Meteorological Organization (WMO)	Office of International Affairs, National Oceanic and Atmospheric Administration

The office's "Fact Sheet" also includes current contact information on some of the most popular international financial institutions as well as regional and Inter-American organizations international job hunters seek information on: Inter-American Development Bank, International Monetary Fund, World Bank, Organization for Economic Cooperation and Development, and the Organization of American States.

Consequently, you may want to get on the State Department roster as well as apply directly to UN agencies and offices for positions.

The United Nations uses a special application form—the UN Personal History Form P-11 (UN P-11)—which is similar to the U.S. federal government's SF-171 or OF-612. Be sure to complete this form and submit it along with a targeted resume for most UN positions.

Your most effective job search strategy will be to target particular agencies and organizations. Personnel offices will provide vacancy announcements and information on the formal hiring process, but you must make contact with the hiring personnel in the operating units. Do informational interviewing so you can uncover vacancies for which you may qualify. You will want to learn about the political environment of offices in order to avoid both wasting your time on positions which are wired and landing what may quickly become a terrible job!

Job Outlook

Many UN jobs are considered "plum" international jobs for those interested in pursuing an international career. This is one of very few organizations that enable one to pursue an international career up a single organizational hierarchy. While the climb up the hierarchy is different from the climb up any other organizational hierarchy—especially given political and nationality considerations in assignments and promotions—the UN can be a very satisfying and rewarding career for many international specialists.

However, the job outlook within the UN is not great these days. The United States, as well as many other nations, has increasingly put pressure on the United Nations to cut costs and implement internal administrative reforms. These pressures translate into more cost conscious personnel practices and leaner hiring for the decade ahead. Indeed, UNESCO and the World Bank have experienced major personnel cuts during the past five years. Cutbacks in other UN agencies are likely to continue over the next five years. As a result, competition for UN positions is very keen as individuals already working in the United Nations are the first to apply for vacancies. Given their inside "connections" and UN experience, they are in the best position to be "qualified" for such vacancies. Increasingly outsiders will have difficulty breaking into full-time professional UN positions. Part-time consulting positions, however, will continue to be a major avenue to other positions within the United Nations.

The long-term job outlook with the United Nations should be good to excellent. With the ending of the Cold War, the United Nations is likely to play an even greater role in international affairs. The United States and many other countries will place greater reliance on multilateral rather than bilateral arrangements for resolving international conflicts and promoting economic development. The United Nations will increasingly become the lead multilateral institution in international affairs. Employment prospects with the UN should increase accordingly.

Multilateral and
Bilateral Organizations

In addition to the United Nations, the United States participates in several other multilateral organizations which also provide job opportunities for enterprising job seekers. Most of these organizations are designed to promote regional security and economic and social development. The major multilateral organizations and corresponding headquarter locations are:

- African Development Bank (Abidjan, Ivory Coast)
- Asian Development Bank (Manila)
- Inter-American Defense Board (Washington, DC)
- Inter-American Development Bank (Washington, DC)
- Intergovernmental Committee for Migration (Geneva)
- International Finance Corporation (Washington, DC)
- International Telecommunication Union (Geneva)
- Organization of American States (Washington, DC)
- Organization for Economic Cooperation and Development (Paris)
- Pan American Health Organization (Washington, DC)
- South Pacific Commission (Noumea, New Caledonia)

The United States is also a member of several regional organizations as well as numerous subsidiary commissions, councils, and committees. Among its many affiliations are the:

- Colombo Plan for Cooperative Economic and Social Development in Asia and the Pacific
- Inter-American Indian Institute
- Inter-American Institute for Cooperation on Agriculture
- Inter-American Tropical Tuna Commission
- International Coffee Organization
- International Institute of Cotton
- International Sugar Organizations
- International Wheat Council
- Interparliamentary Union
- North Atlantic Ice Patrol
- North Atlantic Treaty Organization (NATO)
- North Atlantic Assembly

- Organization for Economic Cooperation and Development
- Pan American Health Organizations
- West African Rice Development Association
- World Tourism Organization

Other international groups hiring international specialists include:

- Andean Group
- ANZUS
- Arab Bank for Economic Development in Africa (BADEA)
- Arab Fund for Economic and Social Development (AFESD)
- Arab Monetary Fund
- Association of Southeast Asian Nations (ASEAN)
- Bank for International Settlements (BIS)
- Benelux Economic Union
- Caribbean Community and Common Market (CARICOM)
- Central American Common Market (CACM)
- The Commonwealth
- Communaute Economique de l'Afrique de l'Ouest (CEAO)
- Conseil de l'Entente
- Co-operation Council for the Arab States of the Gulf
- Council for Mutual Economic Assistance (CMEA)
- Council of Arab Economic Unity
- Council of Europe
- Economic Community of West African States (ECOWAS)
- The European Communities
- European Free Trade Association (EFTA)
- The Franc Zone
- Inter-American Development Bank (IDB)
- International Bank for Economic Co-operation (IBEC)
- International Investment Bank
- International Olympic Committee
- Islamic Development Bank
- Latin American Integration Association (ALADI)
- League of Arab States
- Nordic Council
- Nordic Council of Ministers
- North Atlantic Treaty Organization (NATO)
- Organization Commune Africaine et Mauricienne (OCAM)
- Organization for Economic Co-operation and Development

(OECD)
—International Energy Agency
—OECD Nuclear Energy Agency (NEA)
- Organization of African Unity (OAU)
- Organization of Arab Petroleum Exporting Countries
  (OAPEC)
- OPEC Fund for International Development
- South Pacific Forum
  —South Pacific Bureau for Economic Co-operation (SPEC)
- Southern African Development Co-ordination Conference
  (SADCC)
- Western European Union (WEU)

While the U.S. Department of State can provide information on jobs with some of these regional organizations, you must contact the organizations directly for detailed job information. Keep in mind that U.S. participation on the staffs of these organizations will be limited and, in some cases, nonexistent. Furthermore, most regional organizations hire highly educated, skilled, and experienced professionals. Expect the hiring processes to be somewhat political in most cases.

Useful Resources

Before contacting individuals in the international organizations for informational interviews, you should collect basic data on the organizations. Three directories in particular will give you important descriptions and contact information on all of these organizations as well as thousands of additional international organizations. Most major libraries have the following annual directories for researching these organizations:

- *Yearbook of the United Nations*
- *Europa Year Book*
- *Yearbook of International Organizations*

The *Yearbook of the United Nations* provides detailed information on the operations of each UN agency. This invaluable directory is "must" reading for anyone interested in U.N. operations.

The *Europa Year Book* gives details on the United Nations as well as other political, economic, and commercial institutions throughout the world. This two-volume directory classifies international-al organizations into 21 categories:

- Agriculture, Food, Forestry, and Fisheries
- Aid and Development
- Arts and Culture
- Economics and Finance
- Education
- Government and Politics
- Industrial and Professional Relations
- Law
- Medicine and Health
- Posts and Telecommunications
- Press, Radio, and TV
- Religion
- Science
- Social Sciences and Humanities Studies
- Social Welfare
- Sports and Recreation
- Technology
- Tourism
- Trade and Industry
- Transport
- Youth and Students

The *Yearbook of International Organizations* compiles similar information on over 20,000 organizations. It provides annotated descriptions on all "international" organizations. These are organizations whose membership is comprised of at least 60 member nations. This directory includes all organs, specialized agencies, and related organizations of the United Nations; other international organizations; and individual country profiles of organizations.

You also should acquire annual reports from individual organizations. The World Bank, for example, publishes a comprehensive annual report on its organization, mission, and accomplishments which is required reading for anyone interested in working for this organization. In addition, the World Bank has a publications program which produces numerous special reports and books each year. You can get copies of these reports and publications by writing to or calling the Publications Division of the various organizations.

Most libraries also will have books about international organizations as well as magazines and journals published by different offices within the organization. Reference librarians can usually identify these publications for you.

CONTRACTORS AND CONSULTANTS IN THE DEVELOPING WORLD

Although international organizations and U.S. government agencies have the greatest visibility in the international arena, numerous other organizations pursue public-related international interests. These peripheral institutions consist of consulting firms; trade and professional associations; nonprofit organizations; foundations; research organizations; and educational institutions. These organizations have international interests and interface in both the U.S. domestic and international arenas.

Much of what gets done by government and international organizations is actually done through contractors and consultants. During the past 30 years more and more public services and programs have been contracted-out to private firms. The trend for the remainder of the 1990s appears to be in the direction of even greater use of international consultants and contractors.

Consultants and contractors play important roles in providing services to government and business. Government agencies use consultants and contractors for several reasons:

- They require specialized information not available through their present staffs.

- They need special services and products only available from contractors and consultants.

- It is often more cost-effective to contract-out services than to increase the number of agency personnel to provide the services in-house.

- Many services are short-term and thus can be most quickly and effectively performed by outside consultants and contractors.

At the state and local government levels, contractors may provide sanitation services, road construction, health care, and building construction and maintenance. At the federal level these firms run a variety of federal programs, conduct numerous studies, and regularly supply agencies with every conceivable type of durable and nondurable goods from pencil sharpeners to submarines. At the international level, contractors and consultants are involved in building and maintaining U.S. facilities abroad, implementing the U.S. foreign aid program, and providing information on international developments.

Almost every job in the private sector will be performed in government. Ironically, these government jobs are often performed by private firms on contract with government agencies. Therefore, much of the work of government employees involves obligating funds and administering contracts rather than providing direct government services.

Contractor services are performed at the contractor's or agency's site. In many cases, an agency will provide office space for a contractor's staff which then performs services in offices adjacent to agency personnel. The extreme example of this type of relationship is found in the U.S. Department of Energy where over 80 percent of its personnel are actually private contractors.

The Procurement Process

The work of contractors and consultants centers around the **procurement process**. Procurement is the process by which government acquires goods and services. Well defined rules and regulations govern the process by which agencies can contract-out various services.

The federal government strictly regulates the procurement process through a set of general regulations:

- Federal Acquisition Regulations (FAR)
- Competition in Contracting Act of 1985 (CICA)

In addition, each agency develops more detailed regulations based upon each section of the FAR and in line with the CICA. Altogether, over $400 billion a year flows from the federal government to the private sector through this process.

One major result of the federal procurement process has been to create competition among consulting and contracting firms. For example, all goods and services amounting to $10,000 or more ($25,000 in the case of the Department of Defense) must be procured through competitive bidding or negotiation processes (new pending reform regulations should raise this amount to $100,000). This normally takes the form of sealed bids for equipment or negotiations with agency personnel for services. Once a procurement need is identified and defined by agency personnel, contractors are identified and the procurement process follows specific rules and procedures. If a service is for less than $10,000, contracting officials must contact at least three firms for competitive bids. If the amount for small purchases is more than $10,000, then the officials must issue a Request for Proposal (RFP). An announcement must be published in the *Commerce Business Daily (CBD)* for at least 30 days. During that time firms request copies of the solicitation which outlines the Statement of Work and evaluation criteria for judging proposals. Firms normally have 30 days to develop and submit detailed proposals. Once proposals are received and reviewed by contracting officers and technical personnel, an award is made to the firm receiving the highest evaluation on both technical and cost criteria. This may take from one to three months after the closing date for submitting proposals.

While all federal agencies are supposed to follow these rules for ensuring competition, informal systems also operate to limit competition. Many agencies prefer working with a single contractor and thus they "wire" RFPs to favor one particular contractor. This is done by specifying in both the Statement of Work and the evaluation criteria various requirements which only one firm is likely to meet.

Hiring Structure

It is extremely important to understand this procurement process if you are interested in working for international consulting and contracting firms. The process creates a job market situation which is very fluid, unstable, and unpredictable. A typical consulting firm structure consists of a core staff, associates, and consultants.

Many firms keep a small **core staff** which is employed full-time to respond to RFPs and manage a lean organizational infrastructure. As contracts are won, they hire two types of additional personnel—often on a consulting basis—for implementing the contract. **Associates** normally work closely with the core staff on several projects; these individuals are relatively loyal to the firm and are given a disproportionate amount of contract work as individuals or subcontractors. **Consultants** are less closely linked to the firm; they have specific skills not found with the core staff or associates, and they tend to freelance with several such firms. Therefore, many positions with these firms are short-term positions tied to specific contracts, ranging from one month to one or more years. Most contracts are for one year with options to renew contracts up to two to three years before resubmitting them for open competition.

Given this structure, you must consider whether you want a full-time organization position or a contract-specific position as either an associate or consultant. An organization position may be more stable and predictable, but not necessarily so. For example, most contracting and consulting firms are small organizations employing fewer than 50 individuals. Many specialize in a particular government function or public policy area and work primarily with one or two government agencies. A few firms straddle the public and private sectors by doing contract work for both government and business. Many international consulting firms, for example, only work in the fields of health care, population planning, or rural development. Others specialize in educational development and human resource management. Given the highly competitive nature of their work, many of these firms find they must quickly staff-up and staff-down depending on which contracts they receive. If they receive a large contract, they may need to more than double or triple their staff overnight. If they lose a large contract, everyone except the president may go off the payroll and, instead, work on a daily consulting basis. For many small firms, contracting work is a feast or famine business.

On the other hand, large firms with several large contracts—especially defense contractors—will maintain a relatively large permanent staff. They normally can afford to do this, because their overhead and profits are greater on larger contracts. Furthermore, procurement officials find it difficult to estimate and monitor the costs of large contracts. But recent revelations about alleged contracting abuses by noted Department of Defense contractors as well as numerous contractors doing business with the Department of Housing and Urban Development and highly publicized cases of graft and corruption in the U.S. Agency for International Development (USAID) have created a new element of instability among contractors. Some contractors violated one of the most important unwritten rules of the contracting business—do not get your contracting practices, however legal or illegal, exposed in the news media and thus endanger the careers of agency personnel. Many firms involved in the scandal-ridden Housing and Urban Development (HUD) contracting practices of the late 1980s also took several politicians with them. Contracting abuses within the USAID system—major or minor—often become publicized because of the high public visibility and intense congressional oversight centering on this agency.

Contractors and Consultants in the Foreign Aid System

Several contractors and consulting firms are organized to acquire contracts with federal agencies and international organizations. These include huge firms such as Coopers and Lybrand, which does contract work with both public and private institutions and maintains an international staff of 30,000 in 97 countries; medium-sized firms with staffs of 10 to 50 individuals; and one or two-person firms which primarily rely on short-term contracts with a single agency or office. These firms provide every conceivable service from constructing roads and dams to dispensing food and condoms in Third World countries.

The contracting and consulting business is widespread throughout the international arena. However, its exact dimensions are difficult to measure since much of the work of contractors and consultants is not visible to the public. Government agencies may have responsibility for administering foreign aid programs, but much of what they take credit for is done by contractors. Many agencies primarily obligate funds which are, in turn, dispensed to contractors and consultants who actually get the work done. The agency, in turn, primarily becomes involved in dispensing funds, monitoring contractors, and evaluating contract performance.

The World Bank, United Nations, and several federal agencies are the major funding sources for these contracting and consulting firms. Federal agencies most frequently using international contractors are the U.S. Agency for International Development, Department of Agriculture, Department of State, Department of Defense, and the Central Intelligence Agency.

Take, for example, the U.S. Agency for International Development. This is a good case for getting a sense of how the government procurement process operates in the international arena and how it affects the operation of contractors and consultants as well as several nonprofit or nongovernmental (NGOs) organizations discussed in the next chapter. USAID is one of the largest dispensers of government contracts to large, small, and minority consulting firms. Since USAID is primarily organized to obligate funds for development projects in Third World countries, numerous consulting firms in the United States and abroad are recipients of USAID funding. The contracts deal with every conceivable type of service and project. USAID, for example, classifies all contractors according to 21 activity categories:

- Accounting and Financial Management
- Agriculture
- Architecture and Engineering
- Auditing
- Development Information/Evaluation
- Development Management
- Disaster Assistance
- Education
- Energy
- Environmental/Natural Resources
- Foreign Language Instruction
- Health (Planning and Delivery)
- Housing and Urban Development
- Macroeconomic Analysis
- Management Assistance/Skills
- Management Consulting Services
- Nutrition and Multisectoral Development
- Printing Services
- Procurement Services
- Records Management
- Rural/Regional Income Generation

A USAID contracting officer is assigned to each category. This individual issues solicitations, negotiates, and regularly communicates with the firms doing work under USAID contracts.

USAID does business with nearly 2,000 contractors in the United States and abroad. While many job opportunities are available with U.S. firms, additional opportunities are available with firms located in Third World countries which receive "Host Country Contracts." As part of USAID's emphasis on decentralization, capacity building, and private sector initiatives, more and more USAID contracts are earmarked for consulting firms in Third World countries. Since many of these firms lack basic capabilities to develop proposals and implement projects, some will hire experienced Americans to help them get and manage USAID contracts. The contracting officer attached to each USAID mission should have a list of local firms, which usually will be available upon request.

USAID publishes a wealth of information on U.S. and European-based firms which receive contracts as well as have special relationships with the Agency. Indeed, of all federal agencies, this one is a job hunters paradise. The *Current Technical Services Contracts and Grants* directory, for example, is issued by the Procurement Support Division of USAID's Office of Procurement. This lengthy document identifies most firms receiving contracts and grants from USAID each fiscal year. It includes a statistical summary, a regional directory, and a state and country listing of contractors and grantees. Each contract is identified by contract number, contract name, contract term, dollar amount, contract description, and address of contractor. If you conduct some basic analysis of this document, you will acquire some very useful information for your job search. For example, in the period October 1, 1990 to September 30, 1991, USAID awarded the following number of contracts by region and total dollar amounts:

Area	No. of countries	No. of contracts	Amount in dollars
Worldwide	—	595	$2,085,771,030
Asia	17	493	957,123,967
Latin America	22	626	940,755,583
Africa	41	493	766,506,769
Near East	10	155	507,498,082
Europe	16	113	397,300,520
United States	—	216	356,902,874
South Pacific	7	14	18,203,755
TOTAL	**114**	**2,705**	**$6,030,062,580**

Firms headquartered in eight states received the largest number and dollar value of USAID contracts and grants. These consisted of the following:

Location of Firms	Total Amount
District of Columbia	$1,691,950,762
New York	654,650,802
Virginia	422,202,107
Massachusetts	422,190,357
Maryland	360,513,319
North Carolina	193,944,077
California	172,436,355
Connecticut	140,080,576

Hundreds of firms are located throughout the United States—not just in these eight states. Not surprising, firms in and around Washington, DC—the so-called "Beltway Bandits"—received the largest number of USAID contracts, totaling nearly $2.5 billion. In fact, from 1984 to 1992 the total dollars pouring into contractors and consultants in the Washington Metropolitan area nearly tripled (from $809,806,103 to $2,474,666,188) whereas most other areas in the country experienced about a 60 percent increase. The Washington Metropolitan area remained the central area for these firms which continued to receive the lion's share of USAID funding. Not surprising, this area remains a job hunter's paradise for those interested in doing international contracting and consulting work.

A useful feature of this key USAID document is the index. It identifies which firms received the largest number of contracts and grants during the fiscal year. For example, during Fiscal Year 1991 nearly 1500 foundations, universities, contracting firms, and nonprofit organizations received USAID contracts and grants. Of these, 33 organizations received 10 or more contracts or grants:

USAID CONTRACTORS/GRANTEES
RECEIVING 10 OR MORE CONTRACTS

Firms/ Organizations	Number of Contracts/ Grants Awarded
■ Abt Associates, Inc.	30
■ Academy for Educational Development	24
■ Adventist Development and Relief Agency International	14
■ Africare, Inc.	18
■ Agricultural Cooperative Development International	12
■ Asia Foundation	13
■ Camp Dresser and McKee International	10
■ Catholic Relief Services (CRS)	22
■ Chemonics International Consulting Division	19
■ Cooperative for American Relief Everywhere, Inc. (CARE)	41
■ Coopers and Lybrand	13
■ Development Alternatives, Inc.	20
■ Futures Group	18
■ Helen Keller International, Inc.	11
■ Institute of International Education	10
■ International Executive Service Corps	23
■ International Resources Group, Ltd.	10
■ International Sciences and Technology Institute, Inc.	12
■ John Snow Public Health Group, Inc.	13
■ Louis Berger International, Inc.	12
■ Management Systems for Health	17
■ Management Systems International	11
■ Nathan, Robert, Associates, Inc.	15
■ People to People Health Foundation, Inc.	12
■ Population Services International	10
■ Price Waterhouse	26
■ Private Agencies Collaborating Together	12
■ Research Triangle Institute	10
■ Save the Children Foundation	23

- University Research Corporation   10
- Winrock International   15
- World Vision Relief and Development   13
- United Nations Children's Fund   13

While most firms compete with each other in receiving individual company contacts, an increasing number of contractors receive joint contracts. The major firms joining together in such cooperative efforts include:

- Checchi and Co./Louis Berger International (5 contracts)
- Development Alternatives, Inc./International Science and Technology Institute (6 contracts)
- Development Alternatives, Inc./Nathan Associates, Inc. (5 contracts)
- Development Associates, Inc./Development Alternatives, Inc. (5 contracts)
- Robert Nathan Associates, Inc./Duke University/Louis Berger International/Mid-American International Agricultural Consortium (4 contracts)
- World Wildlife Fund/Conservation Foundation (8 contracts)

Most of these contractors are major firms involved in Third World development projects. They constitute an important network for those interested in working for such types of firms.

Contracting firms, including nonprofit NGOs and universities, receiving $10 million or more in USAID contracts in 1991 included the following:

CONTRACTORS RECEIVING $10 MILLION OR MORE IN USAID CONTRACTS

Contractor	Amount Awarded
A.T. International	$24,873,462
Abt Associates, Inc.	24,611,245
Academy for Educational Development	182,744,998
African-American Labor Center	32,463,868

- African-American Institute   60,119,061
- Africare, Inc.   17,918,011
- Agricultural Cooperative
  Development International   21,484,011
- Aguirre International, Inc.   29,152,780
- American AG International, Inc.   12,908,200
- American Institute for Free
  Labor Development   15,486,269
- American Mideast Educational
  and Training Services   56,151,175
- American Near East Refugee Aid, Inc.   11,043,766
- Ansell, Inc.   29,881,248
- Appropriate Technology International   10,947,527
- Asian American Free Labor Institute   16,228,600
- Association for Voluntary
  Surgical Contraception   48,994,108
- Association in Rural Development   19,674,224
- Berger, Louis, International, Inc.   37,812,049
- Black and Veatch International/
  James M. Montgomery Assoc.   29,238,000
- Camp, Dresser and McKee International, Inc.   44,672,876
- Catholic Relief Services   42,787,203
- Center for Human Services   10,693,624
- CH2M Hill International   10,422,022
- Chemonics International   49,966,974
- Clark University   14,120,608
- Consortium for International Development   40,205,209
- Construction Control Services Corp.   17,373,248
- Cooperative for American Relief
  Everywhere, Inc. (CARE)   36,755,515
- Coopers and Lybrand   18,444,685
- Creative Associates International, Inc.   10,125,992
- Credit Union National Association   20,827,931
- Czech and Slovak American Enterprise   15,000,000
- Deloitte and Touche   14,739,054
- Development Alternatives Inc.   40,104,863
- Development Associates Inc.   33,639,930
- Development Associates/Nathan Associates   11,769,662
- EBASCO Services, Inc.   10,200,000
- Eastern Virginia Medical School   31,407,000

- Educational Development Center, Inc.   13,306,322
- Executive Resource Associates   49,096,094
- Family Health International   117,908,937
- Florida International University   10,708,302
- Florida State University   13,614,196
- Futures Group   61,122,036
- Georgetown University   117,311,055
- Hagler, Bailly and Co., Inc.   12,008,543
- Harvard University   28,883,237
- Harza Engineering Company   21,943,328
- Hungarian-American Enterprise Fund   36,462,250
- Institute for Contemporary Studies   10,325,516
- Institute for Resource Development, Inc.   21,425,542
- Institution of International Education   50,614,403
- International Executive Service Corps   32,296,590
- International Food Policy Research Institute   11,057,168
- International Planned Parenthood Federation   36,775,118
- International Science and
  Technology Institute, Inc.   32,494,726
- JHPIEGO Corporation   37,654,593
- John Snow Public Health Group, Inc.   102,597,711
- Johns Hopkins University   113,867,315
- Labat Anderson, Inc.   11,154,053
- Management Sciences for Health   73,557,130
- Matrix International Logistics   10,538,000
- Medcalf and Eddy International   14,538,891
- Medical Service Consultants, Inc.   16,431,623
- Michigan State University   34,777,800
- Midamerica International Agricultural
  Consortium   16,010,000
- Morrison Knudsen Engineers, Inc.   23,841,449
- National Academy of Sciences   14,193,260
- National Academy of Sciences/
  National Research Council   37,682,702
- National Association of the
  Partners of the Americas, Inc.   25,570,694
- National Capital Administrative Services   17,010,532
- National Endowment for Democracy   22,230,700
- National Rural Electric Cooperative
  Association   28,537,805

- North Carolina State University   19,555,392
- Overseas Bechtel, Inc.   10,135,506
- Partners for International Education
  and Training   86,856,390
- Pathfinder Fund   88,745,614
- People-to-People Health Foundation, Inc.   76,980,735
- Planned Parenthood Federation of America   98,627,591
- Polish-American Enterprise Fund, Inc.   137,692,050
- Population Council   46,293,154
- Population Services International   30,077,589
- Pragma Corporation   23,117,032
- Price Waterhouse   25,575,537
- Private Agencies Collaborating Together   25,795,971
- Program for Appropriate Technology
  in Health   16,433,954
- Project Concern International   11,788,800
- Purdue University   13,639,956
- Ronco Consulting Corporation   17,617,050
- Save the Children Federation   70,919,004
- Scientex Corporation   20,033,603
- Technoserve, Inc.   14,705,058
- Trustees of the American University of Beirut 22,846,828
- Tulane University   14,140,498
- United Nations Children's Fund   15,116,000
- University of Florida   11,829,856
- University of Hawaii   18,996,743
- University of Idaho   11,663,956
- University of Illinois   14,235,320
- University of Kentucky   11,800,988
- University of Maryland   11,460,411
- University of Michigan   11,958,339
- University of Nebraska   26,099,000
- University of North Carolina   11,692,049
- University of Rhode Island   10,899,232
- University of Wisconsin-Madison   17,822,594
- University Research Corporation   24,784,912
- Volunteers in Overseas Cooperative
  Assistance   14,049,811
- Volunteers in Technical Assistance   18,117,759
- Wilbur Smith and Associates   22,871,232

- Winrock International — 39,615,285
- World Resources Institute — 12,091,293
- World Vision Relief and Development, Inc. — 23,451,235
- World Wildlife Fund/Conservation Foundation — 16,560,812

Examples of the type of work conducted by five of these organizations include the following:

CHEMONICS INTERNATIONAL: 2000 M St., NW, Suite 200, Washington, DC 20036, Tel. 202/466-5340. Provides technical assistance services to USAID in the areas of agriculture (policy and planning, farming systems research/extension, on-farm water management, rice production, livestock, seed technology, agricultural engineering), agribusiness (food/fiber processing, marketing, agrochemicals, and business/financial management), natural resources (soil/water conservation/management, range management, and forestry), and rural development (infrastructure, cooperatives, information systems, and public administration). Maintains a full staff in the U.S. of 65 and a long-term staff abroad of 130. Recent international contracts totalled nearly $52 million. Operates in over 40 countries in Africa, Asia, Latin America, the Caribbean, Middle East, and North Africa. Largest projects include $7.2 million for "Central American Non-Traditional Agricultural Export Support" and $7 million for "Egypt Local Development II—Rural Sector."

COOPERS AND LYBRAND: 1251 Avenue of the Americas, New York, NY 10020, Tel. 212/536-2000. One of the oldest (since 1898) and most respected international firms specializing in audit, accounting, tax, information systems, business planning, and resource productivity. Maintains a full-time staff in the U.S. of 15,000 and a long-term staff abroad of 45,000. Operates in nearly 100 countries. Major funding comes from USAID and host country organizations. Sample contracts include: "Assist AID in Studying the Financial Status of the Rural Electrification Program in Bangladesh" (USAID, $245,816) and "Assist USAID Sudan to Conduct Study of Railway Corporations Early Retirement Program" (USAID, $86,000).

DEVELOPMENT ALTERNATIVES, INC.: 7250 Woodmont Ave., Suite 200, Bethesda, MD 20814, Tel. 301/718-8699. A high quality consulting/contracting firm providing technical assistance services in the areas of agriculture, natural resources, finance, management and economics. Maintains a full-time staff in the U.S. of 69 and a long-term staff abroad of 46. Operates in Africa, Asia, Pacific Islands, Latin America, the Caribbean, Middle East, and North Africa. Major clients include USAID, African Development Bank, World Bank, and United Nations Development Programme. Major recent projects include: "Development Strategies for Fragile Lands Project" (Latin America/Caribbean, USAID, $12.9 million), "High Impact Agricultural Marketing and Production" (Eastern Caribbean, USAID, $7.5 million), and "Mahawell Agricultural Development" (Sri Lanka, USAID, $7.7 million).

JOHN SHORT AND ASSOCIATES, INC.: 10226 Wincopin Circle, Suite 400, Columbia, MD 21044, Tel. 301/964-2811. Provides a wide-range of health care management and consulting services, such as public health, primary care, nursing, population and family planning, research, evaluation, health finance, business, and marketing. Maintains a full-time staff in the U.S. of 429 and a long-term staff abroad of 6. Operates in Africa, Asia, Latin America, the Caribbean, Middle East, and North Africa. Major clients include USAID and numerous government agencies and private firms. Recent major projects include: "Increase Allocation of Private Sector Resources to Family Planning and Birthspacing in Private Homes" (Worldwide, USAID, $5.5 million), "Jordan Primary Health Care Nursing Development Program" (Jordan, USAID, $3.4 million), and "Technical Assistance in Family Planning for Enterprise Project" (Worldwide, USAID, $2.4 million).

SCIENTEX CORPORATION: 1750 New York Ave. NW, Suite 200, Washington, DC 20006, Tel 202/347-1515. Specializes in providing management and engineering services. Has 8(a) status. Maintains a full-time staff in the U.S. of 13 and a long-term staff abroad of 2. Major clients include USAID, USDA, Department of Energy, Department of Labor, Department of Transportation, Environmental Protection Agency, and the

Government of Guyana. Operates projects in Africa, Asia, the Pacific Islands, Latin America, the Caribbean, and the Middle East. Recent contract: "Assist in Promoting the Concepts of Divestiture and Privatization" (Worldwide, USAID, $15.8 million).

The names and addresses of these and other organizations, as well as hundreds of individuals who also receive USAID contracts and grants, are included in the section entitled "State/Country Listing of Contractor/Grantee Addresses" of the *Current Technical Service Contracts and Grants* directory. This document is required reading for anyone interested in identifying firms doing international contracting and consulting work. You can get a free copy of this document by requesting it through the Support Division of USAID's Office of Procurement, Procurement Support Division (Tel. 703/875-1270). If you are interested in contracts and grants awarded to colleges and universities, be sure to ask for a copy of the current edition of the *AID-Financed University Contracts, Grants, and Cooperative Agreements* directory.

Another useful USAID document is required reading: *Functional Report: Current Indefinite Quantity Contracts (IQCs)*. Issued on a quarterly basis, this document identifies all firms which have a "special" relationship with USAID. The Indefinite Quantity Contract, or IQC, is a unique contracting mechanism which enables USAID to acquire short-term technical services—normally for 120 days or less—by issuing a "work order" to firms which qualify as eligible for IQCs. In other words, the IQC limits competition to a few USAID approved firms. This special contracting mechanism and agency-contractor relationship ostensibly saves USAID time and avoids lengthy and sometimes difficult negotiation procedures. At the same time, the IQC is highly valued by many firms. These are bread-and-butter contracts which regularly pay salaries and overhead and keep full-time staffs and associates employed especially during periods between large contracts. If you contact firms with IQC status, you may find they have work in your skill and interest areas.

The IQC report identifies every firm which has this special relationship with USAID for the particular quarter. In addition, it classifies firms according to the 21 contracting categories, identifies the number of delivery orders and their dollar value, and includes contact information—name, address, and phone number of the firm.

The November 1991 report identified the following firms with IQC status that also were awarded IQCs for the period 1988 through 1994:

Accounting/
Financial Management:
- DAC International, Inc.
- Price Waterhouse
- Radan Systems, Inc.

Agriculture:
- Winrock International
- Chemonics International
- International Resources Groups
- Agricultural Development Consultants
- Tropical Research and Development, Inc.

Architecture and
Engineering Services:
- Harza Engineering Co.
- Deleuw Cather International

Auditing:
- Price Waterhouse
- Deloitte and Touche
- KPMG Peat Marwick

Development Informa-
tion & Evaluation:
- Management Systems International
- Academy of Educational Development
- TVT Associates
- Devres, Inc.

Development
Management:
- International Science and Technology
- Agricultural Cooperative Development
- Datex, Inc.

Disaster Assistance:
- Jianas Brothers Packaging Co.
- Protective Plastics, Inc.

Education:
- Academy for Educational Development

- Education Development Center
- Meridian House International

Energy:
- International Resources Group, Ltd.
- RCG/Hagler, Bailly, Inc.
- Resources Management Associates

**Environmental/
Natural Resources:**
- Chemonics International Consulting Division
- International Resources Group, Ltd.
- Tropical Research and Development/ KBN

**Foreign Language
Instruction:**
- International Center for Language Studies
- CACI, Inc.—Federal
- Language Learning Enterprises

**Health (Planning
and Delivery):**
- Devres, Inc.
- John Snow Public Health Group, Inc.
- Research Triangle Institute

**Housing & Urban
Development:**
- Nathan Associates, Inc.
- Abt Associates, Inc.
- The Urban Institute
- Research Triangle Institute
- Planning and Development Collaborative

**Macroeconomic
Analysis:**
- Nathan Associates, Inc.
- Development Alternatives, Inc.

**Management
Assistance/Skills:**
- Sheladia Associates, Inc.

**Management
Consulting Services:**
- Coopers and Lybrand
- Deloitte and Touche
- KPMG Peat Marwick

| | ■ Management Systems International, Inc. |
| | ■ Thunder and Associates |

Nutrition and Multisectoral Development:
- ■ Casals and Associates, Inc.
- ■ Pragma Corporation

Printing Services:
- ■ Classic Press, Inc.
- ■ Goodway Graphics of Virginia, Inc.
- ■ Technigraphix

Records Management:
- ■ TASCOnsultation Associates, Inc.

Rural/Regional Income Generation:
- ■ Chemonics International Consulting Division
- ■ Development Alternatives, Inc.
- ■ Devres, Inc.

This document is available in the main USAID library in Rosslyn, Virginia or by calling, writing, or dropping into the USAID Office of Procurement. The USAID library is located and open as follows:

USAID Library
SA18, Rosslyn Plaza
Rosslyn, VA 20523
Tel. 703/875-4818
(Hours: 10am—4pm, Monday thru Friday)

The Office of Procurement is located near the library in the Gannett Building:

Office of Procurement
Procurement Support Division
AGENCY FOR INTERNATIONAL DEVELOPMENT
1100 Wilson, 14th Floor
Rosslyn, VA 20523
Tel. 703/875-1270
Open: 7am to 7pm (reception area), Monday thru Friday

While most government publications are available through the U.S. Government Printing Office, USAID's publications are handled through an in-house documentation center. These and other useful USAID publications, most of which are also found in the USAID Library, can be purchased through the USAID Development Information Services Clearinghouse:

> AID/DISC
> 1500 Wilson Blvd., Suite 110
> Arlington, VA 22209
> Tel. 703/351-4006

You will normally need a document number to order the publication. You can get this number by calling the USAID Library (703/875-4818).

USAID is the only agency we know which compiles such comprehensive and informative documents on contractors. Other agencies either do not organize this data or will not release it unless pressured to do so through a Freedom of Information request.

Information on most USAID-affiliated firms—names, addresses, telephone numbers, and annotated descriptions—is found in a few international job books and directories of consultants:

- *The Almanac of International Jobs and Careers*
- *Careers In International Affairs*
- *Guide To Careers In World Affairs*
- *The Consultants and Consulting Organizations Directory*
- *Directory of Consultant Members*
- *Directory of Management Consultants*
- *Who's Who In Consulting*

The most comprehensive directory to USAID-funded organizations is *Internet Profiles* (Network for International Technical Assistance, P.O. Box 3245, Chapel Hill, NC 27515). This is the "bible" for locating all types of organizations involved in development assistance. It is available in a few specialized libraries. It also can be ordered directly from the publisher for $500. Call (919/968-8324) for details.

You also may want to monitor firms receiving Federal government contracts by regularly reviewing the "Contract Awards" section of the *Commerce Business Daily* as well as the *Federal Register*.

Several minority firms also receive contracts with Federal agencies, but they are less visible to the public. Known as "8(a) firms," these ostensibly disadvantaged businesses qualify for noncompetitive contracts. DAC International, Development Assistance Corporation, Dimpex Associates, Metrotec, Research Management Corporation, Global Exchange, TEM Associates, Energy Systems Engineering, Pragma Corporation, International Development and Energy Associates, Lambet Company, and American Manufacturers Export Group, for example, are 8(a) firms working with USAID. Agencies can reserve certain projects and activities for 8(a) firms. Indeed, many prefer using this contracting mechanism, because it expedites agency spending without requiring a lengthy competitive procurement process for obligating funds. Since agencies keep lists of these firms, contact their contracting office for the names of the 8(a) firms they are using for noncompetitive contracts. The contracting office may or may not willingly release this information unless requested through the Freedom of Information Act. These firms can provide excellent job opportunities, because they often take on projects for which they lack sufficient full-time expertise. They may need additional qualified professionals to plan and implement projects.

International consulting firms should be approached by using networking techniques: conduct your research; call for information; arrange informational interviews; get your resume in their hands and files; and follow-up with telephone calls, letters, and personal visits. Be sure to get your resume in the resume banks of contracting and consulting firms. Many of these firms welcome unsolicited resumes, because they often must quickly staff projects. They frequently turn to their in-house resume banks to locate qualified individuals. If a position requires relocating abroad, the more exotic your skills and the quicker you can relocate, the better your chances of landing a job with these firms. Many firms are always looking for individuals with a combination of technical skills and a willingness to relocate abroad for two or three years.

Personal Services Contracts

If you are interested in doing independent consulting, your best strategy will be to network with government employees who are responsible for contracting-out services. In many cases, agencies prefer giving certain work to individuals rather than incurring the overhead costs involved with contracting-out to an established firm. In addition, agencies can avoid lengthy competitive procedures and maintain closer control when they contract directly with individuals for amounts less than $10,000 or use a special category of contracts—the Personal Services Contract (PSC)—for larger amounts. Many individuals have been able to create consulting jobs for themselves by proposing to agency personnel new projects requiring their expertise.

You should be aware of this category of contracts frequently used in international consulting: Personal Service Contracts. These contracts are convenient ways for an agency to acquire specific expertise as well as additional personnel without disturbing personnel ceilings or increasing the agency payroll. Individuals are hired on one to three year contracts to perform specific services within the agency. Normally these positions are announced in the *Commerce Business Daily (CBD)* and appear similar to classified employment ads. The following announcement appeared in the *CBD*:

HONDURAS: PROGRAM OPERATIONS SPECIALIST.
The USAID/H is accepting CV's (curriculum vitae) and private data from qualified individuals to fill the position of program operations specialist. The position involves assisting the USAID in the analysis, planning, budgeting, monitoring, and implementation of US economic assistance program in Honduras. These programs include economic support funds, development assistance, housing guarantees, and PL 480 Titles I, II, and III. Qualifications include a master's degree in business administration, economics, or a similar discipline. Fluency in Spanish/English at R3, S2 IAW the Foreign Service Institute's standards. Have considerable and proven USAID program office experience relating to the programming, monitoring, reporting, and implementation of the aid program, and a thorough knowledge of aid goals and major programs including NBCCA recommendations. No formal sol will be issued. CV's and biodata from individuals only will be accepted. The contractual relationship will be personal services (PSC) between the USG and the selected individual. Interested applicants should submit CV and salary history NLT mid-Dec. (The Agency for International Development, Contracting Officer, c/o American Embassy, Teguigalpa, Honduras, or USAID Honduras APO Miami, FL 34022)

Notice that like many other international employers, AID requests a Curriculum Vita (CV) rather than a resume. The curriculum vita will place heavy emphasis on educational background, publications, and professional activities. A one to two-page resume normally associated with job-hunting in the United States would be inappropriate for such a position, although we recommend attaching a summary resume to such a curriculum vita.

While agencies are required to announce their intent to conclude a Personal Services Contract, often the positions are "wired" for individuals who already have worked for the agency—especially a former employee who has retired or started a consulting business—or who helped develop a project for the agency and thus created his or her own full-time consulting position with the agency.

Useful Resources

Several useful information sources are available for locating opportunities with various contracting and consulting firms. The single most comprehensive source of names, addresses, phone numbers, and annotated descriptions of firms is found in *The Consultants and Consulting Organizations Directory* and *Who's Who in Consulting* (Detroit: Gale Research Company). Most libraries have current editions of the three-volume *Directory*. It lists over 3,000 consulting firms according to the following categories:

1. Agriculture, Forestry, and Landscaping
2. Architecture and Interior Design
3. Arts and Entertainment
4. Business and Finance
5. Data Processing, Telecommunications, and Information Services
6. Education and Personal Development
7. Engineering, Science, and Technology
8. Environment
9. Health, Medicine, and Safety
10. Human Resources
11. Management
12. Manufacturing/Industrial/Transportation Operations
13. Marketing and Sales
14. Social Issues and Concerns

Since these volumes include all types of consulting firms, regardless of their public or private orientation as well as domestic or international operations, you will need to read through the various annotated descriptions to find which firms are primarily involved in international contract work. Although this is the best directory of such firms, keep in mind it does not include all contracting and consulting firms—only those willing to reveal information on their operations to Gale Research Company. Many firms do not want to publicize their operations through this or other public information resource directories. Consequently, you will have to locate these firms through other resources and investigative efforts.

One of the most useful resources for identifying international contracting and consulting firms doing business with the Federal government is the *Commerce Business Daily (CBD)*, which is available in most major libraries. Issued five days a week, this Department of Commerce publication lists information on all upcoming competitive contracts for $10,000 or more as well as contracts awarded to particular firms for the amounts of $25,000 or more. You should pay particular attention to the "Contract Awards" section. This section identifies which firms received contracts for what amounts. A good job search strategy is to continuously monitor who receives contracts and contact the firm when you see an award made in your area of expertise or interest. But you must do this immediately upon seeing the announcement since there is a lag time between when a contract is awarded and when it is announced in the *CBD*.

We suggest this *CBD* job search strategy because typically firms operate in the following manner. The firm submits a proposal complete with a management structure, job descriptions, and resumes. But once they receive the award, the proposed staff changes due to the unavailability of some individuals proposed. At this time, the contractor must find new personnel and get them approved for the contract. In other words, the contractor now has a personnel problem or vacancy which must be filled immediately. If your qualifications and timing are right, you may find a job very quickly with such a firm. At the same time, you will make an important contact which could lead to having your resume included in other proposals. Most contractors are happy to receive resumes since they are continuously in need of personnel to propose as well as staff new projects. As noted earlier, many contractors maintain in-house resume or talent banks which they continuously refer to when dealing with their personnel needs. Staffing-up is always a problem employers prefer to solve before it becomes a major project implementation issue with clients.

You should also monitor the section of the **CBD** dealing with impending contracts. Once you become familiar with various specialty areas within the consulting business, you can nearly predict which firms will submit proposals for which projects. Knowing this, you can call a firm and mention your interest and availability in being included in their proposal. They may even offer you a short-term contract to help write the proposal should you have such interests and skills. In some cases, individuals manage to get included in two or more proposals for the same contract, thus better ensuring they will get the work once the contract is awarded. Some firms have no problems with your inclusion in competitors' proposals while others frown on such opportunism. But in the contracting game, where competition is heavy, the basic goal is to get the contract and cash flowing.

Another source of information on contractors is the contracts procurement, or acquisitions office in each agency. Some offices, such as the Agency for International Development, gladly provide you with a listing of firms doing contract work with their agency. Others are less organized and willing to provide such information. Also, ask the officials **which** contractors are doing **what** and **whom** you might contact. Sometimes these individuals are very open with such information and will make several useful suggestions. On the other hand, agency officials may guard this information as private and confidential, even though it is public information. In this instance, you may consider formally requesting the information through the Freedom of Information Act.

You will find that some firms largely specialize in one function in a single agency whereas other firms do contract work in one or many functional areas with several agencies. For example, if you are interested in working for a firm in the field of energy or environmental protection, you should contact the Contracts Office at the Department of Energy or Environmental Protection Agency for a list of contractors. Once you have this information, you will know whom to contact. The firms working with these agencies also may be doing similar work in other agencies and in private industry. Call the firms and let them know you are interested in working for them. Try to set an appointment for an interview. Make sure you get your resume in their file. Indeed, many firms refer to this file when they need personnel for new projects. While they may not have a vacancy at the time you contact them, they very well may submit a proposal which results in a position for you.

Many international contracting and consulting firms also periodically place employment ads in either the classified or business sections of major newspapers, especially the Sunday editions of the *Washington Post* and *The New York Times*. You should monitor these sections of the newspaper. However, don't expect to get a job by responding to these ads. Many firms periodically place such ads in order to increase the number of resumes for their files. Sometimes they are in the process of bidding on a project, so they advertise for resumes to put in a particular proposal. If you manage to get your resume in the proposal and the firm wins the contract, you have a job. But more often than not, such ads are "fishing expeditions" with no particular vacancy available at the time of the ad. They want to build their stock of resumes for certain skill areas in the event they need to quickly respond to an RFP.

Professional Positions

Most international contracting and consulting firms hire individuals with strong analytical, communication, and technical skills along with language and area skills and extensive international work experience. Given the nature of consulting work, consultants are hired as problem-solvers. They must quickly analyze situations, devise plans of action, and often implement projects. Such activities require a great deal of analytical skill and the ability to communicate to clients both orally and in writing. Projects continuously require flows of paper— workplans, monthly reports, memos, evaluations, studies—between the consultants and clients. If you are both a good and fast writer, stress these facts to potential employers. They especially need smart, quick thinking, fast writers.

While most firms hire general support staff positions for word-processors, receptionists, secretaries, and accountants, most continuously seek technical specialists. Defense contractors and construction firms hire a disproportionate number of engineers, systems analysts, and computer specialists. Rural development firms hire a disproportionate number of agronomists and agricultural marketing specialists. Research firms hire policy analysts with skills unique to specific programs and agencies. Other firms need specialists in a variety of areas. If you survey the *Commerce Business Daily* notices, you will quickly get a sense of which technical specialties are in demand.

It is much easier to break into an international contracting and consulting firm if you have previous government experience in a specialty area involving contractors. Your special knowledge and contacts with agency personnel will make you very marketable among firms working in your area. Indeed, much of the revolving door with government involves employees leaving an agency and working for the same contractor they previously worked with from within the agency. These individuals become key contact people and informants for the firm. Furthermore, since agency personnel usually think they are "unique"—believing outsiders can't possibly understand their problems, situations, and needs—they prefer working with one of their own who can speak their agency "language."

Educational qualifications also are important with international contracting and consulting firms. They prefer individuals with MAs and PhDs because government places heavy emphasis on educational qualifications of contractors' personnel when awarding contracts. After all, agency personnel working with contracts tend to be well educated—many have MAs and PhDs. When it comes to educational background, they prefer working with consultants who are at least their equal or have higher educations. As the very minimum, a BA degree is expected but an MA or PhD is much preferred. As noted earlier, this is in line with the general emphasis within the international job market on educational qualifications. Education has a much different meaning in terms of "qualifications" in other cultures. The American egalitarian emphasis on "job performance skills" is not widely embraced throughout the world.

But how do you break into the international contracting and consulting game if you don't have experience, technical skills, or advanced degrees? If you have strong analytical and writing skills, along with basic foreign language and area skills as well as some international experience, you should be able to land a position through sheer persistence. These firms continuously need such skills. Often they find their technical personnel with government experience cannot write. Therefore, they must have on their staff individuals who can write and edit. If you get into a firm based on your analytical and writing skills, you may be able to quickly pick up the technical aspects of the work and in time be able to work directly with clients on projects. In the meantime, you will probably stay in the background providing support for technical personnel.

This is a very basic and typical pattern of how individuals break into the government consulting business and become specialists in a short time even though they lack experience as a government employee. In the long run, the best skill to have is an ability to work with agency personnel who are suspicious of outsiders and who feel their agency is unique. They respond best to firms they feel recognize their uniqueness, respond to their problems, and can be trusted. Responsiveness and trust are perhaps the most important elements in developing and maintaining a good contractor-client relationship. On-the-job experience in interacting with clients is the basic requirement for becoming an effective consultant. Education and previous government experience will not be enough.

Independent Consultants and the Networking Game

If you are thinking of starting your own independent international consulting business on either a part-time or full-time basis, you should talk to consultants who have taken this road. They can provide you with useful tips on avoiding the pitfalls of independence as well as suggest useful strategies for becoming successful. You might also read a few of the ever increasing number of how-to books on entering the consulting business. Among the best titles are:

- *The International Consultant*
- *The Consultant's Kit*
- *Cashing In On the Consulting Boom*
- *Consulting: The Complete Guide To a Profitable Career*
- *How to Become a Successful Consultant*
- *How to Succeed As an Independent Consultant*
- *Marketing Your Consulting and Professional Services*

If you are especially interested in the federal contracting process, you should consult Barry McVay's two primers that detail the federal contracting process:

- *Getting Started in Federal Contracting: A Guide Through the Federal Procurement Maze*
- *Proposals That Win Federal Contracts*

If you wish to monitor federal contracts of more than $25,000, you may want to subscribe to the *Commerce Business Daily*. This daily publication is available on an annual subscription basis from the Superintendent of Documents, U.S. Government Printing Office, Washington, DC 20402.

Several professional networks can provide information on consulting job opportunities. Many consultants belong to professional organizations in their specialty areas. These organizations often list job vacancies with consulting firms. Within many of these associations, consultants form their own interest groups or sections to focus on various aspects of consulting work. For example, the American Psychological Association has a Division of Consulting Psychologists. Many local chapters of the American Society of Training and Development have a Consultants' Section. These groups regularly meet to exchange ideas and promote their interests and themselves. Some associations specialize in consulting. For example, several professionals have formed their own professional organizations:

- Academy of Health Care Consultants (Chicago)
- American Association of Hospital Consultants (Arlington, VA)
- American Consulting Engineers Council (Washington, DC)
- American Society of Agricultural Consultants (McLean, VA)
- Association of Management Consultants (Milwaukee)
- Institute of Management Consultants (New York City)
- National Association of Public Employer Negotiators and Administrators (Chicago)
- National Council of Professional Services Firm (Washington, DC)

Several other organizations publish directories of consultants and consulting organizations as well as newsletters in various specialized fields. If you are interested in management consulting, for example, you may want to contact Consulting News, an organization which publishes two newsletters (*Consultant News* and *Executive Recruiter News*) and two directories (*Directory of Executive Recruiters* and *Key European Search Firms and Their U.S. Links*): Consultants News, Templeton Road, Fitzwilliam, NH 03447. These resources also are available through Impact Publications.

NONPROFIT ORGANIZATIONS
AND VOLUNTEER OPPORTUNITIES

Numerous nonprofit and volunteer organizations offer excellent opportunities to break into as well as pursue long-term careers in the international job market. Similar to many contracting and consulting firms, nonprofit and volunteer organizations operating in the international arena are disproportionately involved in social and economic development efforts in Third World countries.

Nonprofit and volunteer organizations are the true missionaries in today's world. They feed the hungry, care for women and children, promote improved health care standards, provide needed medical assistance and education, improve sanitation, evacuate and resettle refugees, develop rural water and sanitation systems, promote family planning and pre-natal care, develop rural lending institutions and cooperatives, assist in marketing crops, and promote community development efforts. They are the major catalysts for change in much of the developing world. They rely heavily on funding from government agencies, especially USAID, and foundations as well as from their own fund raising efforts.

If you are interested in pursuing a cause or making a difference in the lives of others, you should seriously consider working for a nonprofit organization. While most of these organizations pay medium to low salaries, they do provide unique and extremely rewarding opportunities to get involved in development that are largely absent in other types of organizations except for perhaps the U.S. Peace Corps and specialized agencies of the United Nations.

The Organizations

The nonprofit category of international organizations includes organizations frequently referred to as Nongovernmental Organizations (NGO's) or Private Voluntary Organizations (PVO's) which are primarily oriented toward promoting a particular international issue or cause. In contrast to more than 100,000 nonprofit organizations operating within the United States, international nonprofits are fewer in number and operate almost solely in the international arena. They span a broad spectrum of issues and causes:

foreign affairs	relief
education	human rights
energy	religion
economic development	rural development
population planning	children and youth
food	water resources
social welfare	housing
health	community development

Examples of different types of nonprofit organizations and their diverse missions abound throughout the international arena. Most of these organizations cluster around important health, agricultural, social welfare, and disaster issues that are inadequately dealt with in most poor countries: medical services, population planning, agricultural productivity, community development, employment generation, refugee resettlement, and natural disaster relief. Nonprofit organizations such as the International Voluntary Service, Catholic Relief Service, and CARE provide similar development services as the U.S. Peace Corps. The Population Council's involvement in family planning and health issues affects all other development issues in Third World countries. The World Affairs Councils function to increase the awareness of Americans concerning international issues. The Council for International Exchange of Scholars (Fulbright-Hays) and Meridian House International focus on promoting educational and cultural exchanges.

The major nonprofit international organizations which hire international specialists for headquarter and field locations and have full-time staffs of at least 20 and an annual budget exceeding $5 million include:

- Africare
- Agricultural Cooperative Development International
- American Friends Service Committee
- American Institute for Free Labor Development
- American Jewish Joint Distribution Committee
- Association for Voluntary Sterilization
- Cooperative for American Relief Everywhere, Inc. (CARE)
- Catholic Medical Mission Board
- Catholic Relief Services
- Christian Children's Fund, Inc.

- Church World Service
- Direct Relief International
- Family Planning International Assistance
- Food for the Hungry
- Foster Parents Plan International
- Heifer Project International
- Holt International Children's Services
- The Institute of Cultural Affairs
- Interchurch Medical Assistance, Inc.
- International Eye Foundation
- International Executive Service Corps
- International Human Assistance Programs, Inc.
- International Planned Parenthood Federation
- International Rescue Committee
- Lutheran World Relief
- MAP International
- Mennonite Economic Development Associates, Inc.
- Overseas Education Fund
- Partnership for Productivity International
- Pathfinder Fund
- People to People Health Foundation, Inc.
- Population Council
- Salvation Army
- Save the Children Federation, Inc.
- United Methodist Committee on Relief
- Volunteers in Technical Assistance (VITA)
- World Concern
- World Relief
- World Vision International

Many of these nonprofit organizations, including religious-affiliated organizations, are major recipients of USAID contracts. They work closely with the USAID bureaucracy as well as many private contracting firms and universities that are also major recipients of USAID funding. As such, they play an important role in the peripheral network of organizations involved in U.S. foreign policy efforts. From October 1990 to September 1991, for example, the following U.S. nonprofit organizations, or NGOs, were major recipients of USAID funding:

Non-Governmental Organization	Total dollars awarded
■ Adventist Development and Relief Agency International	$ 6,383,863
■ Africare, Inc.	17,918,011
■ Catholic Relief Services	42,787,203
■ Cooperative for American Relief Everywhere, Inc. (CARE)	36,755,515
■ Helen Keller International	9,293,177
■ Pathfinder Fund	88,745,614
■ People-to-People Health Foundation, Inc.	76,980,735
■ Planned Parenthood Federation of America	98,627,591
■ Population Council	46,293,154
■ Population Services International	30,077,589
■ Private Agencies Collaborating Together	25,795,971
■ Save the Children Foundation	70,919,004
■ Volunteers in Technical Assistance	18,117,759
■ World Vision Relief and Development, Inc.	16,560,812

However, many other nonprofit organizations are not linked to the government in this manner. Organizations such as **Oxfam America**, a noted self-help development and disaster relief organization operating in Africa, Asia, Latin America, and the Caribbean, the **Pearl S. Buck Foundation** that works with Amerasian children, and numerous religious organizations doing development-related missionary work abroad have their own funding sources.

Most of these nonprofit organizations are headquartered in the United States—primarily Washington, DC, New York City, and a few other east coast cities—but have field operations in many countries throughout Latin America, Africa, and Asia. Most of the job opportunities will be in the field and thus require individuals with certain technical and linguistic skills along with some international experience.

Volunteer Opportunities

You will also find numerous volunteer groups operating in Third World countries. Many of these groups, such as Amigos de las Americas (5618 Star Lane, Houston, TX 77057, Tel. 800/231-7796), WorldTeach (Harvard Institute for International Development, 1 Eliot St., Cambridge, MA 02138-5705, Tel. 617/495-5527), and Volunteers for Peace (43 Tiffany Road, Belmont, VT 05730, Tel. 802/259-2759), offer students and others opportunities to work on development projects in Third World countries. Many groups require you to pay for your own transportation, food, and housing—which are often minimal—but they do provide excellent opportunities to get international experience without joining the U.S. Peace Corps or some other type of organization. If you lack international experience and want to "test the waters" to see if this type of international lifestyle is for you, consider joining a volunteer group for three to six months that would put you in a work situation abroad. You will acquire valuable experience and learn a great deal about the Third World and the network of government agencies, nonprofit organizations, and contracting firms operating abroad—as well as yourself.

Useful Resources

When conducting research on international nonprofit organizations, you should examine several directories that identify who's who in the international nonprofit arena:

- *Encyclopedia of Associations*
- *Yearbook of International Organizations*
- *USAID Current Technical Service Contracts and Grants*

The first two publications are found in the reference section of most major libraries. The third item is produced by USAID. Information on getting access to this document was outlined earlier in this chapter on contractors and consultants.

Several books on international jobs and careers identify and discuss numerous nonprofit organizations offering job opportunities:

- *The Almanac of International Jobs and Careers*
- *International Jobs*

- *Guide to Careers In World Affairs*
- *International Careers*
- *The Nonprofit's Job Finder*
- *Jobs and Careers With Nonprofit Organizations*

A few other books focus solely on finding jobs with nonprofit organizations regardless of their domestic or international settings. Some of these books may be useful:

- *Careers in the Nonprofit Sector*
- *Doing Well By Doing Good*
- *Good Works: A Guide to Social Change Careers*
- *Great Careers: The Fourth of July Guide to Careers, Internships, and Volunteer Opportunities in the Nonprofit Sector*
- *Profitable Careers in Nonprofit*

Several other books and directories focus specifically on nonprofit international organizations. These include:

The Development Directory: Published by Editorial PKG, 108 Neck Road, Madison, CT 00443, Tel. 203/421-3497.

Internet Profiles: Published by Network for International Technical Assistance, P.O. Box 3245, Chapel Hill, NC 27515, Tel. 919/968-8324. This is the "bible" for locating organizations involved in development assistance. Provides detailed information on all development-oriented organizations. Since this directory costs $500, you may want to check with a major library to see if they have it in their reference section.

InterAction Member Profiles: Published by American Council for Voluntary International Action, 1717 Massachusetts Ave. NW, Suite 801, Washington, DC 20036, Tel. 202/667-8227.

US Non-Profit Organizations in Development Assistance Abroad (TAICH Directory): Published in 1983 by the Council of Volunteer Agencies for Foreign Service, 200 Park Avenue South, New York, NY 10003. Includes 535 nonprofits. Now out-of-print but available in many large libraries.

Overseas Development Network (ODN) Opportunities Catalog: Published by the Overseas Development Network and costs $7. Describes 52 development organizations offering internships, research, and employment opportunities for students. To join ODN ($15), write or call: Overseas Development Network, 333 Valencia Street, Suite 330, San Francisco, CA 94103, Tel. 415/431-4204. ODN also publishes *Opportunities in International Development in New England* ($5) and *Career Opportunities in International Development in Washington, DC* ($7).

Technical Assistance Programs of US Non-Profit Organizations: Published by the American Council of Voluntary Agencies for Foreign Service, New York City, NY.

Several organizations provide clearinghouse, job listing, and placement services for individuals interested in working for nonprofit international organizations. Among these are:

InterAction: American Council For Voluntary International Action (1717 Massachusetts Ave. NW, Suite 801, Washington, DC 20036, Tel. 202/667-8227): Consisting of a coalition of over 100 U.S. private and voluntary international organizations, InterAction provides information and advice on employment with nonprofit international organizations. This is one of the best international networks available.

CODEL (Coordination in Development, 79 Madison Ave., New York, NY 10016, Tel. 212/685-2030): Clearinghouse for over 40 church-related agencies working abroad.

Intercristo, The Career and Human Resources Specialists (19303 Fremont Avenue North, Seattle, WA 98133, Tel. 800/251-7740 or 206/546-7330): This is a Christian placement network which focuses on job opportunities in mission and ministry organizations, many of which are overseas.

If you are in the field of international health, you are fortunate to have a career-aware professional organization to assist you in locating health organizations and job opportunities. The National Council for International Health (NCIH) promotes international health through numerous educational services and publishes the *International Health News*, *Directory of Health Agencies,* and *U.S. Based Agencies Involved in International Health*. It also publishes job listings: *Career Network*. For information on these publications and their job related services, contact:

NATIONAL COUNCIL FOR
    INTERNATIONAL HEALTH
1701 K Street, NW, Suite 600
Washington, DC 20036
Tel. 202/833-5900

If you are interested in international volunteer opportunities, including internships, you will find several useful directories and books to assist you in locating organizations whose missions most meet your interests and needs:

- *Alternatives to the Peace Corps: Gaining Third World Experience*
- *Career Opportunities in International Development in Washington, DC*
- *The Directory of International Internships*
- *Directory of Overseas Summer Jobs*
- *Directory of Volunteer Opportunities*
- *The Directory of Work and Study in Developing Countries*
- *The International Directory of Voluntary Work*
- *The International Directory of Youth Internships*
- *International Internships and Volunteer Programs*
- *Invest Yourself: The Catalogue of Volunteer Opportunities*
- *Jobs Abroad: Over 3,000 Vacancies of Interest to Christians*
- *U.S. Voluntary Organizations and World Affairs*
- *Volunteer! The Comprehensive Guide to Voluntary Service in the U.S. and Abroad*
- *Volunteer Vacations*
- *VolunteerWork*
- *Work, Study, Travel Abroad*
- *Work Your Way Around the World*
- *Working Holidays*

Several professional organizations provide assistance for individuals seeking information on employment with nonprofit organizations. The Society for Nonprofit Organizations, for example, is the only national society organized to promote nonprofit organizations. Its more than 5,000 member organizations constitute an important professional network of nonprofit executives and directors. The Society publishes a bimonthly journal (*The Nonprofit World*, $59 annual subscription) and regularly conducts workshops, provides technical assistance, and publishes resources for strengthening nonprofit organizations. The Society also distributes a *Resource Center Catalog* that includes some books on careers in nonprofit organizations. You can contact this organization at the following address and phone number:

SOCIETY FOR NONPROFIT ORGANIZATIONS
6314 Odana Rd., Suite 1
Madison, WI 53719
Tel. 608/274-9777

However, do not call this organization for information on jobs or for acquiring a directory of its members. They have neither. What they will do is refer you to their catalog as well as a job network organized for nonprofit organizations—*Access*.

The Taft Group, one of the nation's leading information and professional service firms for nonprofit organizations, provides numerous resources and services for individuals seeking employment with these organizations. The Taft Group provides executive search services for individuals seeking positions in development marketing and public relations. If you are interested in executive level positions, you may want to subscribe to their newsletter, *The Nonprofit Executive*, which provides the latest information on executive level developments. However, keep in mind that this organization, as well as the Society for Nonprofit Organizations, is oriented toward all nonprofit organizations which are primarily U.S. domestic organizations. International nonprofit organizations make up only a small percentage of their organizational scope. You can contact this organization by calling (Tel. 301/816-0210) or writing:

THE TAFT GROUP
12300 Twinbrook Pkwy., Suite 450
Rockville, MD 20852

Other organizations can provide information on other types of international experiences, including sponsoring internships and volunteer experiences, that can be useful for developing international skills and experiences. A sample of the many such organizations available include:

World Learning: Formerly known as The Experiment in International Living. Conducts numerous programs in international education, training, and technical assistance, including homestay programs where participants live with families abroad while learning about the local culture. Contact: World Learning, Kipling Road, Brattleboro, VT 05302, Tel. 802/257-7751.

Association Internationale des Etudiants en Sciences Economiques et Commerciales (AIESEC). This international management organization provides students with training opportunities in international business. Most positions are internships with businesses abroad for periods ranging from 2 to 18 months. Contact: Public Relations Director, AIESEC-U.S., Inc., 135 W. 50th Street, New York, NY 10020, Tel. 212/757-3774.

International Association for the Exchange of Students for Technical Experience (IAESTE). Provides students with technical backgrounds opportunities to work abroad for 2-3 month periods. Contact: IAESTE Trainee Program, c/o Association for International Practical Training, Park View Boulevard, 10480 Little Patuxent Parkway, Columbia, MD 21044, Tel. 410/997-2200.

Volunteers for Peace, Inc. Operates a program that places individuals in work camps at home and abroad. Much of the work involves construction, agricultural, and environmental programs. Contact: Volunteers for Peace, Inc., Tiffany Road, Belmont, VT 05730, Tel. 802/259-2759.

Major job listing information services that provide biweekly or monthly information on job vacancies with nonprofit organizations include:

Community Jobs: The Employment Newspaper For the Non-Profit Sector: A "must" resource for anyone looking for a job with nonprofits. This 40-page monthly newspaper is filled with job hunting tips as well as nearly 400 job listings for individuals interested in working in the nonprofit sector. Each issue includes some listings for international nonprofit organizations. Individuals can subscribe by sending $29 for 3 issues or $39 for 6 issues to: Access: Networking in the Public Interest, 9th Floor, 30 Irving Place, New York, NY 10003, Tel. 212/475-1001.

International Career Employment Opportunities: Published biweekly and includes more than 500 current openings in the U.S. and abroad, in foreign affairs, international trade and finance, international development and assistance, foreign languages, international program administration, international educational and exchange programs, including internships. Includes positions with the Federal government, U.S. corporations, nonprofits, and international institutions. Contact: International Employment Opportunities, Rt. 2, Box 305, Stanardsville, VA 22973, Tel. 804/985-6444 or Fax 804/985-6828. Subscriptions for individuals cost $7.95 per issue or $29 for 4 issues, $49 for 8 issues, $69 for 12 issues, $129 for 26 issues, or $229 for 52 issues. Includes money back guarantee.

International Employment Gazette: One of the newest and most comprehensive bi-weekly publications listing more than 400 vacancies in each issue. Includes many jobs in construction and business but also with nonprofit organizations. Offers a custom-designed International Placement Network service for individuals. Contact: International Employment Gazette, 1525 Wade Hampton Blvd., Greenville, SC 29609, Tel. 800/882-9188. $35 for 6 issues; $55 for 12 issues; $95 for 24 issues (1 year).

International Jobs Bulletin: A biweekly publication listing information on hundreds of organizations offering job vacancies overseas. Contact: University Placement Center, Southern Illinois University, Carbondale, IL 62901-4703. $25 for 20 issues.

International Employment Hotline: Monthly listing of job vacancies available worldwide in government, consulting firms, nonprofit organizations, educational institutions, and business. Includes informative articles on the problems, pitfalls, and promises of finding an international job, including useful job search tips. Contact: International Employment Hotline, P.O. Box 3030, Oakton, VA 22124, Tel. 703/620-1972. $39 for 12 issues.

Career Network: A monthly job listing bulletin published by the National Council for International Health, 1701 K St., NW, Suite 600, Washington, DC 20006, Tel. 202/833-5900. Includes jobs for health care professionals only. Costs $10 per month or $60 per year for members; $20 per month or $120 per year for nonmembers. The membership fee for joining NCIH is $40 for students and $75 for regular members.

Options: Published by Project Concern, P.O. Box 85322, San Diego, CA 92138, Tel. 619/279-9690. Includes jobs for health care professionals in the U.S., East Asia, the Pacific, Latin America, and Africa.

PDRC Placement Hotline: Published by the School for International Training, Kipling Road, Brattleboro, VT 03302, Tel. 257-7751, Ext. 258.

Monday Developments: Published by InterAction, 1717 Massachusetts Ave. NW, Suite 801, Washington, DC 20036, Tel. 202/667-8227. Published biweekly (every other Monday), a one-year subscription costs $55.

Modern Language Association Job Information Lists: Published four times a year. 62 Fifth Avenue, New York, NY 10011.

If you are a **Returned Peace Corps Volunteer**, you will want to use the job services available through the Returned Volunteer Services office: Peace Corps, 1990 K Street, NW, Room 7660, Washington, DC 20526, Tel. 202/606-3126 or 1-800/424-8580, Ext. 2284. Please do not contact this office unless you are a returned volunteer. This already over-worked office can only provide information and services to its former volunteers and staff members—both long-term and recently separated. If you left Peace Corps 20 years ago, you can still use this service. It has an excellent library of international resources as well as numerous job listings relevant to its volunteers. It also publishes a biweekly job listing bulletin called *HOTLINE: A Bulletin of Opportunities for Returned Peace Corps Volunteers*. You should also request a copy of *International Careers*, a useful directory summarizing major international employers relevant to the interests and skills of ex-Peace Corps Volunteers. It may well be worth your time and effort to visit this center. After all, Washington, DC is located in the heart of hundreds of organizations offering international job opportunities for those interested in pursuing jobs and careers with nonprofit organizations as well as with consulting firms and educational organizations relevant to the Peace Corps experience. Better still, many of these organizations are staffed by individuals who are part of the growing "old boy/girl network" of ex-Peace Corps volunteers who look favorably toward individuals with Peace Corps experience. Better still, many nonprofit organizations, consulting firms, and educational organizations automatically contact this office when they have impending vacancies.

Job Search Strategies

Use the same strategies for landing a job with an international nonprofit organization as you would for any other nongovernmental organization. This essentially involves networking, informational interviewing, and moving your face, name, and resume among key people associated with these organizations at both the staff and board levels. Success in landing such a job will take time, tenacity, and a positive attitude. Your best locations for literally "hitting the streets" and "pounding the pavement" for nonprofit organizations will be Washington, DC and New York City.

At the same time you will encounter numerous contracting firms and educational organizations that are part of a closely knit network of international development organizations. You may discover that many of these other organizations offer similar job opportunities as the nonprofit organizations. Consequently, we recommend conducting a job search that is **inclusive** of these other counterpart network organizations. All of the books and directories outlined thus far will go a long way in helping you focus your job search on specific organizations for networking, informational interviews, and submitting applications for job vacancies.

Many of the nonprofit international organizations will be organized with headquarters in the United States, especially New York City and Washington, DC, and field operations in developing countries. While most nonprofits hire through headquarters, many also hire individuals in the field. If you are already in the field and neither have the time nor money to travel to Washington, DC or New York City to conduct an intensive job search, make sure you develop contacts with field representatives in your area. Nonprofit organizations tend to be very field oriented and thus many useful job contacts can be made at the field level. Your research on each organization will determine how, where, and with whom to best target your job search within each organization.

8

THE
BUSINESS
WORLD

*S*troll through most any major airport and you'll see who really does the greatest amount of on-the-job traveling—business people, especially those in sales and marketing. As your plane empties, several fellow briefcase-laden passengers head for the row of pay telephones or activate their cellular phones to confirm appointments with clients or check their offices for messages. Then it's into a taxi and on to a hotel and meetings.

This business travel ritual is repeated thousands of times each hour in airports throughout the world. If you love selling and marketing products in distant locations, it's a ritual you may want to join.

BUSINESS TRAVEL

Business travel appeals to many people, especially those who enjoy going first-class. Depending on one's company, you may regularly fly business or first-class, stay in five-star hotels, dine in fine restaurants, enjoy top entertainment and sports activities, and meet interesting and exciting people. This type of work can become addictive as it enables you to participate in a first-class lifestyle.

However, business travel is not for everyone, especially for married, middle-aged individuals with families. If you are constantly on the road, you may become somewhat jaded to this travel lifestyle. Indeed, many businesspeople who must constantly travel in their work discover the joys of travel decline the more they travel. Many now prefer limiting their travels to only a few days each month or a few weeks each year.

Nonetheless, if you want to travel a great deal and get paid for it at the same time, consider finding a job or pursuing a career in business. Your best options are jobs in sales and marketing. A job in international business may give you opportunities to frequently travel and live abroad.

MANAGEMENT

Top management in corporations—corporate chairpersons, presidents, and vice-presidents—frequently travel as part of their corporate responsibilities. They inspect plant and field operations, meet key clients, negotiate contracts, and attend major meetings. They usually travel in style—first-class all the way, from hotels and restaurants to 18-hole golf courses. Getting one of these jobs, of course, requires advancing to the top of a corporate hierarchy.

Many other lower level management and support personnel also travel a great deal. Chief operating officers, chief financial officers, and corporate lawyers travel to field sites, meet with corporate clients, and attend annual meetings. Again, acquiring these jobs requires advancement within a corporate hierarchy. You first must get a job with the business and then advance accordingly within the organization.

SALES

If you want a job involving travel, try sales with a medium to large-sized company. Companies that have regional, national, or international sales territories offer the best on-the-job travel opportunities. Before long you will probably be on the road regularly, visiting numerous cities where you will market your company's products, revisit old clients, prospect for new leads, and cultivate new clients.

MARKETING AT TRADE SHOWS

If your interests lie in marketing, you should consider representing company products at trade shows. Individuals participating in these shows travel a great deal. Representing a first-class image of their companies, they often stay in fine hotels and dine in good restaurants.

Thousands of trade shows are held each year throughout the United States and abroad. The shows last anywhere from three to seven days. In the United States, most of these shows are held in major cities, such as New York, Washington DC, Chicago, San Francisco, Los Angeles, New Orleans, and Miami, which have large conference and convention facilities.

INTERNATIONAL BUSINESS

Businesses employ the largest number of individuals in the international arena. Indeed, as the world economy continues to expand and nations become more economically interdependent, so too does international trade and the role of international businesses.

Opportunities in international business cover a wide range of organizations and jobs. They include jobs with such traditional organizations as banks, oil and chemical companies, manufacturers, importers, and exporters. Positions involve everything from political risk analysis to sourcing for new products and management, sales, and marketing positions.

Breaking In

While businesses may employ many people internationally, don't expect to find many entry-level international business positions except in sales. In contrast to other types of organizations—government and nonprofit—which may hire individuals for entry-level international positions, many businesses promote employees to positions that involve international operations only **after** several years of progressive experience within the organization.

Breaking into international business often requires extensive experience within particular industries—moreso than the knowledge of foreign languages, area studies, or international experience. Most large corporations, for example, assign employees to foreign operations as one step in a promotion hierarchy that requires key personnel to have foreign experience prior to advancing to other positions within the company. Many well established companies have few overseas assignments because they have already developed talented local staffs that have the requisite skills to function locally.

An ideal company providing international travel opportunities would be one just starting to develop overseas operations. During their initial stage of developing new markets and establishing local bases of operations, they normally send expatriates abroad. As more and more companies expand their operations abroad or broaden the scope of operations into new countries, numerous opportunities should be available for working abroad. Many of the positions will involve marketing, sales, finance, and sourcing for new parts and products. Consequently, your best opportunities in international business may be with small companies just starting to enter the international business arena or expanding into new locations. Many large corporations with established operations abroad will be closed to individuals seeking entry-level international positions.

Many small international companies look for individuals with management and marketing skills who also enjoy working abroad. Many of these positions may be in international sales and involve working from a home base in New York, London, Rome, Singapore, Hong Kong, or Tokyo. Breaking into these firms requires having the right kinds of "connections" to people who make the hiring decisions. It involves networking within the international business community. One of the best ways to get such connections is to know people who already work in the international business community. You might, for example, attend a semester abroad program in Europe, Asia, or Latin America which involves studying the local international business community. Alternatively, you might acquire an internship with an international business that puts you in the heart of the international business community where you develop numerous contacts with individuals in many different businesses. The people may later become your ticket to gaining entry to many international businesses.

Several of the organizations and programs outlined in the educational section of Chapter 6 should help you in making connections to the international business community. You should also consider taking international business-related courses in college as well as such bread-and-butter business courses as accounting, finance, and marketing along with one or two foreign languages. If you are a business major, you should consider participating in an international business internship or other international work-related business experience. Three of the best such programs are:

Association Internationale des Etudiants en Sciences Economiques et Commerciales (AIESEC): Public Relations Director, AIESEC-U.S., Inc., 135 W. 50th Street, New York, NY 10020, Tel. 212/757-3774.

Association for International Practical Training (AIPT): American City Building, Suite 217, Columbia, MD 21044, Tel. 301/997-2200.

U.S. Student Travel Service (USSTS): 801 2nd Avenue, New York, NY 10017, Tel. 212/867-8770.

In the case of AIESEC, you will need to be involved in a local chapter in order to participate in this student operated program. Check first to see if your college has a chapter. If not, you might want to contact AIESEC for information on establishing a chapter.

Several companies, such as Chase Manhattan Bank, Salomon Brothers, IBM, Monsanto, United Technologies, General Electric, and Allied-Signal, have established summer internship programs in a variety of business areas. You will have to apply directly to these companies for application information. For information on these and other international internship opportunities, see Will Cantrell's and Francine Moderno's *International Internships and Volunteer Programs* (Oakton, VA: Worldwise Books, 1992) and the Foreign Policy Association's *Guide to Careers in World Affairs* (Manassas Park, VA: Impact Publications, 1993). Both books are available through Impact Publications (see order form at the end of this book).

You might also consider creating your own internship by contacting companies directly and selling them on the idea of letting you work for them as an unpaid or low paid intern. This form of volunteerism within the business community may be well received by some small companies that basically receive an offer they can't refuse!

Not all international business opportunities are with U.S.-based multinational corporations or small businesses. Don't neglect foreign-based businesses that may be interested in American management and marketing skills—two major American business strengths that are highly sought in many countries. Many foreign companies interested in breaking into the American, European, or Asian markets may be interested in your international business skills or your general management and marketing expertise. Again, you learn about these companies through the process of networking within particular countries and selling your skills to potential foreign employers.

Know Your Business

Numerous types of businesses offer a large variety of international job and career opportunities:

- Commercial and investment banking
- Marketing
- Management
- Finance
- Accounting
- Consulting
- News media and broadcasting
- Entertainment (motion pictures, video, games)
- Telecommunications
- Architectural and engineering services
- Construction
- Transportation
- Aerospace
- Shipping
- Insurance
- Publishing and printing
- Retailing and trading
- Sourcing for parts/products
- Mining

- Natural resource production (mining, petroleum, natural gas)
- Manufacturing product lines (food, beverages, chemicals, paper, wood products, fiber, pharmaceuticals, computers, electronics, cosmetics, sporting goods, toys, musical instruments, industrial and farm equipment, apparel, appliances, tobacco, plastics, rubber, motor vehicles, military hardware)

Corporate United States plays a major role in world trade. Thousands of American businesses operate abroad and thousands more will be entering the international arena in the coming decade. Indeed, of the 500 largest world traders, 157—or 31.4 percent of the total—are U.S. corporations; Japan follows next with 150 companies. Collectively, European countries have the largest number of companies in the top 500—161. The U.S. barely remains dominant at present with seven of the 20 largest world traders being U.S. corporations:

Rank	Company	Industry	Sales (billions)
1	General Motors (USA)	Auto	$126.9
2	Ford Motor (USA)	Auto	92.5
3	IBM (USA)	Data	62.7
4	Toyota Motor Corp. (Japan)	Auto	58.3
5	Hitachi Ltd. (Japan)	Elec	46.3
6	Philip Morris (USA)	Bev	44.8
7	General Electric (USA)	Elec	41.0
8	Matsushita Elect. (Japan)	Appl	39.8
9	Daimler-Benz (Germany)	Auto	39.3
10	Du Pont (USA)	Chem	35.5
11	Chrysler (USA)	Auto	34.9
12	Nissan Motor (Japan)	Auto	34.8
13	Siemens (Germany)	Elec	32.7
14	Fiat (Italy)	Auto	32.5
15	Volkswagen (Germany)	Auto	31.7
16	Unilevel NV (Netherlands)	Food	29.4
17	Unilever PLC (UK)	Food	27.9
18	Toshiba (Japan)	Auto	27.5
19	Philips (Netherlands)	Appl	26.6
20	Honda Motor (Japan)	Auto	25.2

SOURCE: *World Trade*, April/May 1990

Other large international companies included in the top 500 are leaders in aerospace, steel, beverage, photo, paper, computer, construction, machinery, health, textile, energy, and building materials industries. Some of the major international businesses include the following:

Company	Major Products
Allied Signal Corporation	aerospace, chemical, oil, gas
Amerada Hess	petroleum exploration/production
American Cyanimid	pharmaceuticals, chemicals
American Home Products	prescription drugs/home products
AT&T	communications
Avon Products	cosmetics
Bell & Howell Co.	business equipment
BellSouth Corporation	communication
Black & Decker	electrical tools and machines
Boeing Co.	aircraft and aerospace manufacturer
Borg-Warner Corporation	automotive parts, chemicals
Carnation Company	food manufacturer
Caterpillar Tractor	earthmoving equipment
Chevron Corporation	oil
Coca-Cola Co.	beverage manufacturer
CPC International	food manufacturer
Dow Chemical Co.	chemical manufacturer
Du Pont Co.	chemicals
Eastman Kodak	photographic supplies and equipment
Eli Lilly & Co.	pharmaceutics and cosmetics
Emerson Electric Co.	electronics manufacturer
Exxon Corporation	oil
Firestone Tire & Rubber	tire producer
Ford Motor Co.	auto manufacturer
General Dynamics	aerospace, chemical, oil, gas
General Motors	auto manufacturer
Goodyear Tire & Rubber	tire manufacturer
Grace Offshore	oil well work-over/completion
Grumman International	aircraft and aerospace
Hewlett-Packard Co.	computers and electronics
Honeywell	computers and automated systems
IBM	computers, electronics

ITT	communications, hotels, electronics
Lockheed Corporation	aircraft and aerospace
Minnesota Mining and Manufacturing (3M)	3M product line
Monsanto	chemicals
Motorola, Inc.	electronics manufacturer
Ogilvy Group	advertising
Pepsi-Cola International	beverage manufacturer
Pfizer International	pharmaceuticals and health-care
Philip Morris	tobacco and beverages
Phillips Petroleum Co.	oil producer
Raytheon Co.	high-tech electronics producer
RCA Corporation	communications/electronics producer
Revlon, Inc.	cosmetics
R.J. Reynolds Tobacco	tobacco products
Rockwell International	aviation and electronics
Sperry Corporation	computers/data processing equipment
Texaco, Inc.	oil producer
Texas Instruments, Inc.	computers and electronics
TRW, Inc.	electronics and equipment producer
Union Carbide	chemical and plastics manufacturer
Unisys Corp.	computers
Weyerhaeuser Co.	wood producer
Xerox Corporation	computers, data processing

Some of the major banks and financial companies operating from the United States and with extensive international operations include:

American Express	Goldman Sachs
Bank of Boston	Manufacturers Hanover
Bank of New York	Merrill Lynch & Co., Inc.
Bank of Tokyo	Mitsubishi Bank
BankAmerica	Mitsui Bank
Barclays	Morgan Stanley
Chemical Bank	Paine-Weber
Citicorp	Prudential Bache Securities
Dai-Inchi Kangyo Bank	Salomon Brothers
Deutsche Bank	Smith Barney
Fidelity Group	Sumitomo Bank
Fuji Bank	Tokai Bank

All of these multinational companies offer numerous international job and career opportunities at home and abroad regardless of one's nationality.

The Best Companies

Many companies are reputed to be the best to work for because of their work environments, management practices, advancement opportunities, and salaries and benefits. According to Robert Levering and Milton Moskowitz in their latest edition of *The 100 Best Companies to Work for in America,* the following companies are the best ones to work for in America:

Company	Headquarters
Acipco	Birmingham, AL
Advanced Micro Devices	Sunnyvale, CA
Alagasco	Birmingham, AL
Anheuser-Busch	St. Louis, MO
Apogee Enterprise	Minneapolis, MN
Armstrong	Lancaster, PA
Avis	Garden City, NY
BE&K	Birmingham, AL
Ben & Jerry's Homemade	Waterbury, VT
Leo Burnett	Chicago, IL
Chaparral Steel	Midlothian, TX
Compaq Computer	Houston, TX
Cooper Tire	Findlay, OH
Corning	Corning, NY
Cray Research	Eagan, MN
Cummins Engine	Columbus, TN
Dayton Hudson	Minneapolis, MN
John Deere	Moline, IL
Delta Air Lines	Atlanta, GA
Donnelly	Holland, MI
Du Pont	Wilmington, DE
A. G. Edwards	St. Louis, MO
Erie Insurance	Erie, PA
Federal Express	Memphis, TN
Fel-Pro	Skokie, IL

First Federal Bank of California	Santa Monica, CA
H. B. Fuller	St. Paul, MN
General Mills	Minneapolis, MN
Goldman Sachs	New York, NY
W. L. Gore & Associates	Newark, DE
Great Plains Software	Fargo, ND
Hallmark Cards	Kansas City, MO
Haworth	Holland, MI
Hershey Foods	Hershey, PA
Hewitt Associates	Lincolnshire, IL
Hewlett-Packard	Palo Alto, CA
Honda of America Manufacturing	Marysville, OH
IBM	Armonk, NY
Inland Steel	Chicago, IL
Intel	Santa Clara, CA
Johnson & Johnson	New Brunswick, NJ
SC Johnson Wax	Racine, WI
Kellogg	Battle Creek, MI
Knight-Ridder	Miami, FL
Lands' End	Dodgeville, WI
Lincoln Electric	Cleveland, OH
Lotus Development	Cambridge, MA
Lyondell Petrochemical	Houston, TX
Marquette Electronics	Milwaukee, WI
Mary Kay Cosmetics	Dallas, TX
McCormick	Hunt Valley, MD
Merck	Whitehouse Station, NJ
Microsoft	Redmond, CA
Herman Miller	Zeeland, MI
3M	St. Paul, MN
Moog	East Aurora, NY
J. P. Morgan	New York, NY
Morrison & Foerster	San Francisco, CA
Motorola	Schaumburg, IL
Nissan Motor Manufacturing	Smyrna, TN
Nordstrom	Seattle, WA
Northwestern Mutual Life	Milwaukee, WI
Odetics	Anaheim, CA
Patagonia	Ventura, CA
J. C. Penney	Plano, TX

Physio-Control	Redmond, WA
Pitney Bowes	Stamford, CT
Polaroid	Cambridge, MA
Preston Trucking	Preston, MD
Procter & Gamble	Cincinnati, OH
Publix Super Markets	Lakeland, FL
Quad/Graphics	Pewaukee, WI
Reader's Digest	Pleasantville, NY
Recreational Equipment, Inc.	Seattle, WA
Rosenbluth International	Philadelphia, PA
SAS Institute	Cary, NC
J. M. Smucker	Orrville, OH
Southwest Airlines	Dallas, TX
Springfield ReManufacturing	Springfield, MO
Springs	Fort Mill, SC
Steelcase	Grand Rapids, MI
Syntex	Palo Alto, CA
Tandem	Cupertino, CA
TDIndustries	Dallas, TX
Tennant	Minneapolis, MN
UNUM	Portland, ME
USAA	San Antonio, TX
U S WEST	Eaglewood, CO
Valassis Communications	Livonia, MI
Wal-Mart	Bentonville, AR
Wegmans	Rochester, NY
Weyerhaeuser	Tacoma, WA
Worthington Industries	Columbus, OH
Xerox	Stamford, CT

Fortune magazine's most recent (March 6, 1995) survey of America's most admired corporations ranks the top 100 as follows:

1	Rubbermaid	9	United Parcel Service
2	Microsoft	10	Hewlett-Parkard
3	Coca-Cola	11	United HealthCare
4	Motorola	12	Gillette
5	Home Depot	13	Boeing
6	Intel	14	General Electric
7	Procter & Gamble	15	Albertson's
8	3M	16	Levi Strauss Associates

17	Johnson & Johnson	59	Roadway Services
18	Corning	61	Compaq Computer
19	AT&T	62	American International
20	Fluor		Group
21	Pfizer	62	Armstrong World
22	J.P. Morgan		Industries
23	Oracle Systems	62	Golden West Financial
24	Merck	66	Abbott Laboratories
25	Walt Disney	66	Banc One
25	Herman Miller	66	Illinois Tool Works
25	Nike	66	Morgan Stanley Group
28	U.S. Healthcare	70	Exxon
29	Du Pont	71	Washington Mutual
29	Publiz Super Markets		Savings Bank
31	Kimberly-Clark	72	PepsiCo
32	Toys "R" Us	72	SBC Communications
33	General Mills	74	AlliedSignal
34	Electronic Data Systems	75	Centex
35	Leggett & Platt	75	Martin Marietta
35	Union Pacific	77	McKesson
37	Enron	78	Intl. Flavors & Grag.
38	Dow Chemical	79	Chevron
38	Shell Oil	79	Schering-Plough
40	Goodyear Tire & Rubber	81	Chrysler
41	Shaw Industries	82	Xerox
42	Norfolk Southern	83	Colgate-Palmolive
42	Southwest Airlines	83	Viacom
44	Columbia/HCA	85	CSX
	Healthcare	85	UST
44	Ford Motor	85	VT
46	Berkshire Hathaway	88	Auto. Data Processing
47	Amoco	88	Bankers Trust New York
47	Nucor	88	Merrill Lynch
49	Unifi	91	Caterpillar
50	Emerson Electric	92	Dow Jones
50	Sysco	92	Reader's Digest Assn.
52	Wal-Mart Stores	92	Time Warner
53	Capital Cities/ABC	95	Anheuser-Busch
53	Mobil	96	ConAgra
55	Sara Lee	96	HON Industries
56	Northwestern Mutual Life	98	MCI Communications
46	Walgreen	99	Burlington Resources
58	Deere	100	Springs Industries
59	PacifiCare Health Systems		

Most of these companies offer excellent domestic and international travel opportunities. Many of them also have overseas operations.

Useful Resources

The following international job and career books describe numerous firms offering international job opportunities for different types of businesses and industries, including important contact information:

- *The Almanac of International Jobs and Careers*
- *Guide to Careers In World Affairs*
- *How to Get a Job In Europe*
- *How to Get a Job In the Pacific Rim*
- *International Jobs*
- *Passport to Overseas Employment*
- *Jobs Worldwide*

However, it is best that you conduct your own research for identifying the many thousands of businesses offering international job and career opportunities. Your best approach will be to initially consult the many business directories available in your local library. Six of the most useful directories are:

American Jobs Abroad, Victoria Harlow and Edward W. Knappman (Detroit, MI: Gale Research, 1994). This 900-page volume provides annotated listings of major U.S. organizations (business, government, and non-profit) that hire individuals for overseas assignments. Organized both by company/organization name and country as well as cross-referenced by job category. Includes information on work permits and living abroad.

Directory of American Firms Operating In Foreign Countries (World Trade Academy Press, 50 E. 42nd St., Suite 509, New York, NY 10017). This three-volume, 2,500+ page directory is invaluable for locating the more than 3,200 U.S. companies operating in more than 120 countries. Provides information on the products/service lines of each company as well as identifies the countries in which they operate. Includes employment statistics and contact information.

Hoover's Handbook of World Business, Hoover's Handbook of American Business, Hoover's Handbook of Emerging Companies, Hoover's Masterlist of 2,500 of America's Largest and Fastest Growing Employers (Austin, TX: Reference Press, 1995). These four directories identify hundreds of major corporations in the U.S. and abroad. Each is filled with facts, statistics, corporate histories, and profiles with contact information.

You can find these directories in most major libraries; the Hoover directories and *American Jobs Abroad* are also available through Impact Publications.

Other useful business directories for researching businesses with international operations include:

- *The International Corporate 1,000*
- *The Multinational Marketing and Employment Directory*
- *Directory of Foreign Firms Operating in the U.S.*
- *Directory of Japanese Firms and Offices in the U.S.*
- *American Register of Exporters and Importers*
- *Dun and Bradstreet Exporter's Encyclopedia*
- *American Encyclopedia of International Information*
- *Trade Directories of the World*
- *Jane's Major Companies of Europe*
- *Principal International Business*
- *Fortune 500: Top 50 Exporters*
- *International Bankers Directory*
- *Who's Who in Banking*
- *Major Companies of Europe*
- *Directory of U.S. Firms Operating in Latin America*
- *Dun & Bradstreet's Middle Market Directory*
- *Dun & Bradstreet's Million Dollar Directory*
- *Standard & Poor's Industrial Index*
- *Standard & Poor's Register of Corporations, Directors and Executives*
- *How to Find Information About Companies*
- *Moody's Industrial Manual*
- *Thomas' Register of American Manufacturers*
- *Ward's Business Directory*
- *Wold Business Directory*

Many embassies also have special directories on international companies operating in their country of responsibility. If you are interested in a particular country, you might call the embassy to find out if they have such a directory or other relevant information. Better still, many embassies maintain libraries which are primarily oriented toward business and commerce. They stock the library with numerous business and city telephone directories as well as magazines, newsletters, and reports that have a wealth of information on their local business community. If you are in Washington, DC, you should definitely plan to visit some of these libraries. They will give you the in-depth information you need on particular businesses rather than just general descriptive and contact information found in the international job books and directories. However, call ahead of time to find out if the embassy of your choice has such a library as well as inquire if and when you can use it.

9

MORE JOBS FOR TRAVEL LOVERS

*I*n this final chapter we briefly examine four additional job and career opportunities for travel lovers. Each provides unique travel and work opportunities both at home and abroad. They range from such structured employment arenas as the military and merchant marine to such relatively unstructured entrepreneurial activities as finding short-term employment abroad and starting your own business. Millions of individuals currently work in these employment fields, and a growing number are becoming self-employed entrepreneurs.

WORKING AROUND THE WORLD

Have you ever thought of just taking off to travel or to work your way around the world? Few people have the free time and financial independence to roam the globe in such a carefree manner. Many young people—especially college students using their summer vacations or taking a semester off to travel abroad—and retirees decide to engage in this type of travel. They're not really interested in the work end of the travel/work equation. What they really want is to enjoy a particular travel style that also enables them to live abroad for short periods of time and experience other cultures by working closely with the locals. Working while traveling helps finance their travel addiction.

Roaming the globe and working at the same time poses numerous challenges. Indeed, we regularly receive inquiries from many young people and their parents who want information on how to both travel and work abroad. Most of these people are primarily interested in finding short-term minimum wage jobs—earn just enough to help meet on-going travel expenses. They do not expect this type of work will lead to long-term jobs or careers abroad. Their primary goal is to make a lengthy trip abroad more financially feasible as well as have an opportunity to meet people from different cultures. Many will seek volunteer opportunities that give them room and board in exchange for their labor.

Restrictions

Finding jobs abroad can be difficult even under the best of circumstances. Most countries have very restrictive work-permit requirements. Except for the European Union (EU) countries where employment in member countries is relatively open (no work permits required for EU citizens) and some Eastern European countries, most countries protect local labor by placing similar restrictions on foreign workers:

1.   Foreigners are forbidden to acquire jobs that compete with local labor and skills. When applying for a work permit and resident visa, employers must provide evidence that the job in question cannot be filled by a local worker with similar skills.

2.   Work permits and resident visas are temporary and thus must be renewed periodically through a Ministry, Department, Bureau, or Office of Labor—every 6, 12, or 24 months. The bureaucracy normally takes its time in processing such applications. You will witness a great deal of bureaucratic inertia in the process of acting on your application—an indication that granting work permits to foreigners is not a top priority government function!

3.   Foreigners must pay local taxes and special resident visa fees. They may be restricted in taking local currency out of the country. Leaving the country even for a short holiday may require tax clearances—including a large cash deposit—and special permissions so you can re-enter without invalidating your work permit and resident visa.

4.   Work permit and resident visa requirements may restrict the number of times foreigners can exit and re-enter a country. In some countries the work permit and resident visas become invalid upon leaving the country. Consequently, the whole application process must be once again initiated upon entering the country.

While many of these restrictions seem illogical and the bureaucratic process can be slow, they are designed with one purpose in mind—discourage foreign workers. Not surprisingly, countries increasingly emphasize "locals only" employment/immigration policies due to a combination of nationalism and high unemployment rates.

However, as numerous young people discover each year as they travel and work abroad, you can by-pass many work permit rules by finding jobs in the "gray market" of each country. If you only plan to work one or two months, and you can find an employer willing to hire your services, you can probably become employed before the local authorities catch up with you and your employer.

Short-Term Employment

Short-term, minimum wage jobs abroad are most abundant in the travel and hospitality industry, agriculture, natural resources, and foreign language instruction. These include such jobs as:

- waiter/waitress
- cook and kitchen helper
- hotel/resort worker
- bartender
- courier
- tour guide
- camp worker
- salesperson
- factory worker
- childcare worker
- ski instructor
- miner
- oil rigger
- fruit and vegetable farmer/picker
- construction worker
- fisherman and fish processor
- English teacher

Three of the best sources providing contact information for acquiring short-term jobs abroad are:

Directory of Overseas Summer Jobs, David Woodworth (ed.) (Oxford, England: Vacation-Work, annual).

Work, Study, Travel Abroad, Del Franz and Lazaro Hernandez (eds.) (New York: St. Martin's Press, biannual).

Work Your Way Around the World, Susan Griffith (Oxford, England: Vacation-Work, annual).

Since each of these books is annually or biannually revised, be sure to examine the most current edition. Each book provides descriptions of potential employers as well as names, addresses, and telephone numbers for contacting them.

Two other useful resources, which primarily focus on short-term or non-career opportunities in the United States, include:

Adventure Careers: Your Guide to Exciting Jobs, Uncommon Occupations, and Extraordinary Experiences, Alex Hiam and Susan Angle (Hawthorne, NJ: Career Press, 1992).

Jobs in Paradise: The Definitive Guide to Exotic Jobs Everywhere, Jeffrey Maltzman (New York: HarperCollins Publishers, 1993).

Kelly Monaghan's *The Insiders Guide to Air Courier Bargains* (New York: The Intrepid Traveler, 1992) shows how to freelance as an air courier and, in the process, travel domestically or internationally for next to nothing. The book provides all the necessary details, including contacts within the industry, to set yourself up as a bona fide air courier.

All of these books are available through Impact Publications (see "Career Resource" section at the end of this book).

In addition to publishing *The Directory of Overseas Summer Jobs* and *Work Your Way Around the World,* which are distributed in the United States by Peterson's, Vacation-Work in Oxford, England (9 Park End Street, Oxford OX1 1HJ) publishes several other useful books for individuals interested in short-term work abroad:

The Au Pair and Nanny's Guide to Working Abroad
Directory of Jobs and Careers Abroad
International Directory of Voluntary Work
Kibbutz Volunteer
Live and Work in Belgium, The Netherlands & Luxembourg
Live and Work in France
Live and Work in Germany
Live and Work in Italy
Live and Work in Spain and Portugal
Teaching English Abroad
The Teenager's Vacation Guide to Work, Study & Adventure
Summer Jobs in Britain
Working in Ski Resorts—Europe

Two other publishers in England—Northcote House Publishers (Harper & Row House, Estover Road, Plymouth PL6 7PZ, United Kingdom, Tel. 0752-705251 or Fax 0752-777603)—and How to Books, Ltd. (Plymbridge House, Estover Road, Plymouth PL5 7PZ, United Kingdom, Tel. 0752-705251 or Fax 0752-695699) publish several how-to travel and work abroad books:

How to Get a Job Abroad
How to Live and Work in Australia
How to Live and Work in Belgium
How to Live and Work in France
How to Live and Work in Germany
How to Live and Work in Hong Kong
How to Live and Work in Japan
How to Live and Work in Saudi Arabia
How to Teach Abroad
Time Off in Australia and New Zealand
Time Off in India and Nepal
Time Off in Spain and Portugal
Time Off in Turkey

Since these books are not distributed in the United States, you must contact the publishers directly for a list of their titles and order information.

You should also review current and back issues of *Transitions Abroad,* which includes numerous informative articles about working abroad; many are written by students who recently completed a summer or semester abroad. The special *"Educational Travel Directory"* issue published each year in June is well worth examining (also available through Impact Publications). This issue provides an invaluable bibliography of travel and work abroad resources. For subscription information, contact:

> Subscriptions
> TRANSITIONS ABROAD
> Department TRA, Box 3000
> Denville, NJ 07834

Published each month, a one-year, 12-issue subscription to this publication costs $39.00.

You may want to consider enrolling in an educational program that takes you abroad in lieu of finding short-term, minimum wage employment that can be more trouble than it is worth. For information on hundreds of such programs, many of which are very inexpensive, examine issues of *Transitions Abroad,* especially the June resource directory. Several of the publications listed in Chapter Six should be helpful.

You might also consider volunteer opportunities abroad. One of the best sources for contact information is David Woodworth's annual *International Directory of Voluntary Work* (Oxford, England: Vacation-Work, 1993). Other useful books that link learning to travel include:

Adventure Holidays (annual)

Learning Vacations, Gerson G. Eisenberg (annual)

Both books are available through Peterson's (Department 2300,202 Carnegie Center, P.O. Box 2123, Princeton, NJ 08543-2123, Tel. 800-338-3282).

If you want to put some work into your travel—but not real serious wage work—be sure to get a copy of Bill McMillan's *Volunteer Vacations* (Chicago: Chicago Review, 1991). This book lists 500 projects and expeditions volunteers can join which will combine their love of the outdoors with learning.

Students interested in studying abroad should get a copy of David Judkins' *Study Abroad: The Astute Student's Guide* (Charlotte, VT: Williamson Publishing, 1989). This book provides information on numerous study abroad programs offered by colleges, universities, and nonprofit educational groups.

If you are determined to travel the globe without any particular job or career in mind, you should be able to find employment along the way in a variety of different fields. However, expect to find relatively low level jobs which do not pay a great deal. Rejected by locals as inferior jobs, many of these jobs tend to go to immigrants and other foreign workers who will work hard for low wages.

Needless to say, this type of employment is not for everyone. But many people find such travel-work to be one of the most interesting and exciting experiences of a lifetime. They meet new people, experience different cultures, and participate in unique lifestyles they would never have encountered had they traveled as ordinary tourists or students.

MERCHANT MARINE

Always wanted to hop on a freighter and travel the Seven Seas? Perhaps the Merchant Marine is for you. While you may not become the captain of the ship, you might become a cook, oiler, deckhand, engineer, mate, or deck officer. You'll be responsible for moving valuable cargo from one port to another.

Water transport workers operate and maintain deep sea merchant ships, tugboats, towboats, ferries, dredges, research vessels, and other waterborne craft on the oceans and the Great Lakes, in harbors, on rivers and canals, and on other waterways. A typical deep sea merchant ship has a captain, three deck officers or mates, a chief engineer and three assistant engineers, plus six or more seamen and oilers. Merchant mariners also have an electrician, machinery mechanics, and a radio officer.

The life of a merchant mariner involves long periods at sea as well as on shore. If you have a family, expect to be gone more than you will be at home. A typical sailor may go to sea for 30 to 90 days and then take 30 to 60 days off before returning for the next journey. Many people enjoy this lifestyle. However, many others quit working the ships after only a few years. This lifestyle appeals to only certain types of individuals.

While many potential merchant mariners may think they will have an opportunity to visit numerous ports, the truth is that few sailors have much time to really visit their ports of call. Typically a ship waits its turn to unload cargo and then proceeds to its next destination. While in port, crew members may spend a few hours on shore—not enough time to really visit the local sites, meet new people, or encounter a new culture. Visiting a port usually means waiting one's turn to unload, turning around, and heading to the next destination.

It's still possible to break into the Merchant Marine with little training or experience, especially if you are willing to start at the very bottom as an ordinary seaman who normally works on deck or in the engineering department. Advancement to the next level—able seaman—requires passing an examination.

If you apply for an engineering or deck officer position, you must be licensed. You acquire this license by graduating from the U.S. Merchant Marine Academy, which is located in Kings Port, New York, or by completing a program offered by one of the six state merchant marine academies. Advancement to officer positions within the Merchant Marine requires a great deal of experience at sea as well as the ability to pass several examinations. An unlicensed seaman needs to be a U.S. citizen and receive a U.S. Public Health Service medical certificate.

Competition for jobs in the Merchant Marine will be keen in the decade ahead as the number of jobs continues to decline in response to a declining U.S. shipping industry. Unions are accepting fewer new members and Merchant Marine academies are facing difficult times placing their graduates. The average annual salary for full-time merchant mariners is just under $30,000. Captains and harbor pilots average nearly $60,000 a year.

For information on merchant marine careers, training, and licensing requirements, contact the following organizations:

CALIFORNIA MARITIME ACADEMY
P.O. Box 1392
Vallejo, CA 94590

MARITIME ADMINISTRATION
U.S. Department of Transportation
400 7th Street, SW
Washington, DC 20590

SEAFARERS HARRY LUNDEBERG SCHOOL
    OF SEAMANSHIP
Route 249, St. Mary's County
Piney Point, MD 20674

U.S. COAST GUARD
Licensing and Evaluation Branch
Merchant Vessel and Personnel Division
2100 2nd St. SW
Washington, DC 20593

U.S. MERCHANT MARINE ACADEMY
Admissions Office
Kings Point, NY 11024

MILITARY

If you are looking for a job that involves travel and you don't mind a great deal of structure and regimentation in your life, the military may be the right place for you. Most Armed Service personnel routinely relocate to new bases every three years. Many assignments will place you abroad in either Europe or Asia. And many jobs within the military involve frequent travel between headquarters and bases as well as between bases and different training and meeting sites.

Despite expected drawdowns in the military over the next five years of over 600,000 military personnel, the Armed Services will continue to hire nearly 400,000 individuals each year. Indeed, as the nation's single largest employer, the Armed Forces employ nearly 2 million active duty personnel in just about every conceivable position.

In 1992 the various services employed the following number of active duty personnel:

- Army   606,000
- Navy   537,000
- Air Force   466,000
- Marine Corps   184,000
- Coast Guard   38,000

Officers in all five services were assigned to the following occupational groups:

- General officers & executives   1,621
- Tactical operations officers   110,270
- Intelligence officers   12,872
- Engineering & maintenance officers   35,530
- Scientists & professionals   12,346
- Medical officers   44,695
- Administrators   19,474
- Supply, procurement, & allied officers   23,568
- Non-occupational   12,279

TOTAL   **273,577**

Enlisted personnel in the five services were assigned to the following occupational groups in 1991:

- Infantry, gun crews, & seamanship specialists   246,702
- Electronic equipment repairmen   151,724
- Communications and intelligence specialists   145,513
- Health care specialists   93,938
- Other technical and allied specialists   35,036

- Functional support and administration   234,740
- Electrical/mechanical equipment repairmen   301,523
- Craftspeople   62,664
- Service and supply handlers   128,609
- Non-occupational   117,810

TOTAL   **1,519,782**

Operating bases which, in effect, function as self-contained communities, the services hire doctors, dentists, medical support personnel, engineers, lawyers, paralegals, accountants, procurement officers, teachers, administrative support personnel, electronic equipment operators and repair personnel, food handlers, transportation and traffic managers, supply managers, correction specialists, police, firefighters, and truck drivers in addition to infantry, demolition, weapons, aircraft, artillery, combat, and rocket specialists.

The general trend is to hire more highly educated and skilled individuals in the Armed Forces. Consequently, entrance requirements into all services are likely to become more restrictive and selective in the decade ahead.

For information on joining the military, contact your local recruitment office or one of the following:

Department of the Army
HQUS Army Recruiting Command
Fort Sheridan, IL 60037

U.S. Air Force Recruiting Service
Directorate of Advertising & Publicity
Randolph AFB, TX 78150

Commandant of the Marine Corps
Headquarters
Washington, DC 20380-0001

Navy Recruiting Command
4015 Wilson Blvd.
Arlington, VA 22203-1991

Commandant (G-PRJ)
U.S. Coast Guard
Washington, DC 20590

For general introductions into careers with the military, refer to the
following books:

Opportunities in Military Careers, Adrian Paradis (Lincolnwood, IL: National Textbook Co., 1989).

Planning Your Military Career, Robert McKay (Lincolnwood,
IL: National Textbook Co.).

The Woman's Guide to Military Service, Texe Marrs and Karen
Read (Liberty Publishing, 1989).

A Young Person's Guide to the Military, Jeff Bradley (Boston,
MA: Harvard Common Press, 1989).

For information on military careers and bases, contact Stackpole
Books (5067 Ritter Road, Mechanicsburg, PA 17055, Tel. 717/796-
0411 or Fax 717/796-0412) for a copy of their most recent catalog.
They publish several useful guides relevant to military careers. Among
them are:

The Armed Forces Guide to Personal Financial Planning
The Air Force Officer's Guide
The Army Officer's Guide
The Enlisted Soldier's Guide
Guide to Military Installations
The NCO Guide

The Naval Institute Press (118 Maryland Avenue, Annapolis, MD
21402-5035, Tel. 800-233-8764) publishes numerous books on the
Navy, including these career-relevant guides:

Division Officer's Guide
Handbook For Marine NCOs
Marine Officer's Guide
Naval Aviation Guide

Naval Officer's Guide
Service Etiquette
Watch Officer's Guide

STARTING YOUR OWN BUSINESS

Working for someone else for occasional travel benefits is not for everyone. Indeed, given the problems of finding employment abroad—legal restrictions and few opportunities as well as the overall unpredictability and instability of many international jobs—working for someone else has numerous limitations. Once established, most U.S. companies with operations abroad, for example, offer few job opportunities for Americans, because they prefer developing local staffs rather than relocating personal abroad. Contractors working in Third World development increasingly find themselves working in some of the world's least attractive places. Many initially got involved in this type of work because they enjoyed the particular countries in which they worked. In contrast to such jobs 10 or 15 years ago, international work in many of today's developing countries is no longer as much fun as it used to be in the countries which are now Newly Industrialized Countries (NICs) and which are primarily expanding their private sectors through foreign investment and trade.

Be Your Own Boss

One way around these problems is to create your own employment with you being the employer. Indeed, why not hire yourself? Why not create a job that will take you to your favorite destinations when **you** decide it's time to travel? Why don't you make the decisions when, where, and with whom you want to work at home or abroad during the next 10 to 20 years? Why not avoid the hassles of finding a job on someone else's payroll and then having to repeat the process again in another two or three years?

For some people the best of all worlds is to have the freedom to travel and work wherever and whenever they want and make a good living at the same time. Given the increased emphasis on business, economics, global trade, and travel in the international arena, the 1990s should be an unprecedented decade for starting small international businesses, especially import/export, consulting, travel, and sourcing businesses. The climate is right for such a move. After all, with the ending of the Cold War and increased emphasis on solving national development problems through economic expansion, more and more countries are eager to develop trade relations and encourage foreign investment and joint ventures.

Whether you are just starting out or changing jobs and careers within the international arena, you may well discover that going into an international business for yourself may be the most exciting and rewarding approach to the international job market.

During the past few years we have met more and more people who have decided to either break into the international arena or change international jobs and careers by starting their own businesses. Some open small shops selling imported arts, crafts, antiques, and home furnishings. Others become wholesalers of jewelry and other products for retail stores offering imported products or function as traders and brokers for other businesses. Some become consultants or agents for U.S. businesses interested in expanding trade abroad. And still others start their own travel business with emphasis on international travel. All quickly become involved in major business activities—purchasing, marketing, trade activities, shipping, and administration.

Getting Started

Going into business is not for everyone. While you will have opportunities to travel abroad and the freedom to pick and choose where you want to work, sustaining a business long-term involves a great deal more than travel. You first of all need to be entrepreneurial and secondly willing to deal with the details of managing a business. This means commitment, hard work, and a willingness to do things you don't necessarily enjoy doing all of the time. You may need to simultaneously be an accountant, marketer, salesperson, administrator, planner, purchasing agent, travel planner, and shipper. If you are primarily interested in import/export business, you need to process two key skills for success—sales and marketing. In addition, you must develop a base of suppliers and customers. To be successful, all of these activities take time, money, and persistence.

While nearly 600,000 new businesses are started each year in the United States, grim business statistics also discourage would-be entrepreneurs: another 400,000 to 500,000 businesses fail; 50 percent fail within the first 38 months; and nearly 90 percent fail within 10 years. Unfortunately, starting your own business is a risky business; the statistical odds are against anyone becoming a successful entrepreneur. Many people fail because they lack the necessary ingredients for success.

Learn to Take Risks

You will find few challenges riskier than starting your own business. At the same time, you may experience your greatest professional satisfaction in running your own business. If done right, an international business can become the perfect solution to the travel and work question.

Starting a business means taking risks. First, you will probably go into debt and realize little income during the first two years you are building your business, even though you had grandiose visions of becoming an overnight success. You may be under-capitalized or have overhead costs higher than anticipated. It takes time to develop a regular group of suppliers and clients. What profits you do realize are normally plowed back into the business in order to expand operations and guarantee larger future profits. Second, business is often a trial and error process in which it is difficult to predict or ensure outcomes. Due to unforeseen circumstances beyond your control, you may fail even though you work hard and make intelligent planning, investment, and management decisions. Third, you could go bankrupt and lose more than just your investments of time and money.

At the same time, owning your own business can be tremendously satisfying. It is the ultimate of independence. Being your own boss means you are in control, and no one can fire you. You are rewarded in direct proportion to your productivity. Your salary is not limited by a boss, nor are your accomplishments credited to others. Unless you decide otherwise, you are not wedded to an 8 to 5 work routine or an annual two-week vacation. Depending on how successful your business becomes, you may be able to retire young and pursue other interests. You can turn what you truly enjoy doing, such as hobbies, into a profitable, rewarding, and fun career.

But such self-indulgence and gratification has costs. You will probably need at least $20,000 to $40,000 of start-up capital, or perhaps much more depending upon the type of business you enter. No one will be sending you a paycheck every two weeks so you can regularly pay your bills. You may work 12 and 14 hour days, seven days a week, and have no vacation during the first few years. And you may become heavily indebted, experience frequent cash flow problems, and eventually have creditors descend on you.

Why, then, start your own business? If you talk to people who have worked for others and then started their own businesses, they will tell you similar stories. They got tired of drawing a salary while making someone else rich; they got bored with their work and hated the 8 to 5 routine. Some were victims of organizational politics. On a more positive note, many started businesses because they had a great idea they wanted to pursue or they wanted the challenge of independently accomplishing their own goals.

There are few things that are more self-actualizing than running your own business. But you must have realistic expectations as well as a motivational pattern which is conducive to taking risks and being an entrepreneur. If you like security, predictability, and stability, you probably are a candidate for a position where someone hands you a paycheck.

Possess the Right Strengths For Success

How can you become self-employed and successful at the same time? No one has a magical success formula for the budding entrepreneur—only advice. We do know why many businesses fail, and we can identify some basic characteristics for success. Poor planning, management, and decision-making lie at the heart of most business failures. Many people go into business without doing sufficient market research; they under-capitalize; they select a poor location; they incur extremely high and debilitating overhead costs; they lack commitment for the long-term; they are unwilling to sacrifice; they can't read or count; and they lack interpersonal and salesmanship skills.

On the positive side, studies continue to identify something called *"drive,"* or the need to achieve, as a key characteristic of successful entrepreneurs. According to Kellogg (*Fast Track*, McGraw-Hill), and others, young achievers and successful entrepreneurs possess similar characteristics:

> *"A high energy level, restless, a willingness to work hard and take risks, a desire to escape from insecurity."*

Successful business people combine certain motivations, skills, and circumstances. Contrary to popular myths, you don't need to be rich or have an MBA or business experience to get started. If you are willing to gamble and are a self-starter, self-confident, or organizer, and you like people, you may be on the right track for business success. These characteristics along with drive, thinking ability, human relations, communication, technical knowledge, hard work, persistence, and good luck are essential ingredients for business success. If these are among your strengths, you may be a good candidate for starting your own business with a high probability of success. If you feel you have recurring weaknesses in certain areas, you may want to consider finding a business partner who has particular complementary strengths for running a business.

Know Yourself

There are many different ways to get started in business. You can buy into a franchise which can initially cost you $20,000 to $500,000. Advertisements in the *Wall Street Journal* are a good source for hundreds of franchise opportunities from flipping hamburgers to selling animals. You can join someone else's business on a full-time or part-time basis as a partner or employee in order to get some direct business experience. You can try your hand at a direct-sales business such as Amway, Shaklee, or Avon. You can buy someone else's business or you can start your own business from scratch.

Your decision on how to get started in business should be based upon a knowledge of your skills and goals. Do not go into business for negative reasons—got fired, hate your present job, or can't find work. Unfortunately, many people go into business with totally unrealistic expectations as well as with little understanding of their own goals, skills, and motivations and how small businesses operate. For example, while it is nice to import clothing and accessories from Hong Kong and work around pretty clothes, owning a dress shop requires handling inventory and personnel as well as paying the rent and doing bookkeeping. Getting all those pretty dresses on the rack is hard work! Many people also don't understand how the business world works. It requires a great deal of interpersonal skill to develop and expand personal networks of creditors, suppliers, clients, colleagues, and competitors.

Therefore, you should do two things before you decide to go into business. First, thoroughly explore your goals and motivations. The questions are familiar:

- What do you want to do?
- What do you do well?
- What do you enjoy doing?
- What do you want to be doing five years from now?

Second, research different types of businesses in order to better understand advantages, disadvantages, procedures, processes, and possible problems. Talk to business persons about their work. Try to learn as much as possible about the reality before you invest your time and money in your own venture. Surprisingly, few people do this. Many people leap into a business that they think will be great and then later learn it was neither right for them nor did they have realistic expectations of what was involved. Indeed, many people would like to get into the import/export business. Perhaps they were traveling abroad and found a particular product they thought would sell well back home. All of a sudden they have great expectations of turning this little discovery into a profitable business. However, reality strikes them once they have to address several nuts-and-bolts business issues involving suppliers, export permits, shipping arrangements, duties, markets, buyers, advertising, and distribution. Failure to address such issues in concrete "who does what, where, and when" terms is precisely why so many businesses fail each year and why the import/export business is filled with numerous dreamers who have difficulty turning an idea into a profitable reality.

You should approach business opportunities the same way you approach the job market: do research, develop networks, and conduct informational and referral interviews. Most business people, including your competition, will be happy to share their experiences with you and assist you with advice and referrals. Such research is absolutely invaluable. If you fail to do it initially, you will pay later on by making the same mistakes that millions of others have made in starting their own businesses in isolation of others. Don't be high on motivation but low on knowledge and skills, for "positive thinking" and "thinking big" are not substitutes for doing the work!

Look For New Opportunities

Most business people will tell you similar stories of the reality of running your own business. Do your market research, spend long hours, plan, and be persistent. They also will give you advice on what businesses to avoid and what business routines you should be prepared to handle.

Numerous international products and services are excellent candidates for a business. Many developing countries, for example, offer excellent quality arts, crafts, and home furnishings that appeal to American buyers either through direct-mail or in small shops and department stores. Indeed, some enterprising individuals have been able to develop businesses as wholesalers and suppliers of such products to mail-order houses and major department stores. They regularly make trips to Africa, Asia, and Latin America seeking products and suppliers for major buyers back home. Others operate their own "international" arts, crafts, antique, home decorative, clothing, or gift shop and periodically make trips abroad to purchase new products as well as work with their suppliers on designs and quality control. Some develop specialty travel businesses that focus primarily on adventure travel to Third World countries.

Whatever your choices, try to select a product or service that you enjoy working with and which has a readily identifiable market.

Prepare the Basics

You also need to consider several other factors before starting a business. Since a business requires financing, locating, planning, developing suppliers and customer relations, and meeting legal requirements, be prepared to address these questions:

1. **How can I best finance the business?** Take out a personal or business loan with a bank? Go into a partnership in order to share the risks and costs? Get a loan from the Small Business Administration?

2. **How much financing do I need?** Many businesses fail because they are under-capitalized and thus unable to gain an appropriate market share for success. Others fail

because of over-spending on rent, furnishings, inventory, personnel, and advertising.

3. **Where is my market?** Just in this community, region, or nationwide, or internationally? Mail-order businesses enable you to expand your market nationwide whereas retail and service businesses tend to be confined to particular neighborhoods or communities.

4. **Who are my suppliers?** How many must I work with? What about credit arrangements? Who handles export and import permits? What about quality control? Can they deliver in a timely and correct manner?

5. **Where is the best location for the business?** Do you need to open a store or operate out of your home? If you need a store or office, is it conveniently located for your clientele? "Location is everything" still best summarizes the success of many businesses.

6. **How should the business be legally structured?** Sole proprietorship, partnership, or corporation? Each has certain tax and liability advantages and disadvantages.

7. **What licenses and permits do I need?** These consist of local business licenses and permits, federal employee identification numbers, state sales tax number, state occupational licenses, federal licenses and permits, and special state and local regulations which vary from state to state and from community to community. What type of insurance do I need? Fire, theft, liability, workers' compensation, auto, disability?

8. **How many employees do I need?** Can I do without personnel initially until the business expands? Should I use part-time and temporary help?

9. **What business name should I use?** If incorporated, is anyone else using the name? If a trade name, is it registered?

10. **What accounting system should I use?** Cash or accrual?
    Can I handle the books or do I need a part-time or full-
    time accountant?

11. **Do I need a lawyer?** What type of lawyer? What legal
    work can I do myself?

12. **How do I develop a business plan?** A business plan
    should include a definition of the business, a marketing
    strategy, operational policies, purchasing plans, financial
    statements, and capital raising plans.

Get Useful Advice

If you decide to go into business, make sure you choose the right
business for your particular skills, abilities, motivation, and interests.
A good starting point is Douglas Gray's *Have You Got What It
Takes?* (Bellingham, WA: Self-Counsel Press). This book provides
you with useful exercises for assessing your suitability for becoming
an entrepreneur. For a good overview of the many decisions you must
make in establishing a small business, see Bernard Kamaroff's *Small-
Time Operator* (Laytonville, CA: Bell Springs Publishing). This book
provides you with all the basic information you need for starting your
own business, including ledger sheets for setting up your books.
Albert Lowry's *How to Become Financially Successful By Owning
Your Own Business* (New York: Simon and Schuster) also outlines
the basics for both small-time and big-time operators.

Several other books provide similar how-to advice for the neophyte
entrepreneur:

The Entrepreneur's Guide to Starting a Successful Business,
James W. Holloran (Blue Ridge Summit, PA: TAB/McGraw-
Hill, 1992)

Going Into Business for Yourself: New Beginnings After 50,
Ina Lee Selden (Washington, DC: American Association of
Retired Persons)

How to Run a Small Business, The J. K. Lasser Tax Institute
(New York: St. Martin's Press)

Starting On a Shoestring: Building a Business Without a Bankroll, Arnold S. Goldstein (New York: Wiley, 1990)

The federal government will help you with several publications available through the Small Business Administration: 1441 L Street, NW, Washington DC 20416, Tel. 800/368-5855. SBA field offices are located in 85 cities. The Consumer Information Center publishes a free booklet entitled *More Than a Dream: Running Your Own Business*: Dept. 616J, Pueblo, Colorado 81009. The Internal Revenue Service sponsors several one-day tax workshops for small businesses. Your local chamber of commerce also can give you useful information.

A great deal of information is also available on specific international businesses. Several books, for example, address the major issues involved in operating an import or export business:

Building an Import/Export Business, Kenneth D. Weiss (New York: Wiley, 1992)

The Export Trading Company Guidebook (Washington, DC: International Trade Administration, U.S. Department of Commerce)

Exportise: An International Trade Source Book for Smaller Company Executives (Boston, MA: The Small Business Foundation of America)

How to Be an Importer and Pay for Your World Travel, Mary Green and Stanley Gillmar (Berkeley, CA: Ten Speed Press, 1993)

Importing Into the United States (Washington, DC: United States Customs Service, Department of Treasury)

Your Own Import-Export Business, Carl A. Nelson (Chula Vista, CA: Global Business and Trade)

Magazines such as *Global Trade Executive* and *World Trade* as well as regional business publications such as *The Far Eastern Economic Review* are well worth reading in order to keep abreast of current international business developments.

Several organizations provide assistance for importers and exporters. The American Association of Importers and Exporters (11 West 42nd St., New York, NY 10036, Tel. 212/944-2230), for example, assists its members with numerous services. Many state and local organizations also provide assistance in the form of regular meetings and seminars focusing on international trade. You may also want to attend international trade fairs where you will have an opportunity to inspect products, attend useful seminars, and network with fellow international business people.

Continue Success

The factors for operating a successful business are similar to the 20 principles we outlined in Chapter 3 for conducting a successful job search. Once your initial start-up problems are solved, you must organize, plan, implement, and manage in relation to your goals. Many people lack these abilities as well as the drive to sustain a business long-term. Some people are good at initially starting a business, but they are unable to follow-through in managing day-to-day routines once the business is established. And others have the ability to start, manage, and expand businesses successfully.

Be careful about business success. Many business people become obsessed with their work, put in 12 and 14 hour days continuously, and spend seven day weeks to make the business successful. Unwilling to delegate, they try to do too much and thus become a prisoner to the business. The proverbial "tail wagging the dog" is a common phenomenon in small businesses. For some people, this lifestyle feeds their ego and makes them happy. For others, the 8 to 5 routine of working for someone else on salary may look very attractive. You must be prepared to change your lifestyle when embarking on your own business. Your major limitation will be yourself.

So think it over carefully, do your research, and plan, organize, implement, and manage for success. The thrill of independence and success of running your own business is hard to beat. Best of all, you'll probably turn your love of travel into an exciting business in which work and play become one and the same!

INDEX

THE
AUTHORS

Ronald L. Krannich, Ph.D. and **Caryl Rae Krannich, Ph.D.** operate Development Concepts Inc., a training, consulting, and publishing firm. Ron received his Ph.D. in Political Science from Northern Illinois University. Caryl received her Ph.D. in Speech Communication from Penn State University.

Caryl and Ron are former university professors, high school teachers, management trainers, and consultants. They have completed numerous projects in the United States and abroad on management, career development, local government, population planning, and rural development during the past twenty years. They have published several articles in major professional journals.

Authors of 31 career books and 11 travel books, the Krannichs are two of America's leading career and travel writers. Their career books focus on key job search skills, government jobs, international careers, nonprofit organizations, and career transitions. Their work represents one of today's most extensive and highly praised collections of career writing with such bestsellers as *The Almanac of International Jobs and Careers, The Best Jobs for the 1990s and Into the 21st Century, Change Your Job Change Your Life, Dynamite Answers to Interview Questions, Dynamite Cover Letters, Dynamite Resumes, Dynamite Tele-Search, Find a Federal Job Fast, From Army Green to Corporate Gray, High Impact Resumes and Letters, Interview for Success, Job Search Letters That Get Results,* and *The New Network Your Way to Job and Career Success*. Their books are found in most major bookstores, libraries, and career centers. Many of their works are now available interactively on CD-ROM (*Job-Power Source*).

Ron and Caryl continue to pursue their international travel interests through their innovative *Treasures and Pleasures of Exotic Places* travel series. When they are not found at their home and business in Virginia, they are probably somewhere in Hong Kong, China, Thailand, Malaysia, Singapore, Indonesia, Papua New Guinea, Australia, New Zealand, Tahiti, Fiji, Burma, India, Nepal, Morocco, Turkey, Mexico, Italy, or the Caribbean pursuing their other passion— shopping and traveling for quality arts and antiques.

CAREER RESOURCES

*C*ontact Impact Publications to receive a free copy of their latest comprehensive and annotated catalog of career resources (hundreds of books, directories, subscriptions, training programs, audiocassettes, videos, computer software programs, multimedia, and CD-ROM).

The following career resources, many of which are mentioned in previous chapters, are available directly from Impact Publications. Complete the following form or list the titles, include shipping (see formula at the end), enclose payment, and send your order to:

IMPACT PUBLICATIONS
9104-N Manassas Drive
Manassas Park, VA 22111-5211
Tel. 703/361-7300
Fax 703/335-9486

Orders from individuals must be prepaid by check, moneyorder, Visa or MasterCard number. We accept telephone and fax orders with a Visa, MasterCard, or American Express number.

Qty.	TITLES	Price	TOTAL
TRAVEL-RELATED JOBS AND CAREERS			
___	Careers for Travel Buffs	$12.95	
___	Flying High in Travel	$18.95	___
___	Jobs for People Who Love Travel	$15.95	___
___	Jobs in Paradise	$12.95	___
___	How to Get a Job With the a Cruise Line	$14.95	___
___	Insider's Guide to Air Courier Bargains	$14.95	___
___	Opportunities in Airline Careers	$13.95	___
___	Opportunities in Travel Careers	$13.95	___
___	Travel and Hospitality Career Directory	$17.95	___

INTERNATIONAL AND OVERSEAS JOBS

___ Almanac of International Jobs and Careers $19.95   _____
___ American Jobs Abroad $19.95   _____
___ Building an Import/Export Business $16.95   _____
___ Complete Guide to International Jobs & Careers $13.95   _____
___ Directory of Jobs and Careers Abroad $14.95   _____
___ Directory of Overseas Summer Jobs $14.95   _____
___ Getting Your Job in the Middle East $19.95   _____
___ Guide to Careers in World Affairs $14.95   _____
___ How to Get a Job in Europe $17.95   _____
___ How to Get a Job in the Pacific Rim $17.95   _____
___ International Careers $10.95   _____
___ International Directory of Voluntary Work $13.95   _____
___ International Jobs $12.95   _____
___ Jobs in Russia and the Newly Independent States $15.95   _____
___ Jobs Worldwide $15.95   _____
___ Study Abroad $18.95   _____
___ Teaching English Abroad $15.95   _____
___ Work, Study, Travel Abroad $13.95   _____
___ Work Your Way Around the World $17.95   _____

BEST JOBS AND EMPLOYERS FOR THE 90s

___ 100 Best Jobs for the 1990s and Beyond $19.95   _____
___ 101 Careers $14.95   _____
___ American Almanac of Jobs and Salaries $15.95   _____
___ America's 50 Fastest Growing Jobs $11.95   _____
___ America's Fastest Growing Employers $15.95   _____
___ Best Jobs for the 1990s and Into the 21st Century $19.95   _____
___ Hoover's Handbook of American Business (annual) $29.95   _____
___ Hoover's Handbook of World Business (annual) $27.95   _____
___ Hoover's Masterlist of 2,500 of America's
     Largest and Fastest Growing Employers $19.95   _____
___ Job Seeker's Guide to 1000 Top Employers $22.95   _____
___ Jobs 1995 $15.95   _____
___ Jobs Rated Almanac $16.95   _____

KEY DIRECTORIES

___ Career Training Sourcebook $24.95   _____
___ Careers Encyclopedia $39.95   _____
___ Dictionary of Occupational Titles $39.95   _____
___ Directory of Executive Recruiters (annual) $39.95   _____
___ Directory of Outplacement Firms $74.95   _____
___ Directory of Special Programs for Minority
     Group Members $31.95   _____
___ Encyclopedia of Careers and Vocational Guidance $129.95   _____
___ Enhanced Guide for Occupational Exploration $29.95   _____
___ Government Directory of Addresses and
     Telephone Numbers $149.95   _____
___ Internships (annual) $29.95   _____

___ Job Bank Guide to Employment Services (annual) $149.95   _____
___ Job Hunter's Sourcebook $69.95   _____
___ Moving and Relocation Directory $179.95   _____
___ National Directory of Addresses & Telephone Numbers $99.95   _____
___ National Job Bank (annual) $249.95   _____
___ National Trade and Professional Associations $79.95   _____
___ Minority Organizations $49.95   _____
___ Occupational Outlook Handbook $15.95   _____
___ Professional Careers Sourcebook $89.95   _____

JOB SEARCH STRATEGIES AND TACTICS

___ Change Your Job, Change Your Life $15.95   _____
___ Complete Job Finder's Guide to the 90s $13.95   _____
___ Dynamite Tele-Search $12.95   _____
___ How to Get Interviews From Classified Job Ads $14.95   _____
___ Joyce Lain Kennedy's Career Book $29.95   _____
___ Knock 'Em Dead $9.95   _____
___ Professional's Private Sector Job Finder $18.95   _____
___ Rites of Passage At $100,000+ $13.95   _____
___ Who's Hiring Who $9.95   _____

CITY JOB FINDERS

How to Get a Job in . . .

___ Atlanta $15.95   _____
___ Boston $15.95   _____
___ Chicago $15.95   _____
___ Dallas/Fort Worth $15.95   _____
___ Houston $15.95   _____
___ New York $15.95   _____
___ San Francisco $15.95   _____
___ Seattle/Portland $15.95   _____
___ Southern California $15.95   _____
___ Washington, DC $15.95   _____

BobAdams' Job Banks to:

___ Atlanta $15.95   _____
___ Boston $15.95   _____
___ Chicago $15.95   _____
___ Dallas/Fort Worth $15.95   _____
___ Denver $15.95   _____
___ Detroit $15.95   _____
___ Florida $15.95   _____
___ Houston $15.95   _____
___ Los Angeles $15.95   _____
___ Minneapolis $15.95   _____
___ New York $15.95   _____
___ Ohio $15.95   _____
___ Philadelphia $15.95   _____

___ Phoenix	$15.95	_____
___ San Francisco	$15.95	_____
___ Seattle	$15.95	_____
___ Washington, DC	$15.95	_____

ALTERNATIVE JOBS AND CAREERS

___ Adventure Careers	$9.95	_____
___ Advertising Career Directory	$17.95	_____
___ Book Publishing Career Directory	$17.95	_____
___ Business and Finance Career Directory	$17.95	_____
___ But What If I Don't Want To Go To College?	$10.95	_____
___ Career Opportunities in Advertising and Public Relations	$27.95	_____
___ Career Opportunities in Art	$27.95	_____
___ Career Opportunities in the Music Industry	$27.95	_____
___ Career Opportunities in the Sports Industry	$27.95	_____
___ Career Opportunities in TV, Cable, and Video	$27.95	_____
___ Career Opportunities in Theater and Performing Arts	$27.95	_____
___ Career Opportunities in Writing	$27.95	_____
___ Careers for Animal Lovers	$12.95	_____
___ Careers for Bookworms	$12.95	_____
___ Careers for Foreign Language Speakers	$12.95	_____
___ Careers for Good Samaritans	$12.95	_____
___ Careers for Gourmets	$12.95	_____
___ Careers for Nature Lovers	$12.95	_____
___ Careers for Numbers Crunchers	$12.95	_____
___ Careers for Sports Nuts	$12.95	_____
___ Careers in Computers	$16.95	_____
___ Careers in Education	$16.95	_____
___ Careers in Health Care	$16.95	_____
___ Careers in High Tech	$16.95	_____
___ Careers in Law	$16.95	_____
___ Careers in Medicine	$16.95	_____
___ Careers in Mental Health	$10.95	_____
___ Careers in the Outdoors	$12.95	_____
___ Environmental Career Guide	$14.95	_____
___ Environmental Jobs For Scientists and Engineers	$14.95	_____
___ Healthcare Career Directory	$17.95	_____
___ Magazine Publishing Career Directory	$17.95	_____
___ Marketing and Sales Career Directory	$17.95	_____
___ Newspaper Publishing Career Directory	$17.95	_____
___ Opportunities in Accounting	$13.95	_____
___ Opportunities in Advertising	$13.95	_____
___ Opportunities in Biological Sciences	$13.95	_____
___ Opportunities in Civil Engineering	$13.95	_____
___ Opportunities in Computer Science	$13.95	_____
___ Opportunities in Counseling & Development	$13.95	_____
___ Opportunities in Dental Care	$13.95	_____
___ Opportunities in Electronic & Electrical Engineering	$13.95	_____
___ Opportunities in Environmental Careers	$13.95	_____
___ Opportunities in Financial Career	$13.95	_____
___ Opportunities in Fitness	$13.95	_____

___ Opportunities in Health & Medical Careers $13.95   _____
___ Opportunities in Journalism $13.95   _____
___ Opportunities in Law $13.95   _____
___ Opportunities in Marketing $13.95   _____
___ Opportunities in Medical Technology $13.95   _____
___ Opportunities in Microelectronics $13.95   _____
___ Opportunities in Nursing $13.95   _____
___ Opportunities in Pharmacy $13.95   _____
___ Opportunities in Psychology $13.95   _____
___ Opportunities in Teaching $13.95   _____
___ Opportunities in Telecommunications $13.95   _____
___ Opportunities in Television & Video $13.95   _____
___ Opportunities in Veterinary Medicine $13.95   _____
___ Outdoor Careers $14.95   _____
___ Public Relations Career Directory $17.95   _____
___ Radio and Television Career Directory $17.95   _____

GOVERNMENT AND PUBLIC-ORIENTED CAREERS

___ Book of U.S. Postal Exams $17.95   _____
___ Complete Guide to Public Employment $19.95   _____
___ Federal Applications That Get Results $23.95   _____
___ Federal Jobs for College Graduates $14.95   _____
___ Federal Jobs in Law Enforcement $15.95   _____
___ Find a Federal Job Fast! $13.95   _____
___ Government Job Finder $16.95   _____
___ Jobs in Washington, DC $11.95   _____
___ Paralegal $10.95   _____

NONPROFIT CAREERS

___ Good Works $24.95   _____
___ Jobs & Careers With Nonprofit Organizations $14.95   _____
___ Non-Profits' Job Finder $16.95   _____

COMPUTER SOFTWARE

___ Cambridge Career Counseling System $349.00   _____
___ JOBHUNT Quick and Easy Employer Contacts $59.95   _____
___ INSTANT Job Hunting Letters $39.95   _____
___ Perfect Resume Computer Kit (Personal) $49.95   _____
___ Quick and Easy Federal Application Kit (Individual) $49.95   _____
___ ResumeMaker With Career Planner $49.95   _____

VIDEOS

___ Find the Job You Want...and Get It! (4 videos) $229.95   _____
___ How to Present a Professional Image (2 videos) $149.95   _____
___ Insider's Guide to Competitive Interviewing $49.95   _____
___ Networking Your Way to Success $89.95   _____
___ Winning At Job Hunting in the 90s $89.95   _____

AUDIOCASSETTE PROGRAMS

___ Creative Job Search Program	$79.95	_____
___ The Edge R For Success	$159.95	_____
___ How to Get a Job Overseas	$79.95	_____

CD-ROM

___ Job-Power Source	$199.95	_____
___ Win-Win Resume 3.0	$69.95	_____

JOB LISTINGS AND VACANCY ANNOUNCEMENTS

___ Federal Career Opportunities (6 biweekly issues)	$38.00	_____
___ Federal Jobs Digest (6 biweekly issues)	$35.00	_____
___ International Employment Gazette (6 biweekly issues)	$35.00	_____
___ International Employment Hotline (12 monthly issues)	$39.00	_____

SKILLS, TESTING, SELF-ASSESSMENT

___ Career Discovery Project	$12.95	_____
___ Discover the Best Jobs for You!	$11.95	_____
___ Discover What You're Best At	$12.00	_____
___ Do What You Are	$15.95	_____
___ New Quick Job Hunting Map	$3.95	_____
___ Three Boxes of Life	$14.95	_____
___ What Color Is Your Parachute?	$14.95	_____
___ Where Do I Go From Here With My Life?	$10.95	_____
___ Wishcraft	$12.95	_____

EMPOWERMENT, SELF-ESTEEM, MANAGING CHANGE

___ 7 Habits of Highly Effective People	$12.00	_____
___ Awaken the Giant Within	$12.00	_____
___ Do What You Love, the Money Will Follow	$11.95	_____
___ Reinventing Your Life	$11.95	_____
___ Seize the Day	$21.95	_____

RESUMES, LETTERS, NETWORKING

___ Dynamite Cover Letters	$11.95	_____
___ Dynamite Resumes	$11.95	_____
___ Encyclopedia of Job-Winning Resumes	$16.95	_____
___ Great Connections	$11.95	_____
___ High Impact Resumes and Letters	$14.95	_____
___ How to Work a Room	$9.95	_____
___ Job Search Letters That Get Results	$15.95	_____
___ *New* Network Your Way to Job and Career Success	$12.95	_____
___ Perfect Cover Letter	$9.95	_____
___ Perfect Resume	$10.95	_____
___ Power Networking	$12.95	_____

___ Resume Catalog $15.95 _____
___ Resumes for the Over-50 Job Hunter $12.95 _____
___ Resumes for Re-Entry $10.95 _____
___ Sure-Hire Resumes $14.95 _____

DRESS, APPEARANCE, IMAGE, ETIQUETTE

___ 110 Mistakes Working Women Make $9.95 _____
___ John Molloy's New Dress For Success $12.95 _____
___ Red Socks Don't Work (for men) $14.95 _____
___ Winning Image $17.95 _____

INTERVIEWS AND SALARY NEGOTIATIONS

___ Dynamite Answers To Interview Questions $11.95 _____
___ Dynamite Salary Negotiations $13.95 _____
___ Interview for Success $13.95 _____
___ Naked At the Interview $10.95 _____
___ Power Interviews $12.95 _____
___ Sweaty Palms $9.95 _____

MILITARY

___ Beyond the Uniform $12.95 _____
___ Does Your Resume Wear Combat Boots? $9.95 _____
___ From Air Force Blue to Corporate Gray $17.95 _____
___ From Army Green to Corporate Gray $15.95 _____
___ From Navy Blue to Corporate Gray $17.95 _____
___ Job Search: Marketing Your Military Experience $14.95 _____
___ Re-Entry $13.95 _____
___ Resumes and Cover Letters for
    Transitioning Military Personnel $17.95 _____
___ Retiring From the Military $27.95 _____

WOMEN AND SPOUSES

___ *New* Relocating Spouse's Guide To Employment $14.95 _____
___ Resumes for Re-Entry: A Handbook For Women $10.95 _____
___ Smart Woman's Guide to Career Success $11.95 _____
___ Smart Woman's Guide to Interviewing and
    Salary Negotiations $11.95 _____
___ Smart Woman's Guide to Resumes and Job Hunting $9.95 _____
___ Women's Job Search Handbook $12.95 _____

MINORITIES AND DISABLED

___ Directory of Special Programs for
    Minority Group Members $31.95 _____
___ Job Strategies for People With Disabilities $14.95 _____
___ Minority Organizations $49.95 _____
___ Work, Sister, Work $19.95 _____

ENTREPRENEURSHIP AND SELF-EMPLOYMENT

___ 101 Best Businesses to Start $16.95   _____
___ Best Home-Based Businesses For the 90s $12.95   _____
___ Entrepreneur's Guide to Starting a Successful Business $16.95   _____
___ How You Got What It Takes? $12.95   _____
___ Starting on a Shoestring $14.95   _____

COLLEGE STUDENTS

___ Complete Resume and Job Search Book
    for College Students $9.95   _____
___ Graduating to the 9-5 World $11.95   _____

SUBTOTAL   _____

Virginia residents add 4½% sales tax   _____

POSTAGE/HANDLING ($4.00 for first
title and $1.00 for each additional book) $4.00

Number of additional titles x $1.00 ----------   _____

TOTAL ENCLOSED ----------------_____

SHIP TO:

NAME _____

ADDRESS _____

_____

_____

❒ enclose check/moneyorder for $ _____ made
    payable to IMPACT PUBLICATIONS.

❒ Please charge $ _____ to my credit card:

    ❒ Visa   ❒ MasterCard   ❒ American Express

    Card # _____

    Expiration date: _____/_____

    Signature _____